Sattwa Café

Meta B. Doherty

LOTUS
PRESS

P.O. Box 325
Twin Lakes, WI 53181 USA

DISCLAIMER

Food can be nourishment, medicine or poison to an individual. The author, contributors and publisher can take no responsibility for the health and welfare of any person in using this book. This book is not intended to treat, diagnose or prescribe. The information contained herin is in no way to be considered as a substitute for your own inner guidance or consultation with a duly licensed health-care professional. We wish the best of health and welfare to all.

First Edition 2006

Printed in the United States of America

ISBN   978-0-9409-8587-2

Library of Congress Catalog Number   2007920562

Published by:
Lotus Press, P.O. Box 325, Twin Lakes, WI 53181 USA
web: www.lotuspress.com
Email: lotuspress@lotuspress.com
800.824.6396

CONTENTS

Dedication

I offer this book to the unity
that is everything.

I dedicate it to my teachers Dr Rajen Cooppan,
T.K.V. Desikachar and his father
Sri T. Krishnamacharya and to
Sri Shivarudrabalayogi Maharaj.

I dedicate it to my family, my two sons Nate and Zack,
who offered many constructive ideas about the recipes,
to my consort Paul, who always receives food with gratitude
and to my family and friends in America.

I dedicate it to Joey (Joanna) E. who turns all food she touches into delicacy.

Receiving the teachings of ayurveda initiates and imprints a person.
Dr. Rajen Cooppan is my teacher and Dr. Sunil Joshi is his and so on back
through the millennia, sustaining a personal energetic link of teacher and
student, sustaining lineage.

~I wish to thank ~
Dr. David Frawley, Dr. Sunil Joshi and their assistants Mira, Cheryl and Mukul
for linking with me
Dr. Sunil Joshi for writing the Introduction
Dr. Rajen Cooppan for his continuing inspiration to us in Perth
Vaidya Bhagyashree Sawrikar for her friendship and instruction
Lotus Press for undertaking publication
Artists for allowing their work to be used:
Helen Robins for "Elemental Woman",
Michele Eastwood for "Dressed"
Geoff Scales for converting slide transparencies to digital format
Paul for my photograph
Those friends in Perth who followed the journey of Sattwa Café
Absolutely Organic in Perth for the provision of biodynamic and organic food

Introduction

Sattwa Café is a great title for a book about ayurvedic food. In ayurveda, we emphasize maintaining a sattvic diet (aahara), a diet that engenders enthusiasm, on a daily basis. This diet enhances sattwa guna, self-awareness, which is responsible for creativity and positive thinking, and these two qualities are essential for keeping an optimal mental balance. This mental balance, in turn, gives one the ability to make good food and lifestyle patterns that support a healthy mind and body. So, the title alone is enough to explain how this book will help enhance a sattwa quality of mind.

This book will take you on an ayurvedic journey. In ayurveda, we know that there are subtle food properties that effect doshic balance. This book beautifully explains the concept of doshic imbalances and how to choose recipes that will restore harmony to your doshas, your body's inherent intelligence. This knowledge gives you an opportunity to enjoy what is good for you and stay away from food that contributes to imbalance, which can lead to disease. In addition to learning about proper food, you will also become aware of proper food preparation. Eating the correct food is your first level of defense against disease.

The first priority of ayurvedic food is that it be fresh. Leftovers and fermented foods are categorically prohibited, which generally means that restaurant food is to be avoided. So you must learn how to prepare the right food with the right spices, consistent with your own particular doshas. This is what makes Sattwa Café such a valuable personal diet book. It will become an invaluable asset to your own library.

Sattwa Café is an easy and accessible introduction to ayurvedic principles. Applying these principles to your diet will allow you to embody and integrate them into your life. I am grateful that Meta has presented this ayurvedic cuisine in multi-cultural Australia, where her seasonal, regional and local references can be of particular value. By doing this she presents a model for eating well while being present to our own specific environments and supporting our own local economies. You will find that cooking ayurvedically with Meta is a pleasurable learning experience, one that will give you the understanding of food as a tool for good health. I am sure you will enjoy reading this book as well as using it as a guide for setting up your healthy ayurvedic kitchen.

My sincere thanks to Meta for exploring ayurveda and presenting her insights to the world in this wonderful book.

Good luck and namaskar.
DR. SUNIL JOSHI
15 –B TILAKNAGAR,
NAGPUR -10
INDIA.

Foreword

Ayurveda is an ancient health science that is making a profound reappearance throughout the world in different cultures.

Meaning "The Science of Life", this holistic and natural system of medicine and health care provides 21st century man with an easily attainable goal of health, despite the gloomy predictions of modern medical science. The power of this medicine lies in the fact that its principles are rooted in the laws of nature. These laws have not changed since the dawn of man. Unlike modern medical science where recent "discoveries" constantly supercede and replace existing knowledge about how to take care of our bodies and mind, Ayurveda provides a consistent and coherent set of principles that allows one to consciously take on the role of caring for oneself.

Food is medicine in Ayurveda. This book is a welcome and timely one that further helps the true seeker of health to put into practice the science and art of food as a medicine and healing tool. Taking a complex science like Ayurveda and bringing it to a simplified level to help people achieve health through proper eating, is a major achievement and I commend Meta in this noble effort. The recipes are true to the science and yet encouragingly simple to use.

I am sure that you will find this a much used book in your life.

Dr. Rajen Cooppan

WELCOME to the SATTWA CAFÉ

You enter through the wide door with your friend and are shown to a table.

"This will be a novel experience, believe me," says Irene.

The cooking space at the open heart of the café has already attracted your attention when someone arrives with a small chair of her own and a pot of just-boiled water.

"Hello. My name is Petra and I'll be your chef today," she says, pouring each person a cup of hot water. "Enjoy some beverage while we talk."

She sits with you for awhile. You talk about how you are feeling and what you've been doing lately. She asks further about your health in general and takes your subtle pulse.

"I'm surprised I'm even here, I've been so lethargic lately, but Irene knew I needed to shift this and brought me to lunch. I feel like I'm slowly turning to concrete," you say.

"Everyone feels stuck at some time or other. How is your appetite?"

"Not really much of that."

It is midday and yet the weather is still cool and damp. In your subtle pulse, Petra feels an excess of earth and water energy. She suggests a meal that is light, dry, warm, spicy, bitter and astringent.

"I recommend firstly an aperitif to stimulate your appetite and then a leafy greens spice medley over millet."

"That sounds intriguing."

"And how are you, Irene?" asks Petra, addressing your friend.

"I feel well and I've been so much more alert. It's as if a cotton wool veil has been lifted off my brain. I'd like a vata-pacifying soup today, with flatbread, what do you think?"

"Warming, grounding and unctuous will do just fine for you right now."
Petra returns to the kitchen and you are served a small drink of aloe vera with

ginger juice and honey at room temperature. Irene is presented a demitasse of hot ginger lemon tea.

Chef prepares your meal from fresh, wholesome ingredients that reflect the quality of the elements in which the food was grown. No ingredient was cooked more than a few hours ago, and so excludes all items from a can or jar. Thus, the vitality, the life force (prana), remains present in the food. On an ongoing basis, this alone will help your energy and clarity, which is what Irene has started experiencing.

Petra is engaged in the service she is providing and is in a loving state of mind, imparting that to your meal. You watch her at work in sacred space where all the chefs move fluidly. Happy sounds and attractive aromas arise.

In the positive ambiance of the café, this light dish is presented to you. Appreciating the physical hunger you now feel as a signal to eat, you do so in relationship and gratitude to all the energy that the food is carrying. There is something to delight each sense and then some. Finally a small cup of digestive tea which smells nice and spicy is set before you. Aromatherapy that you can drink. After your meal and tea, you and Irene sit back, feeling truly nourished.

Petra returns. She advises you to keep yourself warm and dry, especially your head and upper body. She suggests you now have a short stroll to assist digestion and enjoy walking briskly, daily, between meals. She sends you along with a joke:

> "What did the Buddhist monk say to the New York hot dog vendor?
> 'Make me one with everything.' "

> "I know the feeling," you reply, smiling.

Does such a chef exist? The ability is in each of us to cultivate. Does such a café exist? In our own cooking space.

Ayurveda is the wisdom, science and teachings of natural law, of how nature works, gifted to us so that we can support and enhance life as we experience it on earth. Life encompasses the physical body, the senses, the mind and the spirit networking in intelligent coordination. Ayurveda teaches us how to receive what is provided so that we are well, so that we can gather both experience on the more manifest level - our occupation, our relationships, our sense of the outer world and experience of the spiritual domain.

Ayurvedic Cuisine honors your state of being at the present moment, which includes your mental and physical disposition and the environment with which you interact. It recognizes that the person who cooks the meal imparts energy to the food.

Based on ayurvedic principles we nurture a loving state while cooking, use food as nourishment and medicine, which supports and balances the body, senses and mind, and not use it as poison, that which creates dysfunction.

Sattwa is the state we feel as clarity, creativity; it exists in all of nature and in this case the mind. There is a sense of unity and easy balance. Sattwa is influenced by the types of foods we eat, our thoughts, relationships, lifestyle and surroundings because they are also affected by this attribute. There are two other attributes of existence, that of rajas, which produces activity and can lead to excess and that of tamas, which produces dullness and can lead to deficit. Foods that promote sattwa are most fresh fruit and vegetables, almonds, basmati rice, split mung beans, oats, whole wheat, fresh coconut, ghee, milk and unheated honey, with food cooked fresh using those fresh ingredients. Pure water is also included.

Those foods that induce rajas are onion, garlic, chillies, radishes, corn, excessive spicing, eggs, poultry and red meat. Caffeine, too many sweets and fried food can also make the mind restless. Tamas is increased with ingestion of leftovers, fermented products, fungal products, animal products, alcohol and drugs. Eventually fried food and too many sweets also produce a dull mind.

Multicultural Australia is home to people of diverse ethnic origins. We enjoy many styles of cuisine reflecting the ingredients available, the cooking methods used and the wisdom passed through the generations of all countries. Living with people who enjoy cooking with specific foods tend to make those items more readily available and fresh rather than canned. If some of these ingredients are not easily found, as will be the case, embrace the methods and philosophy. Your locally grown fresh produce is always the superior option.

In ascribing a food to a particular region, we are observing a contemporary tenor in agriculture. If we research cultivation of crops back through time, many were not staples in the areas in which they are now popular. Millet was the staple of Asia long before rice was introduced.

In accordance with the teachings of ayurveda, some ingredients and methods may change.

KNOWLEDGE HELPS ACTION

Ayurvedic cooking begins by connecting to what we already know. One of the seven basic concepts in ayurveda is that everything in nature is composed of five densities, space, air, fire, water and earth. If we think about it, we know and interact with the overt manifestation of these elements all the time. We have a firm structure that stands on planet earth, water is a major part of our bodies and of planet ocean, we have inwardly generated warmth and outwardly blazing stars, we interact with the atmosphere which holds the air we breathe by ebb and flow and all of this happens on stage in space. Each element is directed by an archetypal intelligence that is more encompassing, more philosophical, than just its overt manifestation. Together, these great elements orchestrate all physical phenomena. Within humans, these elements influence the size, shape and structure of our bodies, our metabolism as well as other physiological functions and our personalities. A person who has more air looks and acts differently than someone who has more fire or water. The word dosha is defined as a functional intelligence which directs human psycho-physiology and structure. Vata dosha is the conductor of space and air within the body-mind. Pitta dosha orchestrates fire and water and kapha dosha directs water and earth.

We all have all three dosha-s in varying proportions within us. Although we do, there are seven general dosha combinations that people are born with, of which you will exhibit one: vata, pitta, kapha, vata-pitta, pitta-kapha, kapha-vata, and vata-pitta-kapha. With the bi-dosha profile, either one may be a majority.

If you are predominantly vata, your characteristics are dry, light, rough, cold, porous, subtle, minute and mobile. Take note of and recognize them as important factors operating in and influencing your body and mind. They are the characteristics you already have and accumulating more will unbalance your system. When you look for their signatures look into the foods you are eating. For example, crackers are dry and rough. Feel the clothes you wear, are they starched and stiff or soft and insulating with a feeling of some weight? Are their colors cool or warm? What's the weather like right now? Wind dries, unsettles and is mobile like vata. What is the air temperature and humidity? Dry and cold exacerbates vata. How about the environment in your home, is it soft and warm or cold and spartan? Is it drafty? What colors predominate? Mentally, do you find yourself lost in the subtlety of thoughts, spaced out somewhere that exists in the ether or are you present in your actual surroundings? As a dominant vata psycho-physiology

- You will have a lightweight, narrow frame
- Feel the cold

4

- Be prone to dry skin, hair, nails, membranes and constipation, that is, imbalance of a drying nature
- Fidget a lot
- Have variable digestion
- Find that your energy comes and goes
- Be sensitive through the senses of touch and hearing
- Have lots of creative ideas
- Learn and forget things easily
- Be willing to try new things
- Find that there is variability and changeability in your life

Dryness is a characteristic of vata only and if increased, signals vata aggravation.

Pitta psycho-physical characteristics are hot, penetrating, spreading, light, slightly oily, liquefying, acidic and sour smelling. Take note of and recognize those important factors operating in and influencing you. Use your fine mind to recognize in the following examples that which will exacerbate pitta: a 5-alarm spicy-hot dish or a pickled dish which is sour; clothing constructed of materials that retain heat or do not protect you from the heat of the sun; your job and environment such as working the furnace of a steam locomotive or a job with deadlines; and your mental disposition, such as annoyance with the world turning so slow or speech that bites. As predominantly pitta

- You will have a medium size and weight frame
- Feel the heat
- Be prone to imbalance of a hot, sour or acidic nature
- Have sensitive, fair, reddish or freckled skin, hair and membranes
- Detect strong smells in your bodily functions
- Have a sharp, penetrating intellect
- Have good digestion
- Have good stamina
- Be most connected through your sense of sight
- Have a lively, twinkling look in your eyes
- Be courageous and warm
- Like to run the world or at least save it

Heat is a characteristic of pitta only and if mounting, signals pitta aggravation.

If kapha dominates the majority of your psycho-physiology your attributes are heavy, steady, cool, soft, sticky, oily and sweet. Take note of them because they will be the ones that most influence you. If you are in balance you will minimize more of the same, if not, you may be allowing them to increase kapha. Kapha accumulates with heavy, sticky, sweet, cold food and drink; things just too languid and mellow; the stillness of fog, cool, cold, drizzly, damp weather and you just out of the shower and going outside with wet hair. If kapha is the major part of your constitution

- You will have a large frame that must therefore have more weight
- Be less tolerant to the combination of cold and damp
- Have hydrated, slightly oily skin that is cool to the touch
- Have thick, well-rooted hair and nails
- Have a doe-like look to your eyes
- Have slow digestion
- Be prone to imbalance of a congestive and heavy nature
- Take longer to get going but have good stamina
- Take longer to learn things but never forget them
- Be connected to the world through your senses of smell and taste
- Be a steadying, loving influence to those around you
- Relate more to the status quo

Heaviness is a characteristic of kapha only and if increasing, signals kapha aggravation.

It is understandable that the mind-body operates more in the dosha proportion that is genetically inherent and generally tends to overuse the pattern. (There can also be depletion of dosha-s with characteristics not covered in this book.) A vata-dominant constitution will be more sensitive to vata-aggravating influences than pitta-dominant or kapha-dominant people and such an individual would take greater care to minimize them. Yet a vata-dominant individual can still experience a pitta imbalance such as heartburn or a kapha imbalance such as a mucus-blocked nose. It is like this for all the dosha-s. With a bi-doshic pattern, such as vata-pitta, the elements of those two dosha-s influence us, both internally and from our environment. A vata-pitta person would be more alert to keeping their pitta energy balanced in pitta-aggravating circumstances (see below) and their vata energy balanced in vata-aggravating circumstances (see below). This person would also recognize that it is still possible to experience a kapha imbalance in kapha-aggravating circumstances (see below).

That which influences our dosha pattern, keeping it in dynamic equilibrium or unbalancing it, is our diet, lifestyle, the weather, time of day, our age and how much rubbish we have in our system that blocks our natural intelligence from directing normal energy flow. Air (drying), fire (heating) and water (heavy) have their effects in our mind-body so we become pro-active and limit them from over-extending their impact on our natural constitutions; or become reactive, to remedy the disturbances that those factors have caused, the sooner the better.

HOW to CUSTOMIZE THESE RECIPES

The primary focus in these recipes is to promote mental sattwa, assist digestion and allow the dosha-s their normal functions. When sattwa is over-shadowed by rajas and/or tamas, we make inappropriate choices in eating, sense input and lifestyle. This is one way that we disrupt dosha functioning which weakens our digestive fire, leading to mental, emotional and physical ama.

There are methods of removing ama (toxicity) and spoiled dosha function that incorporate diet but changing diet alone cannot remove it. Read about pan-chakarma to find out more about those cleansing methods. On a therapeutic level it is best to remove the ama and spoiled dosha-s first because their presence disrupts the benefit of even good foods and activities.

To use food to promote wellness the short-term goal is to pacify the dosha(s) that is excessive and strengthen the weakened dosha(s). Look over the aspects below to recognize which dosha is in excess. Become aware of what misinformation or lack of prior information may be causing that to happen. Notice which weather pattern exacerbates the imbalance.

Each recipe will inform you to "enjoy less - enjoy some - enjoy more" for each of the three dosha-s. Choose the "enjoy more" recipes for the dosha excess while you are experiencing it. For example, if you have a condition described in the kapha excess list below, best is to look for an "enjoy more" kapha recipe. Second best is to choose any recipe and follow the modifications along the kapha line. This second option is more suitable if you are a kapha in good health.

"Enjoy more" would also translate as enjoy frequently, "enjoy some" as occasionally and "enjoy less" as infrequently.

You will soon notice that the same recommendations repeat themselves for each dosha as they pertain to certain food groups and tastes. You will soon know which foods are good for you and which are not. Keep in mind that if you are bi-doshic or tri-doshic the recommendations will need to find middle ground on a sliding scale according to your present state of characteristics.

For your on-going diet when you are well, eat according to what is best for your birth constitution as you find it described above and support your digestion because it is the key to health.

Some foods, food combinations, or the rushed attitude when eating produces indigestion. It is that broad term of 'indigestion' which indicates that ama is being formed. At a persistent enough level, that ama migrates out of the gastrointestinal tract into the body and lodges in weak, injured, genetically predisposed areas or places in which ama is already present. From there it can disrupt other tissues and organs. This is what causes the majority of degenerative disease that people experience. Support complete digestion because it is the foundation of health.

When you are balanced, what you feel like eating is a message coming from directive intelligence. It is not a craving if it arises, is satisfied, leaves you content and does not arise relentlessly. Even though an 'intake' satisfied you yesterday does not mean it is necessary today.

Some signs of indigestion include nausea, a feeling of tiredness after eating, tiredness in general, early satiety, sour belching, a burning sensation in the chest and abdomen, excess thirst, excess heat after eating, ravenous appetite, abdominal pain, bloating, flatulence, constipation, diarrhea and erratic bowel function.

These recipes began through my ever-present interest in nutrition and a personal propensity for doing things myself so that I know it is the best it can be. Recipes include my own experience of cooking and eating ayurvedic cuisine and research as to which foods are nourishment, medicine and poison (when eaten in excess) for the three dosha-s. I had been using ayurvedic recommendations for twenty years without knowing it while raising two vegetarian children. Since they were mostly in good health, it made that process a lot smoother. We as a nuclear family are mostly well and at the first sign of imbalance, we simplify the diet to vegetable soup and rice and split mung bean porridge. This allows the body to direct more energy into healing by removing the task of digesting complex foods. We also increase rest and decrease activity to help the process.

These recipes also incorporate feedback from gourmet friends who enjoy their food originating from this simple paradigm. Although a vaidya, an ayurvedic physician, will never suggest blueberry lemon mini cakes as found in this book as a remedy, the shift from store-bought, leftover, high sugar, poor quality oils, never-touched-by-loving-hands products to ones you have more input into gives them poetic license. The meals I serve consist of one or two dishes, three at most. If the staple has vegetables in it, that is the meal. If it doesn't, I add them without cooking a separate vegetable recipe. If I cook vegetables or soup, I add flatbread or a savory bakery item. Since we never step into the exact same recipe twice, decide if you liked the result and what improvements could be made. For example, if the herbs you use are very strong in taste, use less. I apologize if any meal from this book turns out less than satisfying.

When you are ready to work creatively with locally grown food you will find dosha-compatible food lists in books in the reading section. You will find that the authors of these lists do not always coincide. Be aware of your own experience regarding each food. Do you experience any signs of indigestion? Allow the possibility that you may be inaccurate in what you perceive. If you feel that is the case, seek out an ayurvedic consultant. When sattwa is in its full measure, we naturally gravitate towards the best foods for our constitution and digestive fire.

If you are feeling well on all levels there is no reason to refuse an invitation to a meal out.

Being obsessed, compulsive or fanatical is not a sign of balance.

THE SIGNATURES of IMBALANCE

Kapha excess:

Overweight and weight gain
Digestion feels sluggish
No appetite
Respiratory congestion/asthma/allergies
Loose-feeling joints
Pallor
Hypothermia (feeling colder than normal)
Sugar intolerance
Diabetes
Elevated cholesterol
Excess oiliness
Cysts and other growths
Pale menstrual fluid with mucus
Lethargy
Heaviness
Procrastination
Feeling unappreciated
Endogenous depression
Unable to think in abstract terms
Kapha is naturally increased:
In cool, cold, damp, still and snowy weather
Between about 6 - 10 AM and PM
In childhood

Some possible causes of Kapha excess:

Lack of exercise
Sleeping after meals
Sleeping during the day
Sleeping too much, especially after sunrise
Excessive attachment to pleasure
Consuming heavy, oily, cold, sweet, sour and salty food and drink to excess
Eating too much wheat and dairy
Drinking cold or iced drinks
Genetic predisposition
Feeling stressed and withdrawing
Being overly indulged or smothered as a child

<u>To rebalance:</u>

Address the possibilities listed above and the recommendations below with zest and ambition

Favor light, dry, warm, pungent, bitter, astringent food

Drink warm to hot beverages

Use most spices liberally

Decrease eating by one meal a day and fast one day a week

Eat a light meal earlier in the evening so it is digested by bedtime

Don't sleep after meals

Decrease eating leftovers more and more as they slow down digestion leading to weight gain

Expose yourself to the wind and sun in a safe manner

Favor warm, open, dry environments and expansive views

Keep warm and dry, especially your head and upper body

Take several brisk walks periodically during the day, weather permitting

Practice stimulating yoga postures and breathing, appreciating that getting started is your challenge

Choose aerobic activities (adipose metabolism) if you are not largely over-weight; if you are, ease your heart up to this

Listen to uplifting music and sing along with it now and then

Take up a mentally challenging pursuit

Receive a strong deep body massage with minimal oil

Use spicy energizing scents in your aromatherapy

Wear robust-colored clothes (rather than pastels) towards the red end of the spectrum with rougher textures

Engage in diversity and experimentation

Find a personal trainer who will provide companionship and the energy to get you going

Seek contact with someone who will not indulge sentimentality and emotional-ity but will encourage non-attachment and action as your expression of service to others

<u>Pitta excess:</u>

Skin rashes, boils, acne

Inflammation, sore throat, colitis, conjunctivitis

Feeling hotter than usual

Fever

Excessive hunger and thirst

Feeling that the food you eat is not converting to substance

A feeling of lightness

Ulcers, hyperacidity, heartburn

Liver and gall bladder disease

Blood dysfunction

Burning hemorrhoids

Increased menstrual flow with bright red menstrual fluid
Fetid body odor and mouth odor
Eyesight acuity decreasing
Hair greying or thinning early
Disturbed sleep
Striving without feeling fully committed
Irritable
Angry
Frustrated
Impatient
Critical
Fanatical
Demanding
Seeing things only as black or white
Pitta is naturally increased:
By hot and humid weather
Between about 10 - 2 AM and PM
From puberty through middle age

Some possible causes of pitta excess:

Humid, hot weather, heat fatigue, sunburn
Excessive and harsh visual intake
Exposure to violence
Working or exercising too hard especially in hot weather
Impure food and water
Excess alcohol consumption
Sexual frustration
Consuming hot, light, spicy, salty, sour, fermented or fried food or drink in excess
Working under pressure from deadlines
Being stressed and reacting with anger
Being overly competitive or experiencing too much conflict as a child

To rebalance:

Address the possibilities listed above and the recommendations listed below intelligently and patiently over time
Favor sweet, bitter and astringent tastes and enjoy food and drink at room temperature
Decrease spices overall
Eat when you are hungry
Seek space, coolness, flowers and nature
Sit or take relaxed walks along calm water and at night
Gaze at the moon and stars
Wear protective, breathe-able clothing in the sun (how about a parasol?) and

favor blue, green, white and other cooling colors

Avoid being in the sun during the hottest part of the day especially during the hottest part of the year

Splash your eyes, face and neck and rinse your mouth with cool water periodically during the day

Take a break from your occupation every hour if possible during the day to decrease intensity of mind

Exercise in the water and with cooling yoga postures and breathing

Experience yoga as something to benefit the body-mind rather than using the body for performance

Listen to sounds like water flowing gently

Receive a low-friction, non-heating body massage with coconut oil, checking out the different massage techniques available

Favor sweet scents in aromatherapy

Engage in "random acts of kindness"

Choose discussion with a person you respect who will not buy into stringent behavior or ideals and who will advocate using intelligence to explore all viewpoints (a sattwic pitta individual)

Vata excess:

Constipation

Flatulence, bloating

Dry, rough or chapped skin and membranes

Intolerance to wind and cold

Aching, noisy or dry-feeling joints

Hypertension

Chronic lower backache not caused by injury

Weight loss and tissue emaciation

Menstrual cramps, dark clotted menstrual fluid

Muscle spasms and twitches

Acute pain, especially nerve pain

Light, restless sleep

Feeling frazzled

Feeling confused

Anxiety

Fear

Memory loss

Vata is naturally increased in:

Cold, dry or windy weather

Between about 2 - 6 AM and PM

In our senior years

Some possible causes of vata excess:

Cold, dry or windy weather

Inadequate clothing protection in the above weather
Any change in body, mind, emotions, weather or circumstances
Any stress and reacting with anxiety and worry
Travel, jet lag or excess local movement in any vehicle or on foot
Overuse of any sense organ and mind
Addictions
Fatigue, overwork
Lack of routine or a change in routine
Insufficient sleep
Excessive or unnatural sexual practice
Fasting, skipping meals or stringent diet
Consuming bitter, pungent or astringent, cold, dried or drying, rough, raw or frozen food or drink in excess
Drinking cold or iced water or any carbonated drink
Insufficient calmness during meals
Being neglected or abused as a child

To rebalance:

Address the possibilities listed above and the recommendations listed below creatively and in depth
In general, increase the warmth, heaviness and unctuousness (oily nature) of your diet and favor salty, sweet and sour tastes; do not increase heavy foods if you feel there is toxicity in your system
Use spices in moderate amounts, without overusing bitter and pungent ones
Seek warmth and more stillness
Sit or walk quietly in nature with companions
Seek routine
Create a safe, soft environment for yourself externally and internally
Listen to calming music, following it mentally
Practice being still, calming your breathing periodically during the day
Practice yoga postures that do not tire you; sustain postures by developing muscle strength and long calm breaths
Appreciate that your physical body will not keep up with the mind's desire to enact all your exciting ideas
Employ sweet, citrus or grounding essential oils in aromatherapy
Gravitate towards wearing tawny, burnished colors (gold, cranberry, rust, copper) that make you feel warm without feeling dry, accenting with other colors; minimise contrasts and angular patterns; choose soft-textured fabrics and wear soft-soled shoes
Receive a gentle sesame oil body massage
Give yourself a sesame oil massage every few days and rest, keeping warm for 15 minutes after it; rinse off in warm water without soap
Seek friends with steadying influence who will help you decrease your mental activity while helping you feel protected, supported and included with others

TO CLEANSE THE PALATE

Our sensitivity to taste can be enhanced by removing the waste on our tongue every morning. A stainless steel, copper or silver tongue scraper can look like a long, narrow horseshoe.

Pressing the edge firmly on the tongue, draw the coating off and out of the mouth. Relax the tongue to do this and reach the scraper all the way to the back. Rinse the scraper and continue until the entire tongue is clean. Use a small spoon until you find a scraper.

Take about one teaspoon of cold-pressed sesame or other cold-pressed oil and swish it in the mouth for five minutes as a mouthwash, activating the face and neck muscles and stimulating waste release. Spit it out in a suitable place and rinse the mouth. If oil is too thick for you, use a small amount of salt and turmeric mixed into tepid water. Brush your teeth.

These ablutions can be performed in whichever sequence is best for you. It is recommended to do so before taking anything by mouth.

An additional avenue by which we can enhance our sense of taste is to take the time to savor our food. We are receiving energy from the taste as long as it is present. Over time, we will know if foods are overly sweet, sour, salty, pungent, bitter or astringent by our own sense of taste, even in these recipes. If you find your mouth very dry this will limit what can be tasted.

And to enjoy taste, we must be able to receive aroma through our sense of smell. There are both yoga and ayurveda practices designed to help clear the nostrils.

FIRE and ICE

To insure the best nutrition on all levels, biodynamic food is supreme. It was brought to our mental reality by Rudolf Steiner in Europe in 1924, although not called biodynamics, when he delivered a series of lectures on agriculture at the request of farmers. He said the ideas were like the letters in an alphabet and that the farmers would be able to make words with them. They have since been doing so as a physical reality by ongoing observation of the principles in action. The words are becoming songs.

This food is grown using natural methods of fertilizing and pest control. In that way it resembles organically grown food. Its storage would be best suited to each item and processing would be minimal or not at all.

Biodynamic food is grown as part of a holistic system using people, animals and plants, which exist in relationship to their environment and influence it and each other. The soil, a living entity, is a most integral aspect of this relationship.

Foremost in a sattwic sense, biodynamic food is grown to promote the health and full incarnation of each person into his/her body, to assist spiritual development and to foster evolution of consciousness. The method uses techniques to attract the energies of the elements, the earth, the moon, the planets and the starry heavens. Eating the animals raised in this system is then a matter of choice. Ayurveda does recommend the consumption of meat in specific circumstances.

We can include a great deal of goodwill into home-grown food, whatever you can grow. Join a biodynamic home gardening group or use natural fertilizers, compost and pest deterrents. Admire plants as they expand your horizon. We observe transformation first-hand and appreciate time as an ingredient. Grow plants in soil in the earth if you can, not hydroponically. As in cooking, what one puts in is what is received. We participate in the process of growth with the plant and then accept its fruits with gratitude.

Read labels and research where your food is coming from. Keep steering towards the most beneficial option. This is part of the practice of removing misinformation as an ongoing process. Would you want to eat the rind of an orange that has been colored, sprayed and waxed?

If you only have access to food grown in the temporary practice of chemical and genetic engineering, bless the food for growing. We still need to eat!

There exists a continuum of the best source of heat to cook over. Straw, wood and dung are recommended first. The burning of these solid fuels brings us closest to the element of fire. Gas flame is next, then electric heat. Humankind has been cooking over fire for a long time and the practices of steaming, boiling, grilling and baking are incredibly well used. Microwaving is a novel invention and is not true heating. Using this type of radiation adversely affects the nutrients and life force in your meal. It fails to provide the link between the fire from the sun that grew the food and your own digestive fire. Using movement to create heat increases vata in a way that is undesirable to any dosha. Many of these recipes are one-pot meals that can be cooked over a camp fire. When it boils down to it, making food more digestible with fire caused a major ripple on this planet.

Reading the contents of your refrigerator is like telling your fortune. The more that is in it, the less energetic you will feel. Most items will probably be leftovers, having had heat or fermentation applied more than eight hours ago. This is how disorder is produced in your system, interfering with proper movement of nutrients and sapping your strength and clarity. In a temperate climate one really only needs a small fridge for most of the year, but don't let me talk you into it.

These recipes will be influenced by the cookware you use. What do you feel is the safest cookware? How well do you know its thermodynamics? Does the pot heat up and cool down fast or slow? The same instructions could cook vegetables into a stew that needs no added water in a heavy-walled pot and burn them to charcoal in a thin-walled one. Adjust the times suggested in these recipes in accordance with your cookware.

The essence of ayurvedic cuisine is to cook vegetables so that on a sliding scale they are neither tough nor disintegrated; to cook grains completely; to cook legumes and beans totally; to extract and heighten the essence of spices into warmed clarified butter, ghee, without scorching; to allow the ingredients to mingle together with warmth for awhile before serving; to add delicate fresh herbs at the end of cooking; to provide a meal that is fresh, warm and slightly oily and to adjust for the six tastes to be present in the right proportions. It takes a person acting with care to craft that.

A pressure cooker is a viable cooking vessel with attention given when using foods that foam. Four good quality pots can cost the price of a stove but the money spent on four pots of poor quality could buy one of good quality. Electrical appliances are not used in most of these recipes. This is because the agitation the food receives with an electrical appliance is visited on your disposition and because the energy that your hands impart is of great nutritional value. In Southeast Asian cuisine, we are specifically guided not to use electric blenders over hand methods because the texture will become boring. The choice is yours and your attitude towards what you are doing needs to be considered. If you are yet impatient with manual methods, use an appliance. A few kitchen gadgets will be used in the following recipes and simpler is better.

One important utensil is a good quality knife that is honed for its function before every use. It is more dangerous to use a blunt knife with force than a

17

sharp knife with ease. Chinese wisdom advises us that when we are finished with it, store it out of sight.

The proper storage conditions for foods vary for different items. Some foods do best with light, heat and moisture excluded. Grains of wheat recovered from inside the Egyptian pyramids were still capable of sprouting. It could be because of the dark, dry, insulated conditions within or it may be because of pyramid energy! Some foods need humidity, some need light. It is a practice of observation and experiment. If your ginger root goes moldy in the refrigerator, don't store it there. We refrigerate only what absolutely needs it because refrigeration increases kapha. If you buy carrots once a week and wrap the waiting-to-be-used ones each in brown paper, leaving them in the cool dark, they will remain fine and fresh unless you live in the tropics (where carrots do not like to grow anyway).

Some foods cause others to ripen quicker. Use that to your advantage by your ever-changing food arrangements. Whole foods will store longer than milled. A home grain mill can make fresh flours, nut butters and ground spices. Whole foods also have more life force than milled or split counterparts do. To exclude moths, ants and other small consumers, bay leaves in the jars may help. Whole cloves scattered in the cupboard may help. Let the shopkeeper know if you feel the integrity of the food is being compromised. In many countries, the merchant provides you a pantry and the cook buys food daily. As a better approach, ayurveda teaches us to investigate and then remove the cause of any dysfunction.

Ingredients are traditionally measured by hand, by weight in hand, by eye, by experience, by intuition. Since this is not a commercial cookbook, exact scale measurements are not critical and are included if they minimize discrepancy. We don't approach cooking in the same way as rocket science. In this book, one teaspoon equals five milliliters and one tablespoon is fifteen. If you add a tablespoon of salt instead of a teaspoon, you will know for next time.

The art of food combination and food non-combination is important. Firstly, there are few animal products (considered primary proteins) in these recipes to non-combine so that simplifies things. Fruits are best eaten by themselves or cooked to make them more compatible to eat with other foods. Raw milk is a complete food and the recommendation is to drink it, always boiled and spiced, then at room temperature if desired, on its own. Many westerners have become accustomed to mixing milk with other foods. Equally, there is no dairy to be found in Asian cuisine. Best not to combine milk with banana, cherries, melon or sour fruit even if all have been cooked. Mango and cucumber is not an affable combination. Ayurvedic texts indicate that combining starches with milk or dates is not good. That the nightshade family, including Cape gooseberry, tamarillo, eggplant, potato and peppers (capsicum), does not combine well with milk or cucumber. That eating foods from the nightshade family is not recommended at all by some ayurvedic lineages. That lemon should not be mixed with cucumber. That cooked and raw food should not be eaten in equal quantity at the same meal, but only when one is of a majority and the other a minority. That hot and cold food eaten at the same meal confuses digestion. That cold food retards digestion. And from this moment on, please do not heat honey or buy heat-processed honey or combine honey with an equal weight of ghee.

Leftovers are not recommended as food but medicinal food preparations may have had heat, time and blessings applied, making them elixirs. Items that are mostly of a sweet nature such as fruit jams are acceptable to store for a short time and other procedures such as parboiling are accepted as well.

You will come across other food combining recommendations in your reading and these presented could have exceptions, depending on the individual and the situation.

One of the guidelines in macrobiotics is to eat foods in season in your environment. This is a simple way to know what to choose to cook. If you don't yet know what is in season observe what is plentiful and offered at a lower price, which would probably reflect the local harvest. What is expensive may be imported from the other hemisphere. It would be unnatural if you had the ingredients for all of the following recipes in your home at any one time.

Also consider that even though an ingredient is available year round in your area it may be coming from a climatic zone that does not reflect your situation at the moment. For example, coconut grows only in hot climates and is cooling so wait until summer to use it or if you are a natural-born pitta or when you are experiencing pitta excess.

The closer we eat towards a whole food diet, the healthier it is. On the continuum of whole foods to compromised foods, take wheat as an example. Firstly, 'hard' wheat contains higher gluten protein. The majority of this variety is used with bran and germ removed in bread making. There are whole wheat varieties of hard wheat flour as well. Unyeasted baked goods made with this flour become tougher the more they are handled. Flat, unleavened breads are the ayurvedic alternative to yeasted breads and use 'soft' wheat, atta flour, which can be kneaded without becoming tough. Whole wheat flours have more character than sifted ones but can be coarse. Experiment with your variety of wheat flour.

Wheat is best eaten by pitta and vata constitutional people and even these people want to decline wheat for breakfast, snack, lunch and dinner. Best is to sprout (or not sprout) and cook whole wheat berries well with digestive spices. Or crack the wheat, ideally just before cooking. This lessens cooking time. Still add some pungent spices or herbs to aid digestion and balance its earthy nature. Bulgur wheat has already been partially cooked and is not then sattwic. Rolled wheat and most other rolled grains have been steamed in order to make them soft enough to flatten, so we minimize these too. Wholemeal flour is ground from whole wheat berries and if milled on that day it is good nutrition. The longer it is stored, the more the wheat germ deterioration is compromising its safety. Some industrial milling of whole wheat flour does remove the wheat germ, the sattwic component. This gives it longer shelf life but less wholeness. Check out your brand.

When flour is made into flatbread, cake and shaped wheat and gluten products it falls from grace if heat was applied and you eat it days later. The amount of processing it has been subject to is also a consideration. Extracting gluten protein and shaping it into products that look and taste like meat seems unnecessary.

Flour and water combine as pasta and if not pre-cooked, is appropriate. Best is to prepare it fresh. Traditional couscous begins like pasta and is hand-rolled and dried. How long it remains like that influences its desirability. Instant couscous is steamed and dried again, therefore not sattwic.

Now imagine a food enterprise turning dry, stale bread into breadcrumbs, coating vegetables with it, cooking them, freezing them and selling the product to you with instructions to heat in a microwave. That is ultimate insult to the most noble of grains and to us.

Deep-frying with fresh oil is appropriate in theory only for vata constitutional people with strong digestion. This in itself is a rare occurrence. Mentally it causes restlessness reflecting the subjection of the food to a procedure of very hot and fast. Physically it is taxing to the digestive process. Anyway, is it not absurd to take fresh cold-pressed organic oil, use it just once for deep-frying, and then use it to polish furniture or something? Steer away from this method of cooking.

In using oil for baking, sautéing and salad dressings, cold-pressed organic oils in dark glass bottles are the superior option. Toasted and blended oils have been subject to adverse measures.

Smile if you recognize that like all other diet plans, ayurveda has a point of view. In understanding ayurvedic recommendations, we appreciate diet, lifestyle and mental disposition as major contributors to health. One diet is not appropriate for everyone.

This is because the different dosha constitutions need different amounts of the five elements that foods contain in different amounts. Vata needs less airy foods, pitta needs less fiery foods and kapha needs less earthy foods.

The foods that produce sattwa are praised over others. When rajas and tamas override their natural percentages and no longer support sattwa, the mind either leads us to wilfully perverse choices or loses the plot altogether.

The majority of these meals are pure vegetarian so how do milk, soft cheese and ghee hold such an honored position? Why do we include these animal products? Is it because the cow is sacred in India, a manifestation of the divine mother?

One explanation is offered through biodynamics, which developed in Europe without any religious bias to the cow. The cow is the supreme metabolic miracle. Most of the energy it takes in is converted to useful products for others. (On the other side of the metabolic spectrum is the wee mouse. Most of what it takes in is dissipated in movement and nervous energy.) Granted the cow is rumored to have little on its mind except for eating, thus the humorous hypothesis that it has but one neuron and when that neuron is occupied one can do anything to it. That's not really true. Whilst the animal is mellow and unthreatening, its excellences can be spoiled by the treatment and environment it experiences. As with all foods, we ingest the chemicals/practices that have been concentrated up the food chain into them. Only fresh raw milk from well-treated cows is purely sattwic. Even this milk should be brought to boil and have digestive spices added which offset mucus formation.

Ghee is another sattwic food. It interweaves all the components of a dish together. It helps both digestive and tissue metabolism. It soothes the nerves and mind.

Yogurt is not included in this cookbook because it is fermented. In essence and taste, it is compatible to vata constitutions taken at room temperature or warmer during daylight hours but its fermentation may produce indigestion. If you did want a cultured milk product, allow 3 hours maximum incubation with the yogurt culture. In that way, it can help digestion.

There are as many reasons to support the use of milk and its products as there are disputing it. Ultimately the choice is yours, based on your actual experiences and as free from mental bias and media debate as possible. If you wish to make use of pure milk, it will take time to allow the body to become non-allergic to what commercial milk products have caused to happen. Ayurveda recommends pure cow's milk for vata and pitta and pure goat's milk for kapha individuals.

Then there is that wonderful medicine, garlic. As with all foods that are good for us in the right quantity at certain times, these same foods can become unbalancing if taken in excess or at the wrong times. Some schools of ayurveda recommend garlic for daily intake, others do not. Have you noticed in the list of foods producing restlessness of mind, rajas, that garlic is included? Garlic's action begins as aggressive and penetrating and eventually produces dullness, tamas, in one's disposition. To harness garlic's useful penetrating quality, a small amount of garlic can be used in basil pesto (using earth salt instead of cheese) in cold weather. And historically, garlic has been given a wide berth by religious orders, in part because it is an aphrodisiac. In some circumstances that's a good thing!

Ayurveda promotes the fulfilment of a happy, healthy, productive life. Still, it does not happen just by reading these words, it happens through actions. All people improve in some degree when using ayurvedic recommendations. Sattwic diet is one of them.

If you find that the foods you eat are not included in these recipes it could be as follows. It is fine to eat: it is a fresh fruit, vegetable, grain, legume, seed, nut, liquid, herb or spice which doesn't produce rajas or tamas; it is simple to prepare and if all tastes are present with it in a meal it is great to eat with proper cooking and spicing; I haven't discovered or had access to it yet; it does not pass the sattwa test in the way it has been processed; it may interfere with complete digestion.

APPRAISING RECIPES

Take any recipe in this cookbook and feel free to interchange vegetables, pulses, grains, herbs and spices on occasion. It is not that "Potatoes, Peas and Lettuce" always needs to have peas. It could come out as potatoes, green beans and spinach. If you use any food often, it is worthwhile looking up its reported effect on your dosha/s and being alert to its actual effect.

In learning anything new, it takes recapitulation to understand what has been suggested. When I come back to a recipe I have not used in awhile, I need to begin again and sort the steps out along with the ingredients. Perhaps writing the recipe down would be helpful so that hand, eye and mind have taken it in.

Take any recipe in any book and scan for already-cooked ingredients. Can you procure the fresh option? Use that. Perhaps you can use a substitute. Scan for onions and garlic and unless prescribed by your ayurvedic physician, use pungent asafoetida instead, a little goes a long way. Asafoetida is the dried sap from a plant related to fennel. It helps all downward movements in our bodies. If you choose to eat animal products consult dosha food lists for the best options. Red wine, is it really consumed for its anti-oxidant properties? There are anti-oxidants in fresh fruit, vegetables, spices and herbs. Ayurveda provides recipes for diverse medicinal herbal wines, taken for health in specified situations. Scan the recipe for other rajasic or tamasic ingredients and ask what part they play in the recipe as far as taste and substance. Explore how you can better approach that. Practice a willingness to liberate some recipes from your repertoire.

Vata constitutional people use oil in cooking and can use cooking methods such as sautéing that produce moist and unctuous results. Covered oven casseroles and thick soups are other examples. Their meals are eaten warm and can be comprised of savory foods more than purely sweet ones. Pitta constitutional people can use cooking methods such as steaming which produce a less heated or oily meal, generally allowing food to cool down before eating. Baking is another good method. Ghee is the best oil for them. Their best meals are sweet and slightly bitter. Kapha constitutional people can choose cooking methods which dry or lighten the food such as uncovered baking or puffing/popping and use minimal oil. Notice that even though beans are cooked in boiling water, when drained their texture is dry. Kapha meals are taken warm and can be comprised of pungent and bitter foods.

Think in terms of six tastes. Scan the recipe and notice if all are present. The sweet taste is in all foods grown that have chlorophyll and does not just mean sugar. Milk, cream, ghee and meat are also sweet. It is the basic taste in what we eat and is sattwic when unprocessed and no harm has been caused to the animal source. Sweet is the taste of love. We seek to be sweet, but an excess for some people can lead to desire and possessiveness.

The salty taste is found mainly in salt and a few grains provide it. Salt helps the other tastes express their character. Earth salt has less sodium and more additional minerals than sea salt and is useful in all savory dishes. The salty taste promotes digestion, is moistening and softening if used in the proper amount. If used in excess by some people, it causes them to behave like an 'old salt', a sailor on leave, greedy for gratification.

The sour taste is in citrus and many stone fruits, sorrel, tamarind, sumac berry powder, green mango powder and rose hips. Its action in moderation promotes digestion and increases strength and invigoration. An excess of this taste can produce the mental states of criticism, dissatisfaction and envy, 'sour grapes'.

The pungent taste is the sharpness of black pepper on the tongue and is found in particular herbs, spices and vegetables. Taste for that sharpness in thyme, oregano and ginger and apply that sensory understanding to evaluate other foods. The actions of this taste include relieving stagnation and promoting digestion. In excess for some people, it can cause hostility.

The bitter taste is available in leafy greens like dandelion and endive. The bitter part of citrus peel is useful in small amounts. Aloe vera gel-juice (certified stable for optimum therapeutic strength) provides the bitter taste. It does not take long to recognize the bitter taste in vegetables, herbs and spices and in small amounts is to be sought after. It provides the action of detoxification. Psychologically, an excess can produce aversion and fear.

The astringent effect in the mouth is a drawing, drying, contracting feeling and is present to some degree in all fruits and vegetables, more so in under-ripe ones. Taste an unripe banana to get the feeling. Or become aware of the feeling while drinking a cup of green tea. The astringent action in the proper amount in the body is drying, firming and contracting. It promotes absorption of body fluids and healing. An excess can cause fear, anxiety and depression.

Therefore, a drop of lemon juice satisfies the sour requirement and a grate of its zest and pith the bitter requirement. Easy, eh? In addition, most foods, herbs and spices have more than one taste. Cinnamon bark is sweet, pungent, bitter and astringent. Can you detect them all? If the recipe just would not work with all the tastes, include the missing taste(s) in a side dish or beverage at the same meal.

Also note that major contributors to dosha balance include whether the food's effect on the body is light, easy to digest (good for all doshas) or heavy (taxing to digestion); moistening (good for vata, neutral for pitta) or drying (good for kapha); unctuous (good for vata) or less oleating (good for pitta and kapha) and heating which stimulates digestion and metabolism (good for kapha, by and large good for vata) or cooling (good for pitta). Be aware that there are some foods that behave independent of expected effect. Applaud them for prompting us to release ourselves from following instructions mindlessly.

Was that too much information? Then use the recipes intrepidly and ask questions later.

Bakery, Savory

BROCCOLI PASTRIES

We gain experience and exercise creativity through action.

The Pastry	The Filling	
2 cups wheat flour	flowerets of 1/2 broccoli	asafoetida
1/4 tsp nutmeg	1 tbsp fresh parsley	1 tsp paprika
1/2 tsp earth or sea salt	1 tsp fresh thyme	1/2 tsp earth or
150 gm = 5 oz butter	1 tbsp ghee	sea salt
6 tbsp cold water	1 tsp cumin seed	1 tsp lemon juice

1. To prepare pastry combine flour, nutmeg and salt. Cut in sweet butter to the size of peas. Add cold water, mixing until water is just absorbed. Add up to 30 ml = 2 tablespoons additional water if needed. Gather into three spheres, cover and keep cool. Pastry bakes flaky if the dough is cool, the oven is hot and we don't homogenize the butter into the flour.
2. To prepare filling mince broccoli. In a separate pile mince parsley to 1 tablespoon and rub thyme leaflets off stems to 1 teaspoon.
3. Warm the tablespoon of ghee in a medium skillet over medium heat. Add cumin seeds, sauté 1 minute and lower heat.
4. Add broccoli, a sprinkle asafoetida and sauté until broccoli is tender.
5. Add fresh herbs or half the amount of dried herbs.
6. Add paprika, salt and lemon juice. Let cool thoroughly.
7. Some time in the next two steps preheat oven to 425°F (220°C, Gas 7). Collect 2 large baking trays.
8. To assemble: work with one sphere of the dough. Divide it into 8 sections. On a lightly floured surface roll out one section with minimal handling into a 7.5 cm = 3 inch round.
9. Place 2 teaspoons of drained filling just below the center and fold in half. Seal opening and trim. (Total excess pastry will make three more wrappers.)
10. Place completed pastries on lightly oiled baking sheet and keep cool. Proceed until the first baking sheet is full and place in oven on the lower shelf. Bake for 12 - 15 minutes until pastry is light brown. Prepare pastries for the second sheet and bake.
11. Let pastries cool on the baking sheets. Arrange carefully to serve.

Makes 27. North American Influence, Southern U.S.

Of this recipe,	To fine-tune,
Kapha, enjoy less	enjoy the filling without the pastry
Pitta, enjoy some	nutmeg, thyme and paprika can be decreased
Vata, enjoy more	cooked broccoli in this amount is O.K.

BAKED IN HALF MOON SHAPES.

CORNBREAD

Maize is the grain of Saturn.

The Wet
1 tbsp dried chives
1 tsp dried sage
1 cup water
1/2 tsp earth or sea salt
1/2 tsp palm or unrefined cane sugar
2 tbsp sunflower oil

The Dry
3/4 cup fine cornmeal
3/4 cup millet flour
1/2 cup wheat flour, any variety
pine nuts, optional

1. Preheat oven to 400°F (200°C, Gas 6). Oil a 20 cm = 8 inch square.
2. Combine the dried herbs and water and let the herbs rehydrate. Add the salt, sugar and oil. If you have fresh herbs use 2 teaspoons chopped sage and 2 tablespoons chopped chives.
3. Combine cornmeal and flours in a bowl.
4. Begin adding liquid to dry ingredients with minimal mixing, perhaps observing the ability of liquid to aid cohesion.
5. Add additional water until a moist, non-runny batter is achieved.
6. Bake 25 minutes until tester is dry and edges are golden.

Serves 6. The Americas - Italian Influence.

Of this recipe,   To customize,
Kapha, enjoy more .... oil in this amount divided amongst 6 people is O.K.
Pitta, enjoy less .... maize is not recommended; have a wheat-based baked savory with cumin, coriander and mint
Vata, enjoy less .... delete the millet flour and replace with wheat flour; use ghee instead of sunflower oil; the pine nut option is for you with which to decorate the top

SIMPLE MIX, BAKING WHILE YOU PREPARE VEGETABLES OR SOUP.

FILLED FLATBREAD

The modern supermarket sells very little real food.

Flour, 4 cups: rye-barley for kapha; wheat, any variety, for pitta and vata
Earth or Sea Salt: 1/4 tsp for kapha and pitta; 1/2 tsp for vata
Olive Oil: 1 tsp for kapha; 1 tbsp for pitta; 3 tbsp for vata
Water: about 1 1/4 cups

1. Place flour and salt on flat surface or in bowl. Rub in oil.
2. Form a hollow in the flour and work water in to form soft, smooth dough. Knead for 5 minutes and let rest covered with a damp cloth while the filling is prepared.

Potato Pea Filling:

> 1 kg = about 2 lbs small potatoes
> 300 gm = 10 oz peas in pod yielding 1/2 cup or 1 handful snow
>   peas

> <u>The Seasonings</u>
> 2 tbsp olive oil and extra for baking
> 1 tsp fennel seed
> 1 tbsp oregano
> 1 tsp basil
> 3/4 tsp mint
> 1 tsp orange zest
> 3/4 tsp earth or sea salt
> black peppercorns

1. Boil potatoes whole, covered, until soft, about 20 minutes.
2. Shell the peas. Add to the potatoes in their last 8 minutes of cooking. Or trim and finely cut snow peas to 1/2 cup and add for 5 minutes.
3. Drain peas and potatoes. Cool potatoes and remove skins.
4. Warm oil in a large skillet over low heat. Add fennel and sauté half a minute. Add peas and potatoes. Mash potatoes adding oregano, basil, mint and zest. Sauté several minutes.
5. Mix in salt, a few turns of fresh ground pepper and remove from heat. Let cool, uncovered.
6. Preheat oven to 400°F (200°C, Gas 6). Olive oil 2 large baking sheets.
7. To assemble, divide dough into 10 pieces. Roll out one at a time into a circle, not too thin, and fill with one tenth of the vegetables. Place the vegetable mound in the lower half of the circle leaving some dough free to seal. Seal by folding into a semi-circle, wetting and pressing edges together and trimming excess dough. If the rye-barley dough is too crumbly either add more water or let rest for longer next time.

8. Set flatbreads on trays, prick tops with fork and oil tops lightly.
9. Bake 20 minutes, or until golden around the edges and bottoms.

Makes 10. European Influence, Greece.

Of this recipe,   To accommodate your dosha,
Kapha, enjoy more
Pitta, enjoy more ....decrease oil, oregano and pepper
Vata, enjoy some ....decrease filling as potatoes are drying

BAKED POCKETS WITH SAVORY FILLING.

OATCAKES

As soon as we do not require dough to rise, we regain all grain flours for flatbread.

1/2 cup water

1 tbsp sunflower oil
1/2 tsp ginger powder
2 tsp coriander seeds, crushed, or 1 tsp powder

1/2 cup coarse oatmeal
1/2 cup medium oatmeal
1/2 cup fine oatmeal or a total of 1 1/2 cups fine oatmeal

1/2 tsp earth or sea salt

1. Preheat oven to 300°F (150°C, Gas 2).
2. Put water to boil.
3. Warm oil in a small skillet over medium low heat. Add ginger and coriander, swirl and heat 2 minutes.
4. Place oats in a mixing bowl and add skillet mix.
5. Dissolve salt in the boiling water.
6. Slowly add 4-7 teaspoons of the water to the oats to make a firm mix.
7. Dust a flat surface with oats and roll dough into a circle with a sprinkle of oats on top, 1.5 cm = 1/2 inch thickness.
8. Cut into 8 wedges and place on ungreased baking sheet.
9. Bake in the center of the oven for 30 minutes. The wedges will still be pale and the center will be dry. Avoid browning these little gems.

Makes 8 small wedges. Scottish Influence.

Of this recipe,   To modify,
Kapha, enjoy more
Pitta, enjoy some ....instead of oil use 1 1/2 tbsp ghee
Vata, enjoy less.............use 1 1/2 tbsp ghee; top with something rich and unctuous and still enjoy only on occasion

OAT WEDGES ARE BAKED IN A SLOW OVEN.

PINE and THYME

What shall be communicated with the preparation and presentation of this food?

2 ample tbsp fresh thyme or 1 tbsp dried

The Batter
2 cups water
2 tbsp olive oil
1/2 tsp earth or sea salt
1/2 tsp black pepper
1/2 cup buckwheat flour
1 1/2 cups wheat flour, any variety

The Topping
1/2 cup pine nuts
a sprinkle of paprika

1. Back comb the thyme off its stems.
2. Preheat oven to 375°F (190°C, Gas 5). Oil a 22 x 32 cm = 9 x 13 inch baking dish.
3. Place water into a mixing bowl; mix in oil, salt, pepper and thyme.
4. Add flours and mix until just combined.
5. Add batter to baking dish, spreading thin, imbedding the nuts into the top and dusting with paprika.
6. Bake for 35 minutes, until the edges and bottom are golden.

Serves 6-8. European Influence, Italy.

Of this recipe,   Enjoy more if you,
Kapha, enjoy less .... use rye instead of wheat flour and less nuts
Pitta, enjoy some .... choose more wheat, less buckwheat; decrease thyme, pepper and nuts; just a sprinkle of anything is O.K.
Vata, enjoy some.. .... choose more wheat, less buckwheat

HERB INFUSES THE BATTER, PINE NUTS TEXTURE THE TOP.

POTATO CAKES

*In noticing an unknown item at the market, ask the vendor
how to prepare it, then buy it and try it.*

3 large potatoes
2 tbsp ghee
1/2 cup wheat flour, any variety
1/2 tsp earth or sea salt

Sweet	Savory
1 apple	1/2 tsp black pepper
1 tsp unrefined sugar	fresh or dried herbs
1 tsp cinnamon	a few seeds, nigella for example

1. Boil the potatoes in their skins until soft, peel and mash.
2. Combine potatoes with ghee, flour and salt, making a soft 'dough'.
3. Preheat oven to 350°F (180°C, Gas 4).
4. Rub some ghee in the bottom of 8-12 individual baking or muffin cups. Push aside one third of the potato dough in the bowl for the topping. Apportion the rest into the baking cups.
5. For the sweet variation, place a 1 cm = 1/2 inch thick slice of peeled apple over the potatoes, sprinkling with sugar and cinnamon. Top with potato dough to cover.
6. Sprinkle again with cinnamon and ghee.
7. Bake for 35-40 minutes, or until golden around the edges and bottom.
8. For the savory variation, place the potato dough in the baking cups, sprinkle with black pepper and herbs, top with the remaining dough and imbed a few seeds. Bake as above.

Serves 4. Scottish Influence.

Of this recipe,	To enjoy more,
Kapha, enjoy some	use rye flour or no flour at all; use less sugar and ghee
Pitta, enjoy more	use less of the savory ingredients if they are pungent
Vata, enjoy some	potato and apple are O.K. on occasion, the ghee and wheat balance their drying tendency; slice the apple thinner so that it cooks through

POTATO DOUGH ENCLOSES TWO FILLINGS.

RYE ROUNDS

The colon absorbs life force from well-digested food.

2 cups rye flour
2 tsp ghee
1/2 tsp earth or sea salt
1/4 tsp fennel seed
less than 1 cup water

1. Combine flour, ghee, salt and seeds on a working surface or in a bowl, making a well in the center.
2. Add water to the center a little at a time, drawing in flour, making pliable dough. As in all dough recipes, the nature of the flour and the humidity of the environment affect how much water to add.
3. Knead for 3 minutes and let rest for 15 covered with a damp cloth.
4. Preheat oven to 400°F (200°C, Gas 6). Have ready one baking tray.
5. Roll dough out to 2 cm = just under 1 inch in height. Cut out 6 cm = 2 inch circles and remove an inner circle, about 2 cm of dough with an apple corer. Reshape the remnants to make a total of 8 rounds. Prick holes in each donut with a skewer.
6. Bake for 20 minutes, until the bottoms are just starting to become golden.

Makes 8 rounds. Scandinavian Influence, Sweden.

Of this recipe,   To fine-tune,
Kapha, enjoy more
Pitta and Vata, enjoy less, use wheat flour instead and more ghee

SOMETHING TO SINK YOUR TEETH INTO, COMPANY TO SOUP
OR VEGETABLES.

SAFFRON CRACKERS

Our internal system is always accommodating change.

1/4 cup water
1/4 tsp lightly measured saffron
   threads
1 tbsp palm or unrefined cane sugar
3/4 tsp earth or sea salt

2 cups wheat flour, any variety

The Skillet Mix
1/4 cup ghee
1 tbsp beige and/or black sesame seeds
3 tsp allspice
3/4 tsp nutmeg
3/4 tsp ground white or black pepper

1. Warm the water and soak the saffron threads in it for 30 minutes, swirling now and then. Get closer to the unfolding with a magnifying glass. In the last several minutes stir in and dissolve the sugar and salt.
2. In a small skillet warm the ghee over medium heat. Add the sesame seeds and sauté until the beige ones are light brown. Remove skillet from heat, let cool somewhat and swirl in the allspice, nutmeg and pepper, developing their digestive properties.
3. Preheat oven to 375°F (190°C, Gas 5). Have ready 2 baking sheets.
4. In a mixing bowl combine flour, the skillet ingredients and saffron mix. Knead into soft dough. If too crumbly add more water.
5. Roll out on a lightly floured surface to 7.5mm = 1/4 inch thick. Cut shapes of choice. Place on baking sheets and prick holes with a fork. Bake 20 minutes until golden. Let cool to become crisp.

Makes 24 crackers, 4cm = 2 inch. Mediterranean Influence, Greece.

Of this recipe,   To enjoy more,
Kapha, enjoy less ....the spice blend is the best part of this for you; use it over vegetables or staples or in the Rye Rounds recipe
Pitta, enjoy some ....decrease the allspice, pepper, nutmeg and sesame
Vata, enjoy more...........as well as being heating the spice mix is drying, decrease allspice and pepper

UNUSUAL BLEND OF PUNGENT.

SAVORY CAKE with HERBS

Sattwic food nourishes the body and mind, association with sattwic people nourishes the mind and soul.

The Herbs
4 cm = 1 1/2 inches rosemary
1 tbsp packed fresh chives
1 tbsp packed coriander stems

1 1/2 cups water, maybe more
3/4 tsp earth or sea salt

The Flours
1/4 cup rye flour
1/2 cup millet flour
1 1/4 cups wheat flour, any variety
1/4 cup olive oil
1/4 tsp ground black pepper

1/4 cup linseed

1. Preheat oven to 400°F (200°C, Gas 6). Coat a 22cm = 9 inch round with olive oil.
2. Back comb rosemary for memory from its branch. The aroma and properties of the camphorous component clear the brain. Chop it with the chives and coriander stems.
3. Place water in mixing bowl, dissolving in salt.
4. Add flours, oil, pepper and herbs with minimal mixing. Although not a batter, this is a moist mass that holds together. Add more water if too dry.
5. Add linseed.
6. Spread in prepared round baking dish and bake for 35 minutes, or until a tester in the center denotes the cake is done and the edges and bottom are golden.

Makes 8 slices. The Americas and Italian Influence.

Of this recipe,   To fine-tune,
Kapha, enjoy some .... use sunflower oil and rye flour instead of wholemeal; decrease the linseed
Pitta, enjoy some .... use mostly wholemeal flour and less rosemary, chives, black pepper, linseed and oil
Vata, enjoy some .... use mostly wholemeal flour

HERBS AND GRAIN FLOURS PROVIDE NOVEL TASTE.

SEED CRACKERS

Home cooking is stacking up better and better.

between 1 and 4 tbsp wattle, portulaca, amaranth, linseed,
a small amount of poppyseeds (they induce drowsiness),
other small mild seeds or a combination of your choice
1 1/2 cups wheat flour, any variety
1/2 tsp black peppercorns
1/2 tsp earth or sea salt
2 tbsp ghee
1/2 cup water

1. Crush large seeds and peppercorns coarsely and blend with flour, salt and small seeds in a bowl or on a flat surface.
2. Add ghee and slowly add water, kneading until a pliable dough is formed.
3. Knead for 5 minutes. Let rest 15 minutes, covered with a damp cloth.
4. Preheat oven to 325°F (170°C, Gas 3). Oil 2 medium baking trays with a thin film of ghee.
5. Divide into quarters.
6. Roll each on a lightly floured surface into a 150 cm = 6 inch square or equivalent.Cut 6 crackers, shapes of choice.
7. Place on baking sheets and bake 15 minutes. Flip and bake until light brown, perhaps another 10 minutes.
8. Cool on racks.

Serves 4. Antipodean Influence, Australia.

Of this recipe,   To refine,
Kapha, enjoy less ....use rye, barley and/or millet flours instead of wheat; use 1 tsp sunflower oil and 1 tsp ghee and only a sprinkle of seeds; the dry baked texture is good
Pitta, enjoy more ....decrease black pepper and use less seeds
Vata, enjoy some ....although ghee and seeds are used, the crackers are still dry: you could butter them

SEEDS PROVIDE TEXTURE FOR SIGHT AND SOUND.

BAKERY, SWEET

BLUEBERRY LEMON MINI CAKES

When J enter the door, J do so in peace.

1 lemon
1/4 cup ghee
1 tsp ginger powder
1/4 tsp sea salt
1 1/2 cups water
a generous 1/4 cup palm or unrefined cane sugar
1 1/2 cups wheat flour, any variety
1 cup blueberries, fresh are best, stems removed

1. Preheat oven to 350°F (180°C, Gas 4).
2. Grate the rind releasing the lemon oil, collect the rind and then juice the lemon.
3. Warm ghee in small skillet over medium low heat and add ginger powder. Remove from heat, swirl and add salt. Swirl again.
4. Mix together water, sugar and 2 teaspoons lemon zest in a bowl.
5. Add flour until just combined. Add skillet mix and just over half the berries. Fold in gently, thoroughly, with minimal mixing.
6. Oil 8 muffin cups with a film of ghee.
7. Spoon batter in and distribute remaining berries on top, pressing in.
8. Bake 30 minutes until done, the edges turning golden.
9. Add a few drops of lemon juice on top of each while still warm.

Serves 6-8. English Influence.

Of this recipe,   Alternatively,
Kapha, enjoy less .... use much less ghee or sunflower oil; use millet, rye and/ or barley flour instead of wheat; use less lemon juice on top
Pitta, enjoy some .... delete lemon juice and then enjoy more
Vata, enjoy more .... starch plus fruit may produce wind, in which case delete the fruit next time; starch plus lemon juice may also produce indigestion, in which case delete the juice

MOIST, COLORFUL, BEAUTIFUL TASTE.

COCONUT COOKIES

It is satisfying to find creative solution.

Skillet Ingredients
1 1/2 cups dried coconut
3/4 cup ghee or coconut oil
1 tsp cinnamon
1/2 tsp ginger powder
1/4 tsp nutmeg

1/2 cup palm or unrefined cane sugar
1/2 tsp sea salt
3 1/4 cups flour, any variety
a generous 1/2 cup water
8 whole cloves

1. Preheat oven to 350°F (180°C, Gas 4). Have ready several baking sheets.
2. Toast coconut in medium skillet over medium low heat watching the change of color. Transfer to holding bowl.
3. Dissolve ghee or oil in the skillet and add cinnamon, ginger and nutmeg. Sauté at low heat for 1 minute.
4. Combine most of the sugar, salt and flour in a bowl. Add skillet contents and mix with a flat paddle.
5. Add coconut. Add water. Gather into a firm, pliable, unctuous dough.
6. Oil your palms up to the fingers and form 8 large cookies, 1.5 cm = 1/2 inches high, shapes of choice.
7. Imbed a whole clove into each or sprinkle powdered cloves on the center.
8. Sprinkle the cookies with the remaining sugar and press in.
9. Bake for 25 minutes or until bottoms are light brown.

Yields 8 with 10 cm = 4 inch diameter. Caribbean Influence.

Of this recipe,   To modify,
Kapha, enjoy less .... it can't be done without altering the design
Pitta and vata, enjoy one of these biscuits, maybe less

VERY RICH WITH TROPICAL SPICES AND COCONUT ROLLED TOGETHER.

DATE SLICE

In biological terms the specimen is always right. In human experience the mind can influence the outcome.

1 generous cup dates

<u>The Base</u>
1 cup wheat flour, any variety
3/4 cup rolled oats
2 tbsp water
1 1/2 tsp ginger powder
1/4 tsp sea salt
1/4 cup ghee

1 orange
1/4 cup walnut pieces

1. Chop the dates into small pieces and let soak in a small saucepan with water to cover while preparing the rest of the slice.
2. For the base, combine flour, oats, water, ginger and salt. Knead in the ghee until the mass sticks together. Set aside.
3. Grate the orange zest to the amount of 2 teaspoons.
4. Bring dates and water to boil and simmer 10 minutes, covered.
5. Add 2/3 of the orange rind and cook uncovered until texture is spreadable without being dry. Remove from heat and add a sprinkle of salt.
6. Meanwhile, preheat oven to 350°F (180°C, Gas 4). Have ready a 20 cm = 8 inch baking square.
7. Press the base into the baking square and etch it into 9 pieces. Deliver a dollop of the date sauce over each square and embed the walnuts into the top.
8. Bake for 30 minutes.
9. Let cool a few minutes and then decorate with the remaining orange zest.

Serves 6-9. Middle Eastern and Western World Influence.

Of this recipe,
Kapha, enjoy less, just a taste if you fancy it
Pitta, enjoy more
Vata, enjoy more............recall that dates and starch may not be a good combination

STICKY ORANGE DATE PURÉE BAKED ONTO AN OAT PASTRY BASE.

FILLED ORANGE CRESCENTS

One can find blossoms and fruit on an orange tree at the same time but not all grapes in a bunch ripen together.

The Dough
3/4 cup water
12 orange blossoms, optional
2 cups wheat flour
1/2 tsp sea salt
2 tbsp sunflower oil

The Filling
3/4 cup almonds
1/2 tsp cinnamon
2 tbsp orange water or pure water
2 tbsp palm or unrefined cane sugar
1 tsp finely grated orange zest

1. Combine the 3/4 cup of water and the orange blossoms. Infuse 6 hours at room temperature. If blossoms unavailable just use the water in subsequent steps.
2. Meanwhile, soak almonds for the filling separately.
3. When you are ready to prepare the crescents, heat almonds in a small amount of warm water until skins swell. Cool, remove skins. Grate or blend into meal and cover to keep moist.
4. For the dough, combine flour and salt and work in oil with fingers.
5. Remove blossoms and add orange water to the flour mix to form a soft mass, starting with half a cup. Save 2 tablespoons of orange water for step 9.
6. Knead for a few minutes and set aside, covered, while you prepare the filling.
7. Dissolve the sugar in 2 tablespoons of (orange) water.
8. Combine all filling ingredients to a soft paste.
9. Preheat oven to 375°F (190°C, Gas 5) and oil 2 small baking sheets.
10. Roll dough out thinly on a lightly floured surface to a 40 x 34 cm = 18 x 14 inch rectangle. Cut into 7 cm = 3 inch squares.
11. Form 1 teaspoon filling into a cylinder about 5 cm = 2 inches long and place along the lower edge of each square, leaving outer edges unfilled. Complete this step for all squares.
12. Roll dough up around the filling and seal the outer edges together by rolling back and forth with gentle pressure. Mold into a crescent. Trim excess dough from edges if necessary. If dough and filling do not come out even, you have a chance to create something different. Some flours will make softer doughs than others and temperature and humidity will influence the crescents.
13. Bake 20 minutes, or until bottoms are becoming golden. Cool and serve.

Makes 24. North African Influence, Morocco.
Of this recipe,   To modify,
Kapha, enjoy less .... use rye flour, which will be coarser to work with, and less filling per crescent
Pitta, enjoy some
Vata, enjoy more

DELICATE ORANGE-ALMOND FILLING, BITE-SIZE WRAPPERS.

HAZELNUT BISCUITS

Listen to us Father, Grandfather. We ask thought, heart,
love, happiness. We are going to eat.
  – Arapaho Prayer

1 cup hazelnuts
1 cup ghee or sweet butter
1/2 cup palm or unrefined cane sugar
1/2 tsp sea salt
1/4 tsp nutmeg
1 1/2 cups wheat flour, any variety
2 tbsp carob powder, optional

1. Heat oven to 400°F (200°C, Gas 6). Roast hazelnuts for 3 minutes. Remove
   and lower heat to 325°F (160°C, Gas 3). Place nuts between 2 towels. Rub
   off and blow away whatever bran you can, crush nuts and set aside.
2. Have ready 2 medium baking sheets.
3. Combine sugar, salt, nutmeg, flour and carob. Add ghee and knead into
   dough. Add nuts.
4. Pinch off 1 tablespoon pieces, roll into spheres and place on dry, cool baking sheet.
5. Press the bottom of a glass into some flour and lightly press biscuits flat with
   it. You could etch designs in the top.
6. Bake 30 minutes until edges are darkening.
7. Cool on baking sheets.

Makes 30 biscuits. European Influence, Ireland.

Of this recipe,	Can it be modified?
Kapha, enjoy less	not without changing the recipe
Pitta, enjoy some	decrease the nuts and still enjoy just some
Vata, enjoy more	without over-indulging

CAROB AND NUTMEG COMPLEMENT HAZELNUTS IN THESE RICH
BISCUITS.

LOQUAT TART

Ride the wave of energy that a new start provides.

The Base
1 1/4 cups almonds
1 medium lemon
1/2 cup ghee or sweet butter
1/4 cup palm or unrefined cane sugar
2 tsp cinnamon
1/4 tsp sea salt
1 cup wheat flour, any variety

The Fruit
24 loquats, 16 apricots or other fruit
extra sugar
cinnamon
almond oil

1. Heat almonds in a small amount of warm water until skins swell. When cooler, remove skins. Grate or process the nuts into medium-fine meal and cover to keep moist.
2. Preheat oven to 325°F (160°C, Gas 3).
3. Grate the rind of the entire lemon. In a mixing bowl cream ghee and sugar. Add lemon rind, cinnamon and salt and create an even-colored consistency.
4. Add almonds.
5. Add flour, creating a rich dough.
6. Spread some ghee or butter onto the bottom of a 20 cm = 8 inch baking dish. Press dough to cover the entire bottom of the dish.
7. Bake for 30 minutes.
8. Meanwhile, peel and seed fruit and cut into medium-small dice. Toss with some cinnamon, sugar and oil. If using firmer fruit like apples, cook first for 10 minutes on the stovetop.
9. Distribute fruit on top of base after the half hour and bake 10-15 minutes more.
10. Let cool completely, then cut and serve with your choice of garnish.

Serves 8-10. European Influence, Austria.

Of this recipe,   To customize,
Kapha, enjoy less .... this is best enjoyed only as a taste if you choose
Pitta, enjoy some .... decrease almonds; use well-ripened fruit
Vata, enjoy more .... if fruit and starch produce wind, have either the base or the topping

LINZERTORTE PASTRY BAKES WHILE THE MEDLAR TOPPING IS PREPARED.

MULBERRY TARTS

Who was it who said if we spent the time cooking instead of watching a cooking program, we'd actually get to eat the food?

The Pastry
2 cups wheat flour, any variety
1/2 tsp sea salt
150 gm = 5 oz sweet butter
2 tsp minced orange zest
90-120 ml = 6-8 tbsp cold water

The Filling
1 cup almonds
4 cups mulberries or other berries
1 tbsp palm or unrefined cane sugar

1. Prepare pastry by combining flour and salt and cutting butter in until it resembles coarse cornmeal. Add zest.
2. Add water to flour mixture and mix until water is just absorbed. Wrap and keep cool.
3. Warm almonds, heating in water until the skins swell. Cool.
4. To prepare filling, remove mulberry stems and sprinkle on sugar.
5. Remove almond skins, grate or process into fine meal. Cover to keep moist.
6. Preheat oven to 425°F (220°C, Gas 7) and have ready 8 custard cups 8 cm = 3 inch diameter, 5 cm = 2 inches high.
7. Divide pastry into 8 sections. Roll out the first on a lightly floured surface to a 15 cm = 6 inch circle, no thinner. Ease it into a custard cup pleating but not stretching the dough. Proceed with the other seven.
8. To prepare for baking, apportion most of the almond meal on the base of the pastries, about 2 tablespoons each, and the berries on top. Bend remaining pastry from the sides towards the center.
9. Bake for 20 minutes in the hot oven, then lower heat to 350°F (180°C, Gas 4). At this time sprinkle the remaining almond meal on the tart tops and bake 15 minutes more or until bottoms are becoming darker.

Makes 8. European/North American/Northern Pakistan Influence.

Of this recipe,   To accommodate your dosha,
Kapha, enjoy less .... enjoy the mulberries and zest, uncooked
Pitta, enjoy more
Vata, enjoy more .... stay aware to the possibility of more internal wind due to the starch and fruit combination in which case enjoy the base or the fruit separately

AN OCCASION TO WEAR YOUR MULBERRY PICKING- COOKING- EATING CLOTHES.

NUT SLICE

The first and ultimate concept is to leave the mind
unencumbered by concept.

12 dried figs	**The Batter**
1 cup water	1/4 cup almond oil
	2 tsp allspice
1 cup shelled hazelnuts	1 tsp nutmeg
1 cup shelled pecans	1/2 tsp sea salt
	1 cup water
1/2 cup coconut	1 cup wheat flour, any variety

1. Cut figs into small pieces, removing stems, and soak in the water in a small saucepan for an hour. Later on, heat for several minutes to create a smooth slurry. Set aside.
2. Meanwhile, roast hazelnuts in a medium hot oven for 10 minutes. Place the nuts between 2 tea towels and rub, then blow away the bran.
3. Lower oven temperature to 350°F (180°C, Gas 4) and oil a 22 x 34 cm = 9 x 13 inch baking dish with ghee or extra almond oil.
4. Chop, grate, pulse or grind by hand or in a food mill both varieties of nut separately until there is both meal and nut pieces.
5. In a small skillet, lightly toast the coconut over low heat until golden and aromatic, judging time by color and fragrance. Transfer to a mixing bowl.
6. Do the same with the pecans.
7. In the same skillet warm the oil over low heat and infuse the allspice and nutmeg essence into it, swirling as you remove the skillet from the heat. Let cool a few minutes and add to the mix.
8. Add the fig slurry, hazelnuts, salt and last cup of water.
9. Add the flour, stirring only until mixed. Spread thin into the baking dish.
10. Bake for 35 minutes.

Serves 8-10. European/Caribbean Influence.

Of this recipe,	To change it,
Kapha, enjoy less	any change alters the recipe significantly
Pitta, enjoy less	decrease pecans and hazelnuts, decrease spices and almond oil
Vata, enjoy some	if figs or figs plus starch produce wind use palm sugar

THREE VARIETIES OF TOASTED NUT WITH FIGS.

OAT BISCUITS

Sustaining our link to indwelling intelligence can protect our inner nature and our health.

1/2 cup almonds

The Skillet Mix
1/4 cup ghee
1 tbsp ginger powder
2 tsp cinnamon
1 tsp cardamom
1 tsp nutmeg
1/2 tsp ground cloves

The Dry
1 cup wheat flour, any variety
1 cup rolled oats
1/2 cup unrefined cane or palm sugar
1/4 cup coconut
1/4 tsp sea salt

3 - 6 tbsp water, depending on humidity
1/4 cup sunflower seeds
1 tbsp linseed

1. Heat almonds in a small amount of warm water until skins swell. When cooler, remove skins. Chop fine, cover and set aside.
2. Preheat oven to 325°F (160°C, Gas 3).
3. Warm ghee in small skillet over low heat. Dust in all the spice powders, swirling them evenly into the ghee. Remove from heat and let cool several minutes.
4. Combine flour, oats, sugar, coconut and salt in a mixing bowl.
5. Add skillet ingredients into dry ingredients.
6. Add 3 tablespoons of water and give the mix a preliminary stir. Add the linseed, sunflower seeds and almonds (L-S-A). Oil or ghee your hands and knead to blend ingredients. It will seem a bit crumbly. Add more water if really too dry.
7. With light re-oiled hands form dough into 24 spheres. Place on baking trays and flatten slightly. Press split edges in.
8. Bake for 30 minutes or until the bottoms are golden. Let cool on baking sheets.

Makes 24 biscuits. Antipodean/European Influence. Australia and New Zealand biscuits with Dutch spicing.

Of this recipe,   To modify in your direction,
Kapha, enjoy less .... use the spice blend to make spice tea for 8 people
Pitta, enjoy some .... the amount of spice powders going into the ghee can be substantially reduced; decrease almonds
Vata, enjoy some .... substitute oily nuts instead of sun seeds on occasion; the spices in this amount and the oats can be drying

SPICY L-S-A ANZACS.

ORANGE MUFFIN CAKES

What is the weather like today? It influences us and our cooking.

1/2 cup dried apricots or 4 fresh
1 1/4 cups water
1/8 tsp saffron threads
1 tsp orange or mandarin zest
1/4 cup palm or unrefined cane sugar
1/2 tsp sea salt
2 cups wheat flour, any variety
ghee

1. Dice and soak dried apricots in 1 cup of the water for 60 minutes.
2. At the same time sprinkle saffron onto the 1/4 cup of water, warmed, and let cool, swirling periodically.
3. Preheat oven to 350°F (180°C, Gas 4).
4. Combine the above liquids. Chop or grate zest and add with sugar and salt.
5. Add flour with minimum mixing to form batter. If the dried fruit has absorbed a lot of water it may be necessary to add more water.
6. Divide batter into 10 oiled or ghee-d muffin cups. If using fresh apricots peel if necessary and dice. Embed fruit into the batter in each cup. Top each muffin with a small amount of ghee.
7. Bake for 20 minutes, until skewer inserted into a muffin comes out moist only from apricot and the edges are golden.

Makes 10 flat muffin-cakes. Mediterranean Influence, Spain.

Of this recipe,   To customize,
Kapha, enjoy less .... decrease wheat flour, substituting barley, rice and/or millet flour; use minimal ghee on top
Pitta, enjoy more
Vata, enjoy more .... observe if combining fruit and starch produces wind

APRICOT, SAFFRON AND ORANGE ZEST.

PEACH CAKE

Which senses do you use while cooking?

5 large peaches or equivalent
1/2 cup palm or unrefined cane sugar
1/4 cup ghee
1 tsp ground coriander
1/2 tsp nutmeg
1/2 tsp sea salt
2 cups wheat flour, any variety
1/4 cup macadamia nuts, halved

1. Preheat oven to 350°F (180°C, Gas 4).
2. Mash well 4 peeled peaches and the sweetener, providing about 2 cups of purée. Natural aroma surpasses any manufactured copy.
3. Warm the ghee in a small skillet over medium low heat. Add the coriander. Infuse 1 minute and remove from heat. Add the nutmeg. Let cool a bit.
4. Add to the peach purée with the salt.
5. Fold in the flour without over-mixing.
6. Ghee/oil a 20 cm = 8 inch baking square or equivalent. Dust the bottom with some sugar and nutmeg and slice the last peeled peach around that. Intersperse the nuts in any spaces, round side down.
7. Spoon the batter over and smooth the top.
8. Bake for 40 minutes, until cake batter tests dry. Remove from dish by inverting onto an oven-safe serving dish and bake or grill until top is cooked, about 10 minutes.

Serves 9. American Influence, Southern U.S.A.

Of this recipe,   To further refine,
Kapha, enjoy less .... as with all baked goods, decrease wheat and oil (see other bakery recipes) and decrease the peaches; use sunflower seeds instead of macadamias and less of them
Pitta, enjoy some .... use less peaches and nuts; use sun seeds
Vata, enjoy more .... try this sometimes with macadamia oil instead of ghee; decide if your digestion is as happy with nuts, fruit and starch in combination as your mouth is

AN UPSIDE DOWN CAKE.

PEAR CAKE

The stomach is a mixing vessel the size of one's fist but if filled too full, thorough mixing cannot take place.

1/4 cup ghee
1/2 tsp fennel seed, crushed
1 tsp coriander powder
1/2 tsp ginger powder
1 1/2 cups water
1/4 cup palm or unrefined cane sugar
1/4 tsp sea salt
3 pears
1 1/2 cups wheat flour, any variety

1. Preheat oven to 350°F (180°C, Gas 4). Oil a 20 cm = 8 inch square or equivalent of your choice with additional ghee.
2. In a small skillet warm ghee over medium low heat and add fennel, coriander and ginger. Swirl for 2 minutes, take off heat and cool a few minutes.
3. In a mixing bowl combine the water, sugar and salt.
4. Cut pears into chunks, peeled or unpeeled, and add.
5. Add the flour until just combined.
6. Fold in the skillet mix.
7. Pour batter into baking dish, sprinkle on a few extra fennel seeds and bake for 30 minutes, or until a tester comes out dry and the edges are golden.

Makes 9 squares. North American, European and Indian Influence.

Of this recipe   Better yet,
Kapha, enjoy less .... use a millet-barley-rye flour blend instead of wheat; decrease ghee
Pitta, enjoy more
Vata, enjoy some .... pears are best not eaten often and fruit may combine adversely with starch for anyone

PEARS AND COMPLIMENTARY SPICES.

BEVERAGE

ALOE APERITIF

Slowly accustom yourself and those who you feed to this cuisine.

Per Person
1/4 tsp ginger juice
1/2 tsp unfired honey
3 tbsp pure water
3 tbsp stabilized, certified aloe vera juice or gel

1. Grate enough fresh ginger to squeeze out 1/4 teaspoon of the juice.
2. Mix with honey and water.
3. Add aloe.
4. Sip before meals.

Of this recipe,   To make it better,
Kapha, enjoy more
Pitta, enjoy less .... delete the ginger juice and honey; the aloe
can be mixed with the water and a little unrefined cane sugar and is then
digestive and cooling; aloe is good for pitta but may produce too loose a
bowel with its natural laxative action; if so, decrease aloe
Vata, enjoy some .... decrease the ginger juice and use palm sugar
sometimes instead of honey; add a squeeze of citrus juice and a very small
amount of earth salt

ALOE REGULATES PHYSICAL FUNCTION AND CAN BE SIPPED WITH OTHER INGREDIENTS.

BARLEY TEA

Ayurvedic teachings convey ways and means to maintain wellness.

Per Serving
1 tbsp barley and 250 ml = 1 cup pure water

1. Roast barley in small skillet, shaking over medium heat until the grains start to darken, swell and spin.
2. Bring water to boil, add roasted barley and simmer 15 minutes.
3. Leave grains in tea and sip when preferred temperature.

Japanese Influence. All dosha-s, enjoy on occasion.

ROASTED BARLEY PROVIDES FULL-BODIED TASTE.

BARLEY TONIC

It is the subtlest shift of mind that allows personal change.

Per Serve
1 1/2 tbsp barley
2 cups pure water
1 shave of licorice root or 1/8 tsp powder
1/4 tsp crushed coriander seeds or powder
a very small amount of earth or sea salt
1 small red-skinned apple

1. Wash the barley and soak for 8 hours.
2. Combine with the water, licorice root and coriander seeds.
3. Bring to boil and simmer, uncovered, for at least 1 hour, until the liquid is condensed by half.
4. Stir in salt, licorice and coriander powders if using.
5. Let steep 10 minutes.
6. Peel and grate fine the apple. Squeeze out 1/4 cup juice.
7. Strain the solids from the tonic; add the apple juice. Use the barley with the next meal that day.

Makes 1 1/2 cups. American-Asian-European Influence.

Of this recipe,
Kapha, Pitta, Vata, enjoy this as a beverage when you wish to fortify yourself.

INTERPLAYING OF BARLEY WATER AND APPLE JUICE.

CAROB GINGER

Please don't think of matter in terms of chemical notation. It is more liberated than lines connecting letters.

For Kapha
1 tbsp carob powder
1 tsp ginger powder
1 tsp honey
3/4 cup warm water
1/4 cup hot goat's milk

For Vata
1/2 tbsp carob powder
1/2 tsp ginger powder
2 tsp palm or unrefined cane sugar
3/4 cup hot cow's milk
1/4 cup cream

For Pitta
1 tbsp carob powder
1/8 tsp ginger
1 cup boiled, then cooled, cow's milk
2 tsp palm or unrefined cane sugar

1. Combine carob, ginger and sweetener with 1 tablespoon of water to make a syrup.
2. Bring milk to boil and mix with other liquid.
3. Add to syrup and stir smooth. When using honey allow liquid to be warm rather than hot before adding to the syrup.

A FAVORITE TAILORED TO YOUR CONSTITUTION.

DIGESTIVE and DOSHIC TEAS

The digestive capacity is measured not in the size of the stomach but in the balanced efficiency of the digestive enzymes and supportive secretions.

Cardamom, Fennel, Coriander
1 litre = 1 quart pure water
1 tsp cardamom seeds
1 tsp fennel seeds
1 tsp crushed coriander seeds

1. Dry roast or toast seeds over medium low heat.
2. Bring water to boil, remove from heat and add all seeds.
3. Cover and infuse until drinking temperature.
4. Strain and sip with or after your meal.

Serves 6. Good for all dosha-s

Bay, Ginger, Cinnamon, Cardamom
1 litre = 1 quart pure water
1 bay leaf
1 tsp ginger powder
1 tsp cinnamon powder
1 tsp cardamom powder

1. Bring water and bay to boil and simmer, covered, 5 minutes.
2. Remove from heat and add the powders. Cover and infuse until drinking temperature.
3. Sip with or after your meal and for respiratory congestion.

Serves 6. Pitta, enjoy less.

For Vata
1 litre = 1 quart pure water
1 tbsp loosely packed grated fresh ginger
1 tbsp lemon juice
less than 1/4 tsp rock salt

1. Bring water to boil, add the ginger root, remove from heat, cover and infuse 10 minutes.
2. Add juice and salt and mix well.
3. Sip before meals.

Serves 6.

For Pitta
1 litre = 1 quart pure water
4 fresh aromatic roses
2 dandelion or other bitter green leaves
1 teaspoon unrefined cane sugar

1. Bring water to boil.
2. Remove from heat and add roses and leaves.
3. Infuse until room temperature. If leaves unavailable add 1 teaspoon of aloe vera juice here.
4. Add sugar, stir and strain and sip as a beverage.

Serves 6.

For Kapha
1 litre = 1 quart pure water
1 tsp cumin seed
1/2 tsp nutmeg
1/2 tsp turmeric
1 tsp honey

1. Bring water to boil.
2. Dry roast or toast cumin seed.
3. Remove water from heat and add all spices except nutmeg.
4. Infuse until body temperature and then add nutmeg and honey.
5. Sip with meals or as a beverage.

Serves 6.

HERBS AND SPICES ARE A CULINARY PHARMACY.

FLOWER WATERS and INFUSIONS

The time that elapses before ingesting the next meal has a bearing on digestion. Be hungry before eating.

1 litre = 1 quart of pure water in a clear pitcher

Per litre-quart add one of the following:
petals of one fragrant pink, red, yellow or other color rose
10 cm = 4 inches sprig fresh mint
several sacred basil leaves
3 sliced rounds of a lemon, orange, grapefruit, mandarin or lime
zest of half a lemon, orange, grapefruit, mandarin or lime
top flowers nipped off 20 lavender spikes
3 nasturtium flowers, colors of your choice
a handful of jasmine flowers
a handful of orange blossoms
a handful of chamomile flowers
a handful of honeysuckle flowers

1. Prepare several separate pitchers and add one of the colored ingredients.
2. Let infuse at room temperature for an hour or infuse with the heat of the sun, rocking gently.
3. Also experiment with color and texture combinations. The season will provide the flowers.
4. Carry your own bottle of infusion instead of plain water and use within 6 hours.

These waters would be lovely for any constitution, however Kapha and Pitta, minimize the citrus juice.

DELICATE COLORS AND FLAVORS.

GINGER TEA

Ginger is considered a primary supporter of health.

Per Person
1 tsp fresh ginger
2 tsp lemon juice
2 tsp unfired honey
1 cup water

1. Bring the water to boil.
2. Grate ginger in and let steep 15 minutes.
3. When cooler, strain and add lemon juice and honey.

This elixir will produce perspiration and is most helpful in sweating an incipient cold out of your system.

A TRADITIONAL REMEDY.

HOT WATER

Deleting substance from our bodies, however toxic, must be done slowly. We become attached to even destructive influences.

Per person
1 cup fresh and quality water, not previously boiled

1. Bring water to the boil and remove from heat.
2. Serve and sip while still hot.

Of this,
Enjoy two to three cups a day

Kapha, drink hot and please don't waterlog yourself
Pitta, allow to cool if you feel it is too hot
Vata, hot is good

JUST-BOILED WATER HAS A LOWER SURFACE TENSION AND
REMOVES TOXINS.

GRAPE-FRUIT JUICE

Being able to procure all fruits and vegetables at all times due to global economy dissociates us from harmony with the seasons.

1 kg = 2 lbs ripe grapes
1-2 grapefruit
a very small amount of earth or sea salt
cinnamon powder
whole cloves
fresh mint
a strip of grapefruit zest

1. Crush the grapes and sieve out the skins and seeds. Traditionally the crushing would be done with your feet. They pop easily that way.
2. For each cup of grape purée, dry roast over low heat, grind and add 1 clove along with 1/8 teaspoon cinnamon, a few grains of salt and 3 fresh mint leaves, minced.
3. Add 4 tablespoons grapefruit juice per cup and mix.
4. Serve in clear glass and garnish with a few slivers of grapefruit zest and a mint leaf.

Makes about 2-3 cups. Middle Eastern Influence, Israel.

Of this beverage,   To further personalize,
Kapha, enjoy less
Pitta, enjoy some .... decrease the grapefruit juice
Vata, enjoy more

A REFRESHING COMBINATION OF GRAPES AND GRAPEFRUIT.

LIME-AIDE

The place where one is eating, the environment, has a bearing on digestion.

Per serve
2 limes
1-3 tsp unrefined cane sugar or honey
1/2 cup water
a few grains of sea salt

1. Grate the zest of one half a lime.
2. Combine water, juice of limes, sugar and salt.
3. Garnish with zest. Drink at room temperature.

Caribbean-Indian-African Influence

Of this recipe,
Citrus juice is best for vata, however Indian lime juice is O.K. in moderation
for Pitta and Kapha.
Kapha, use honey instead of sugar

LIME JUICE ENHANCED BY SWEET AND SALTY QUENCHES THIRST.

SPICED HONEY DRINK

Consuming anything too hot or cold limits the sense of taste.

4 whole cardamom pods, just opened
8 cm = 3 1/2 inches cinnamon quill
2 tsp grated fresh ginger
1 tsp grated lemon rind
1 tsp dried mint or 14 fresh leaves
8 whole cloves
a very small amount of earth or sea salt
8 cups water

a pinch of nutmeg
2 tbsp unprocessed honey
milk, optional

1. Bring all the ingredients to boil except the nutmeg, honey and milk.
2. Reduce to half by simmering uncovered, aromatic in your space.
3. Cover and let cool. Strain out spices, add nutmeg and honey.

Serves 4. Russian Influence.

Of this recipe,   To refine,
Kapha, enjoy more
Pitta, enjoy less .... use less spices overall so that means enjoy less;
use palm or unrefined cane sugar to sweeten
Vata, enjoy some .... use some honey and some sugar

Pitta and Vata, decrease the concentration of these heating and drying spices
by adding some boiled milk; vata constitutional people can add some cream
instead if desired.

SPICE ESSENCES SIMMERED AND SWEET.

DAIRY

BASIC GOURMET MILK

Mental indigestion alters the mind in this lifetime.

> 4 almonds, optional
> 1 cardamom pod or 1/8 tsp powder
> 1 cup milk, preferably raw
> a few threads of saffron or a sprinkle of turmeric
> a grating of nutmeg
> 1 tsp unfired honey, palm or unrefined cane sugar or maple
> syrup

1. Heat almonds in a small amount of warm water until skins swell. When cooler, remove skins. Soak in water until needed.
2. Dry roast cardamom pod until fragrant. Remove seeds and crush.
3. Bring the milk to a rising boil and remove from heat.
4. Stir in cardamom, saffron or turmeric. Let cool a few minutes.
5. Add nutmeg. Swirl occasionally.
6. Finely grate or process almonds into meal.
7. Add almond meal to the milk with the sweetener. Stir before drinking.

Makes 2 servings. Indian Influence.
This beverage can help a person sleep. It is nutritive and enhances immunity.

Of this beverage,   To personalize,
Kapha, enjoy less .... use goat's milk, honey when cooler and less almonds
Pitta, enjoy more .... decrease nutmeg and almonds; use cane sugar or maple syrup
Vata, enjoy more .... use any sweetener

SPICING AND BOILING MAKES MILK MOST DIGESTIBLE.

CARROT and MILK PUDDING

If we practice balance when the going is easy, we will have its support when the going is tough.

> 2 large carrots
> 1 1/2 cups milk, preferably raw
> 2 tsp grated orange peel
> 1 cardamom pod, opened
> 1 tbsp cashews
> 1/4 cup palm or unrefined cane sugar or maple syrup
> 1 tbsp ghee
> 1/4 cup raisins

1. Grate the carrots and cook at a slow boil, uncovered, in the milk with the orange peel and cardamom, beholding the tones of the color orange.
2. Toast the cashews and let cool.
3. As the carrots soften, in about 10 minutes, add the sugar and ghee.
4. Cook another 5-10 minutes, adding the raisins.
5. Serve both the carrots and liquid garnished with the toasted cashews.

Serves 4. Middle Eastern/Indian Influence.

Of this recipe,   To modify,
Kapha, enjoy less .... use goat's milk, less nuts, no sugar and honey when cooled
Pitta, enjoy more
Vata, enjoy more

CARROTS COOKED IN MILK, CAROTENE GALORE.

CHYAWANPRASH and MILK

J take this food as effective medicine to keep my body in good health.

1/4 tsp ghee
2 tsp Chyawanprash
1 cup milk, preferably raw
a sprinkle of turmeric

1. Add ghee to Chyawanprash and consume.
2. Thirty minutes after having the above, bring milk to a rising boil. Float the turmeric powder on top and drink when it reaches desired temperature. Look for Chyawanprash in Indian food shops. It is made with Vitamin C-stable fruit and many herbs and is ideal to support immunity in the winter.

Makes 1 serving. Indian Influence

Of this recipe,   To enhance,
Kapha, enjoy less .... take Chyawanprash and ghee without the milk
Pitta, enjoy some .... use 1 tsp Chyawanprash with the ghee, it is pungent
Vata, enjoy more

THE FRUIT PURÉE KNOWN AS HAPPY JAM IS THE INDIAN MAINSTAY TO WELLNESS.

CONDENSED MILK

Thanksgiving for food and for the people who put food on the table.

4 cups milk, preferably raw, full cream or not
1/2 vanilla bean
palm or unrefined cane sugar
other spices optional

1. In a large and high pot heat the milk and vanilla pod to boil and boil uncovered until condensed, about 20 minutes, stirring the top down, the bottom up and the sides in often. How far you condense this can vary. The milk turns from milky white to cream-colored even if there is no cream in it. One cup can condense down to 2 tablespoons of pudding or have more volume as a beverage.
2. Towards the end of condensing, remove the vanilla bean and open. Gather seeds by running a small spoon along the inside. Add seeds back to pot.
3. Add a small amount of sweetener if needed and spices such as cinnamon or cardamom if desired.

Yield is dependant on cooking time.

Of this recipe,   Even better,
Kapha, enjoy less .... enjoy less
Pitta and vata, enjoy more

RICH CONSISTENCY DOTTED WITH VANILLA SEEDS.

GHEE

One requirement if food is to provide nutrition is that we want to eat it.

1 kg = 2 lbs choicest grade sweet butter

1. Melt butter over medium heat in heavy saucepan until it boils.
2. Lower heat and simmer uncovered until it stops foaming, until there are no globules of opaque butter welling up from the bottom. This can take 40 minutes. When the ghee is ready what will be seen under the foam is a transparent golden liquid and some darker fine sediment.
3. Collect the foam separately. Use it for flavoring. Collect the golden oil and store in a clean, dry, lidded glass container. Discard the meagre sediment.
4. Ghee stores unrefrigerated. It does not store well if water mixes with it (although in some medicinal or cosmetic applications water is mixed with it); use a dry spoon when you use ghee.

Yield: close to an equal quantity as the butter used.

Ghee is a healthful substance for all in moderation, best for pitta, kapha using the least. It does not elevate normal cholesterol levels.

BUTTER IS CLARIFIED AND ENHANCES FOOD FLAVOR AND QUALITIES.

GHEE MÂITRE D'HOTEL

We practice the yoga of Patanjali when the mind attends to the occupation at hand.

3 tbsp ghee
2 tbsp each, fresh only, lightly packed, tarragon, parsley, chervil, chives; other herbs can be used
a sprinkle of rock or sea salt
1 tsp lime or lemon juice

1. Warm ghee in a heatproof ramekin or other vessel with low heat and then remove from heat. Keep warm.
2. Mince all herbs together, soon to impart their essence.
3. Add herbs to ghee and keep warm. Let infuse a quarter hour.
4. Mix in salt and citrus and infuse a few minutes more.

Spoon over plain vegetables, grains, soups, flatbreads, etc.

Serves 6. European Influence.

Of this recipe,
Kapha, enjoy less; ghee is good for you in smaller amounts; the herbs are great with a lesser amount of ghee
Pitta, enjoy some; ghee is best for pitta but the herbs may be too heating; mint, coriander dill or fennel are more suitable
Vata, enjoy some; no one consumes ghee in large quantity

DRAWN BUTTER CAN EXTRACT THE ESSENCE OF HERBS.

SAVORY MILK CASSEROLE

3 small sweet potatoes
2 sticks celery
2 cups milk, preferably raw
1 tsp ghee
1/2 tsp turmeric
black peppercorns

1. Peel and dice vegetables.
2. Place milk and vegetables into a medium saucepan.
3. Bring to boil and simmer, covered for 20 minutes or until vegetables are cooked.
4. Dissolve the ghee in a pool on top of the vegetables. Add the turmeric to this pool and infuse for several minutes.
5. Mix the turmeric ghee through the casserole and mash some of the potatoes to blend in the ghee and milk. Add a turn of the pepper grinder.

Serves 4. European-North American Influence.

Of this recipe   To refine,
Kapha, enjoy less .... use goat's milk and less sweet potato (enjoy less)
Pitta, enjoy more .... use less pepper, more ghee
Vata, enjoy more

ORANGE POTATOES BECOME CREAMY COOKED IN MILK.

SOFT CHEESE

How close do we get to our food when preparing and eating it?

8 cups cow's milk, preferably raw
4 tbsp lemon juice

1. In a large covered pot bring milk just to boil.
2. Remove from heat and add lemon juice.
3. Stir through minimally and let rest 15 minutes.
4. Pour through a lined sieve and let drain.
5. Press the curds together by leaving the cheese in the sieve and placing a clean weight evenly over the top, e.g. water in a plastic bag.
6. After 1 hour cut into cubes. Enjoy as is or proceed as below.

Serves 4 as garnish. Worldwide practice in dairy-friendly countries. Ayurveda does not recommend mixing milk with anything sour, so enjoy only on special occasion.

To make it better,
Kapha, use goat's milk

KITCHEN CHEMISTRY FEATURING LEMON JUICE COALESCING MILK PROTEIN.

SOFT CHEESE with SPICES

Once we recognize a culprit, we do everything to defend it.

2 tsp ghee
1/4 tsp turmeric
1/2 tsp cumin
less than 1/4 tsp ground black pepper

1. Warm ghee in a medium skillet over medium low heat.
2. Add all spices and swirl together.
3. Add the cubes of 'paneer' and cook several minutes on 2 sides.
4. Remove from heat and cool to firm them again.
5. Serve with greens or green peas.
6. As a visual alternative leave some cubes white.
7. As a non-cooking alternative, combine the spices and roll cubes of paneer in them. Experiment with other spice blends.

Only on special occasion,
Kapha, decrease the ghee; both greens and peas are appropriate
Pitta, use less pepper; use bitter greens; peas are fine
Vata, enjoy less greens; cooked peas are fine

ADDING YELLOW WITH TURMERIC AND GREEN WITH PEAS.

DESSERT

There is no teaching in ayurveda that promotes fruit or heavy sweets at the end of a meal. Fruit is best eaten on an empty stomach and left to clear the stomach during the next half hour or so. If it is eaten at the end of a meal it will be caught up with the rest of the meal and ferment due to its higher sugar content and extended confinement in the stomach. Sweet desserts would disrupt digestion if eaten at the end of a meal and are best eaten in small quantity at the beginning. What are we waiting for!

Traditional ayurveda recommends the harder-to-digest foods be eaten first, when appetite indicates that our digestive enzymes and secretions are ready to work. The sweet taste, comprised of the earth and water elements, points us to those foods that require the most digestive strength. The best time to eat sweeter, heavier foods is around midday, when the energy of fire is strongest in the internal and external environment.

In some parts of the world people eat only sweet things for the morning meal, in others both sweet and savory. In having the six tastes in each meal, savory foods would be recommended for breakfast as well.

The following recipes would classify as sweets.

<u>From the Bakery, Sweet</u>
all and especially
Date slice
Nut slice
<u>From Dairy</u>
Carrot and Milk Pudding
Condensed Milk
<u>From the Fruit Selection</u>
Broiled Pineapple
Custard Apple
Lily-Pillie and Mulberries
Pear and Anise
Pineapple and Coconut
Plum Sauce
Quince Spread
Seeds, Figs and Apples
Steamed Apples
<u>From Nuts and Seeds</u>
Honey Shapes
Nut Porridge
Sesame, Almonds and Dates
Sweet Walnuts
<u>From the Soup Selection</u>
Sweet Mung Soup
<u>From the Staples Selection</u>
Dark Rice and Sweet Potato
Cream of Rice
Rice and Sweet Aduki Beans
Steamed Buns
Steamed Yam Cake
Sweet Pine Nut Porridge
Sweet Rice Dumplings

FRUIT

AVOCADO

Admire your ingredients.

2 medium avocados
1 tbsp orange juice
1 tsp palm or unrefined cane sugar
a sprinkle of sea salt
a sprinkle of ginger powder
1/2 tsp coriander powder
orange zest

1. Cut smooth, soft, heavy avocado into pieces.
2. Combine the remaining ingredients and pour over the fruit.
3. Garnish with a few shavings of orange peel.

Serves 4. Mesoamerican Influence, Mexico.

Of this recipe,   To fine-tune,
Kapha, enjoy less .... notice that the attributes of avocado and kapha
are similar
Pitta, enjoy some .... use less dressing
Vata, enjoy more

CUBED AVOCADO AND DRESSING.

BERRY STEW

We offer reverence to the energy that sustains the body.

>4 cups strawberries, raspberries, other berries or sour cherries
>2 cups water
>1 cinnamon quill
>2 tbsp palm or unrefined cane sugar or maple syrup
>1/4 tsp sea salt
>1/4 cup raw milk, the upper portion or warmed cream,
>   optional

1. Remove stems, seeds, etc. as necessary from the fruit. Slice into 1 cm = 1/4 inch lengths or bite-sized pieces as necessary, collecting the sweet juices.
2. Combine water and cinnamon in a medium saucepan and bring to boil. Simmer, covered, 5 minutes.
3. Add berries or cherries and juices and cook over low heat, covered, 5-10 minutes, or until just soft.
4. Add salt. Let cool and taste for sweet and sour. Add up to the 2 tablespoons sweetener, maybe less.
5. Serve at room temperature. Decorate with a tablespoon of warmed cream or creamy milk brought just to boil.

Serves 4. European Influence, Hungary.

Of this recipe,   Better yet,
Kapha, enjoy less .... use honey instead of sugar when cool and forego the milk or cream
Pitta, enjoy some .... use sweet berries or sweet cherries and a small amount of just-boiled milk
Vata, enjoy more............ with cream or milk

FRUIT COOKED BRIEFLY IN CINNAMON TEA.

BROILED PINEAPPLE

Outer events are as they are; each person's mind puts its own spin on them.

1 fresh sweet pineapple
1 tbsp ghee
1 tsp coriander powder
1/2 tsp ginger powder
1/4 tsp nutmeg
1/4 tsp turmeric
a sprinkle of sea salt
fresh tarragon, mint, coriander, and /or Thai basil

1. Remove rind and eyes of your pineapple and slice into 1 1/2 cm = 3/4 inch thick lengths or rounds, removing core.
2. Broil or barbecue, turning each over to cook through, possibly turning them over several times or just once.
3. Meanwhile, warm ghee in a small skillet over medium low heat. Add spices and swirl. Heat for 1 minute and add salt. Remove from heat and keep warm. An option here is to cook the pineapple in the skillet with the ghee and spices, using a larger skillet.
4. When pineapple is soft, stir up spices into the ghee and drizzle on. Use fresh chopped herb/s as garnish.

Serves 8. Central American Influence.

Of this recipe,   To fine-tune,
Kapha, enjoy less .... enjoy a little if your body is asking for
pineapple
Pitta, enjoy some .... use less ginger and nutmeg
Vata, enjoy more

USING FRESH HERBS AND SPICES.

CUSTARD APPLE

How does the trickster show up in your cooking?

Per Person
1 custard apple or soursop
1/2 tsp palm or unrefined cane sugar or maple syrup
 a few grains of sea salt
1 Brazil nut or blanched almond, chopped
a grating of nutmeg

1. Open white-fleshed custard apple with black seeds and remove inner stem.
2. Scoop fruit from shell and place in colander over a collecting bowl.
3. Rub fruit through holes until the seeds remain above and the purée below.
4. Add the sweetener, more to taste if necessary, and salt to fruit.
5. Cut nut into coarse pieces. Lightly toast.
6. Place fruit purée into serving dish and garnish with nutmeg and nut pieces.

Caribbean Influence.

Of this recipe,   Better for your dosha,
Kapha, enjoy less .... add extra nutmeg, omit sweetener or use honey;
have a small serving
Pitta, enjoy more
Vata, enjoy more

SMOOTH DELECTABLE FRUIT WITH NUT GARNISH.

DATE-MINT CHUTNEY

To admire creative presentation browse through other
cookbooks, look at natural landscapes, visit the arts museum.

12 whole dates
water
3/4 cup mint leaves or strong mint tea made with
    1 tbsp dried mint and 1 cup water

<u>The Skillet Mix</u>
1 tsp ghee
barely 1/4 tsp cumin seed
a sprinkle of asafoetida
barely 1/4 tsp earth salt
1/4 tsp black pepper
1/2 tbsp tamarind or lemon juice
a few curls of lemon rind

1. Remove seeds and cut dates into small pieces. Soak in water to cover for about 1 hour. If you cannot obtain fresh mint, make a mint tea and soak dates in this.
2. In a medium skillet warm the ghee over medium low heat and add the cumin seeds and asafoetida, sautéing for a few minutes.
3. Add the dates and their soaking liquid and continue cooking.
4. Mince the mint leaves and add to the skillet, mashing the dates while you're there.
5. As the liquid starts to decrease add the salt and pepper. The chutney will firm up on cooling so leave some moistness.
6. Add the sour juice.
7. Transfer to small serving dish and garnish with lemon curls.

Makes 1/2 cup, serves 6-8 people. Indian Influence.

Of this digestive chutney,
Kapha, Pitta and Vata, enjoy a tablespoon.

ALL TASTES CONCENTRATED BY COOKING.

DRIED FRUIT IN GREEN TEA

For most people sleeping after meals and during the day is not advantageous to health.

> 1 cup strong green tea
> 2 cups mixed dried fruit
> fresh ginger
> 1/2 tsp grated citrus zest
> a few grains of sea salt
> fresh mint, tarragon or other herb

1. Prepare green tea and let cool.
2. Cut fruit into spoon-sized pieces and place in a bowl. Add the tea.
3. Grate ginger and squeeze out 1/2 teaspoon of juice. Grate citrus zest, medium texture. Add both to the fruit with a few drops of citrus juice.
4. Stir on occasion until the tea is absorbed, between 2 and 4 hours. This taste gets better with time.
5. Add the salt.
6. Garnish with fresh mint, tarragon or other herb.

Serves 4-6. Worldwide Contribution.

Of this recipe,   To improve for your dosha,
Kapha, enjoy some
Pitta, enjoy more
Vata, enjoy less.............. dried fruit is apt to produce excess wind

SWEETNESS IS MELLOWED BY TEA, GINGER JUICE AND CITRUS.

FEIJOAS

There is opportunity to adjust our digestive fire higher or lower if need be much like adjusting a flame for cooking.

fresh ginger
2 teaspoons unfired honey
a few grains of sea salt
12 feijoas (pineapple guavas) or other guavas
a squeeze of lemon juice

1. Grate a small amount of fresh ginger and squeeze out the juice. Collect 1/4 teaspoon.
2. Combine ginger juice with honey and salt and add enough water to make a syrup. Set aside.
3. Prepare fruit by cutting in half crosswise and scooping out the pulp with a spoon. Toss in the lemon juice.
4. When all the fruit is prepared, add syrup, mix well and serve.

Serves 2-3. South American Influence, Argentina.

Of this recipe,   For your dosha,
Kapha, enjoy some
Pitta, enjoy some .... ginger juice and honey is a potent toxin-reducing mix but it is also heating; substitute cinnamon and sugar
Vata, enjoy some

THESE IRON AND VITAMIN RICH FRUITS ARE COATED WITH LIGHT HONEY-GINGER SYRUP.

FRUIT in AGAR-AGAR

If we are willing, love can override any other emotion.

3 3/4 cups water
10 gm = 1/3 oz agar-agar
1/2 cup palm or unrefined cane sugar
a sprinkle of sea salt
1/2 tsp galangal or ginger powder
1 tsp fresh or 1/2 tsp dried mint
fruit pieces such as lychee, guava, papaya, persimmon,
    cherries, dragon fruit, mango, etc.

1. Bring water to boil in a medium saucepan.
2. Add agar-agar, return to boil and lower heat. Cover. Stir occasionally for
   10-15 minutes until agar-agar is totally dissolved.
3. Meanwhile cut about 3 cups of fruit into bite-sized pieces, saving any juice
   in the process.
4. Add sugar to agar-agar mix and heat until dissolved.
5. Add salt, galangal, mint and available fruit juice, stir and pour into a 33 x
   20 cm = 13 x 8 inch baking dish or equivalent. (Experiment with the flavor
   of the 'tea' that the agar-agar will set.)
6. Embed fruit while still warm, using color and shape to artistic advantage.
7. When firm, about 20 minutes, cut into shapes.

Serves 6. Asian Influence, China.

Of this recipe,   To fine-tune,
Kapha, enjoy less .... omit the sugared jelly; use the spices on apple
Pitta, enjoy some .... omit the galangal/ginger and choose less papaya
and cherries
Vata, enjoy some .... decrease sugar and persimmon and choose well-
ripened fruit

COLORFUL FRUIT AND MINT IN A SEAWEED-THICKENED BASE.

LEMON RIND CHUTNEY

We use intelligence to guide us in using our bodies and senses.

1 large lemon, thick skinned
1 tsp mustard seed
1 tsp coriander seed
a generous tsp of fresh-grated ginger
1 tsp ghee
a sprinkle of sea salt
1 1/2 tsp honey

1. Slice rind and white layer from the lemon with a small amount of juice globules adhering and dice small.
2. Dry roast mustard and coriander seeds in a small skillet over medium heat for 1 minute. Cool and grind to powder. Ideally all powders are made from freshly ground seeds.
3. Grate ginger finely.
4. Warm ghee in the skillet now over low heat and sauté spice powder briefly. Add rind, then ginger and some water, cooking 5 minutes. Stir occasionally.
5. Add salt, mix and let cool. Add honey and additional lemon juice if needed.

Serves 6-8. Indian Influence.

Of this recipe,   To enjoy more,
Kapha, enjoy more .... without additional lemon juice
Pitta, enjoy some .... decrease mustard and ginger; use cane sugar and no additional lemon juice
Vata, enjoy less .... decrease lemon rind which means a small serving and add the extra lemon juice on that serving

USING THE BITTERNESS AND VITAMINS IN CITRUS RIND AND CONVEYING ALL TASTES.

LILY-PILLIES and MULBERRIES

Let the kitchen rest now and then during the day.

> 1 cup water
> 1/2 cup palm or unrefined cane sugar
> 4 cups lily pillie berries or other berries
> 2 cups ripe purple mulberries or other berries
> 1 tsp coriander
> a sprinkle of sea salt

1. In a small saucepan over medium heat bring water and sugar to boil, stirring at the beginning to dissolve the sugar.
2. Boil uncovered for 10-15 minutes to syrup stage. Add coriander and salt. Let cool.
3. Score the lily-pillies in half, twist apart and remove seeds.
4. Combine with mulberries in a serving bowl.
5. Pour syrup over the fruit, mix gently and serve.

Serves 6. Antipodean Influence, Australia.

Of this recipe,   To enjoy more,
Kapha, enjoy some .... omit the syrup and sprinkle the coriander on the fruit
Pitta, enjoy more
Vata, enjoy more .... use less sweetener

A STRIKING COLOR VISUAL THE YEAR BOTH FRUITS RIPENED TOGETHER.

MANGO

Ayurveda teaches us to recognize others as representatives of the elements they are carrying.

2 mangoes
a few grains of sea salt
1 tsp ground coriander
small handful coriander leaves
1 lime

1. Slice the cheeks off the mangoes and score into cubes, just short of the peel. Invert the peel to expose the cube bottoms and slice off into a serving dish.
2. Cut the rest of the mango off the seed if you can and into pieces.
3. Mince coriander leaves to about 2 teaspoons, leaving a few intact.
4. Grate 1 teaspoon of lime rind and collect 1 teaspoon of the juice.
5. Toss the fruit with these other ingredients.
6. Garnish with a few whole coriander leaves.

Serves 4. Mesoamerican Influence, Mexico.

Of this recipe,   To fine-tune,
Kapha, enjoy some .... mangoes are O.K. occasionally in season
Pitta, enjoy more .... use sweet ripe mangoes, delete juice
Vata, enjoy more

BOTH SEEDS AND LEAVES OF CORIANDER, BOTH ZEST
AND JUICE OF LIME.

MARMALADE SYRUP

The dosha-s bridge the gap between energy and matter.
When functioning unimpeded they are directive energies,
when impeded they precipitate into disruptive matter.

1/4 cup orange, lemon, lime, grapefruit, mandarin, and/or tangerine zest
1 cup water
1/2 cup palm or unrefined cane sugar
a sprinkle of earth or sea salt
2 tbsp citrus juice, best for vata

1. Pare the peel from organic fruit. Further shape into threads or dice. Vary the citrus or use all of one variety.
2. Combine with the water in a small saucepan, bring to boil and simmer, covered, on low heat for 15 minutes.
3. Add the sugar and stir until dissolved. Cook, uncovered, on low heat about 40 minutes or until the liquid is syrupy but not thick.
4. Add the salt. When cooler, add the optional juice.
5. Spoon over fruit, unsweetened baked items or pancakes. Or use in recipes calling for citrus and sugar.

Makes a generous half cup. Mediterranean, European, North American Influence.

Of this recipe,   To refine,
Kapha, enjoy less .... the peel is the best part of this, grate it raw over your food
Pitta, enjoy some .... sweet and bitter is good, enjoy in moderation; use less juice
Vata, enjoy less .... this is mostly cooling; add some ginger, fresh or powdered, in the last 5 minutes of simmering; add the juice and still enjoy less

THE BITTERNESS OF CITRUS RIND IS EQUILIBRATED BY SLOW
COOKING WITH SUGAR.

MELON

The physical-psychological-spiritual unity we experience consists of The Knower, The Process that affords Knowing and That which is Known.

1/4 cup loosely packed mint leaves or 2 tsp dried
1 tbsp loosely packed basil or 1/2 tsp dried
3 cups melon(s) of choice
a sprinkle of sea salt

1. Mince mint and basil together.
2. Slice, cube or ball melon and place in serving dish.
3. Sprinkle on a few grains of salt and mix. If using dried herbs, allow time for them to rehydrate in the melon juice.
4. Add greens and mix. Eat melons on their own to allow best digestion.

Serves 4-6. African Influence, Republic of South Africa.

Of this recipe,   To enjoy more,
Kapha, enjoy less .... substitute apricots, pears, peaches for melon
Pitta, enjoy more
Vata, enjoy some

WE BENEFIT FROM THE MERIT OF EATING MELON WITH MINT AND BASIL.

PAPAYA

Appraise results and proceed from there.

1 tbsp raisins
750 gm = 1 1/2 lbs papaya
a small piece of fresh ginger
a sprinkle of cinnamon
1/2 cup orange juice
a sprinkle of sea salt

1. Soak raisins in a small amount of water.
2. Peel, cube papaya, remove seeds in any order you wish.
3. Grate ginger finely to the amount of 1/4 teaspoon.
4. Squeeze orange and collect 1/2 cup juice.
5. Combine all ingredients together,
6. Decide if you fancy a few papaya seeds with your serving.

Serves 4. Caribbean Influence, Cuba.

Of this recipe,   To enjoy more,
Kapha, enjoy less .... use peaches, pears or apricot instead of papaya
and just a squeeze of orange juice; use a few papaya seeds on your fruit
Pitta, enjoy some .... papaya is O.K. occasionally; decrease ginger,
orange juice and papaya seeds
Vata, enjoy more

FRUIT CUBES IN ORANGE JUICE SLURRY.

PAPAYA and CAPE GOOSEBERRIES

We have the capacity to change using logic and inspiration.

1 kg = 2 lbs papaya
1 cup cape gooseberries
a sprinkle of palm or unrefined cane sugar or a small amount of maple
    syrup
a sprinkle of sea salt
1 tbsp aloe vera juice

1. Peel and cube papaya, slippery as it is, and reserve 1/2 teaspoon of the
   seeds.
2. Remove the papery lantern covers and quarter the gooseberries.
3. Mix the fruit with the sweetener, salt and aloe liquid.
4. Garnish evenly with the papaya seeds, they are peppery.

Serves 6. African/Mesoamerican Influence.
Tamarillo can substitute for the gooseberries, or use strawberries.

Of this recipe,	To enjoy more,
Kapha, enjoy less	these aren't your best fruits so have less
Pitta, enjoy some	O.K. occasionally; decrease papaya seeds
Vata, enjoy more	

SWEET AND SOUR ORANGE FRUIT SALAD.

PEACH and CHERRY COMPOTE

We imbue our bodies with the energy of the food we eat.

2 cups water
1/4 cup unrefined cane sugar
1/2 stick cinnamon or 1 tsp ground
1/2 tsp whole cloves, crushed
a sprinkle of sea salt
1 kg = 2 lbs peaches
250 gm = 1/2 lb cherries

1. In a medium saucepan combine water, sugar and cinnamon stick. Bring to boil and simmer for 20 minutes, uncovered. Add remaining spices and salt.
2. Peel and slice peaches and pit the cherries into halves.
3. Add the fruit to the cooking syrup. When it returns to boil, simmer 3 minutes, stirring the syrup through.
4. Remove cinnamon stick and serve.

Serves 4-6. Mesoamerican Influence, Guatemala.

Of this recipe,   Enjoy more if you
Kapha, enjoy some .... sprinkle the spices on a small portion of uncooked fruit
Pitta, enjoy less .... decrease the peaches, make sure the cherries are sweet; decrease the cloves
Vata, enjoy more

A COLORFUL COMBINATION OF LIGHTLY COOKED FRUIT.

PEARS and ANISE

What we don't change with intelligence, nature rectifies through less desirable means.

>**4 pears**
>**1 tbsp ghee**
>**2 tsp aniseed**
>**1 tbsp linseed**
>**1/4 tsp sea salt**
>**1 tbsp grapefruit juice**
>**2 tsp grated grapefruit zest**

1. Peel and core pears, cut into lengthwise pieces and poach in a small amount of water in a covered saucepan over medium low heat, stirring now and then.
2. Crush the anise and linseed.
3. In a small skillet warm the ghee over medium heat. Add the seeds, lower heat and cook 1 minute. Add the salt and let cool.
4. When the pears are cooked yet intact, about 10 minutes, stir the ghee, juice and zest into them gently.
5. Serve warm well before any meal.

Serves 4. European Influence.

Of this recipe,	To further benefit,
Kapha, enjoy some	use less ghee, linseed and juice
Pitta, enjoy some	use less anise, linseed and juice
Vata, enjoy some	pears are not recommended on a regular basis

POACHED WITH GRAPEFRUIT JUICE AND RIND.

PEPPER FRUIT SYRUP

Ayurvedic methods aim to be mostly as gentle as possible and sometimes more aggressive.

1/2 level tsp black peppercorns
1/2 level tsp allspice berries
1/4 tsp ground cinnamon
a few grains of sea salt
1 tbsp honey

1. Dry roast the pepper and allspice in a small skillet over medium low heat. Transfer to mortar and grind to powder.
2. Combine all ingredients using water if needed to thin the syrup.

Serves 2. Caribbean Influence.

Of this recipe,   To modify,
Kapha, enjoy more
Pitta, enjoy less .... all of these ingredients are heating
Vata, enjoy some .... these ingredients are also drying

A SPICY-SWEET BLEND THAT COMPLIMENTS FRUIT.

PINEAPPLE and COCONUT

Be satisfied with the way your kitchen allows you to work.

> 1 tsp fresh grated ginger
> 1 cup fresh sweet pineapple
> 1/2 cup fresh coconut or 2 tbsp dried
> fresh coriander leaves
> 1/4 tsp turmeric
> a scant 1/4 tsp sea salt
> 1 tbsp palm or unrefined cane sugar or maple syrup

1. Grate ginger.
2. Remove peel, slice lengthwise, remove core and dice pineapple, collecting juice as well.
3. If using fresh coconut, grate the white finely.
4. Cut fine the coriander leaves to the amount of 2 tablespoons. Nice colors.
5. In a small skillet over medium low heat, toast the dried coconut until golden and aromatic. If using fresh, add below with the pineapple. Remove toasted coconut from skillet.
6. Add the pineapple, juice, ginger, turmeric and fresh coconut, if using, to the skillet. Simmer about 10 minutes.
7. Add the salt and sweetener. Cook several minutes more.
8. When cooler toss through the coriander and garnish with the toasted coconut. It may be appropriate to drain the excess liquid which will make a tasty beverage.

Makes about 1 cup. South East Asian/Caribbean/Philippine Influence.

Of this recipe,   To modify,
Kapha, enjoy less .... increase ginger and coriander, decrease all else
Pitta, enjoy some .... decrease ginger
Vata, enjoy more

A TROPICAL CHUTNEY.

PLUM DUMPLINGS

Accept the generosity of the plant kingdom.

The Wrappers

1 tbsp ghee

1 tsp fennel seed

1/2 tsp cumin seed

1/4 tsp caraway seed

1 1/2 cups whole wheat flour, any variety

1/2 cup water

1 tbsp palm or unrefined cane sugar

1/4 tsp sea salt

1 1/2 tsp orange rind

12 cherry plums or 3 whole plums

extra fennel seed

extra sugar

1. Warm ghee in a small skillet over medium low heat. Add all seeds and sauté for 2 minutes. Remove from heat and cool.
2. Place flour in a mixing bowl.
3. Dissolve sugar and salt in water.
4. Add ghee mix and water mix to the flour, with the orange rind, making soft pliable dough. Knead for 5 minutes and let rest, covered with a damp cloth, while you prepare the plums.
5. Cut the cheeks off the cherry plums. Dip one cheek in the extra fennel seeds and the other in the extra sugar. Realign the halves. If using whole plums, cut each into quarters. Dip each quarter both into the sugar and seeds.
6. Set a medium saucepan of water to boil, covered.
7. Divide dough into 12 pieces. Roll each out to 9 cm = 3 1/2 inches diameter, more of an ellipse than a circle. Make sure it is not too thin.
8. Into the lower half of each ellipse, place the realigned cherry plum halves or plum quarters and fold dough over, creating half circles. Seal the edge well and trim excess dough.
9. Place all dumplings into the water at a low boil, uncovered, stirring occasionally.
10. When they rise to the surface, cook 3 minutes more.
11. Drain and dry on cooling racks. Serve with plum and orange remnants and something green for the visual sense.

Makes 12 dumplings. European Influence, Croatia.

Of this recipe,	To modify in your direction,
Kapha, enjoy less	you would change the fruit and flour, decrease the sugar and ghee; this means enjoy less
Pitta, enjoy more	make sure the plums are sweet
Vata, enjoy more	make sure the combination of starch and fruit does not produce wind; everyone can heed this possibility

PLUM FILLING COOKED IN BOILED DOUGH WRAPPERS.

PLUM SAUCE

We learn to trust our own guidance.

6 firm, ripe plums
2 tsp ghee
2 tsp fresh ginger
1 tsp coriander powder
1/4 tsp cardamom
1/4 tsp sea salt
2 tbsp palm or unrefined cane sugar or maple syrup, maybe
    less

1. Slice plums in half lengthwise to remove stones. Remove skins if necessary.
2. Warm ghee in small saucepan over medium low heat. Grate in ginger (or use 1 tsp powder), add coriander and cardamom and swirl. Heat for 1 minute.
3. Add plums and cook, covered, 15 minutes, stirring occasionally.
4. Incorporate salt and sweetener and cook uncovered another 5 minutes.
5. Serve at room temperature.

Serves 4. European - Indian Influence.

Of this recipe,	Better yet,
Kapha, enjoy less	use apples instead of plums and when cool, honey instead of sugars
Pitta, enjoy some	use sweet plums only and decrease the ginger
Vata, enjoy more	with less sugar, which unsettles vata

SPICES SUPPORT FLAVOR AND DIGESTION. FRUIT CAN BE A
MEAL IN ITSELF.

PRUNE CHUTNEY

I serve the Divine in preparing this food.

1 cup prunes
water
1 orange
1 tsp ghee
1 tsp ginger powder
a sprinkle of asafoetida
1/2 tsp sea salt
1 tbsp sunflower seeds

1. Soak the prunes in water for several hours.
2. Work in the soak water to remove the prune seeds. Coarsely chop prunes and recombine with the soak water in a small saucepan.
3. Cook uncovered over medium low heat, stirring occasionally to evaporate the water, about 15 minutes.
4. Grate the peel of the orange to the amount of 2 teaspoons and pare off a few thin threads for garnish. Collect the juice.
5. Add 2 tablespoons of juice and the grated rind to the prunes.
6. Dissolve the ghee on top of the cooking prunes, adding the ginger and asafoetida to the molten pool. Infuse for one minute and mix in.
7. Add the salt to the chutney and cook a few minutes to blend energies. Let cool.
8. Toast or dry roast the sun seeds.
9. Garnish with toasted seeds and orange rind threads.

Serves 8-10. European - Indian Influence.

Of this recipe,
Kapha, Pitta and Vata, enjoy some
PRUNE AND ORANGE, A LITTLE GOES A LONG WAY.

QUINCE SPREAD

If one is predominantly pitta, they won't do their best work in a hot and steamy kitchen.

2 tbsp almonds
1 kg = 2 lb fresh quince
2 tbsp pistachios

The Seasonings
1 tsp sesame oil
1 tsp cinnamon
1/4 tsp nutmeg
1/2 tsp sea salt
2 tbsp unprocessed honey

1. Heat almonds in a small amount of warm water until skins swell. When cooler, remove skins. Cut into large pieces and soak in water while proceeding with the recipe.
2. Have a steamer going. Cut quinces into narrow sections, breathing in the aroma. Steam for 10 minutes until soft. The peel agreeably flavors the fruit but not if overcooked.
3. Cool. Remove core and peel and mash the fruit.
4. Warm a small skillet over medium heat. Lightly toast pistachios and remove.
5. Remove skillet from heat and add the oil, warming it with the remaining heat. Swirl in the spice powders.
6. Pat almonds dry.
7. Combine fruit, salt, almonds and spices. As it is no longer hot, add honey and garnish with pistachios.

Serves 6. North African Influence, Egypt.

Of this recipe,   To modify,
Kapha, enjoy less ....decrease the nuts
Pitta, enjoy some ....use less nuts and nutmeg and use cane sugar instead of honey
Vata, enjoy more

THE PERFUMES OF QUINCE, CINNAMON AND NUTMEG.

RHUBARB and STRAWBERRIES

A simple combination of food is easier to cook and easier to digest.

3/4 cup sultanas
3 sticks of rhubarb
375 gm = 13 oz = 1 1/2 punnets strawberries
1 orange
1 tsp ghee
1/4 tsp cloves
1/4 tsp sea salt

1. Soak sultanas in water to cover for 1 hour.
2. Cut rhubarb and strawberries into small pieces.
3. Collect the zest from one half of the orange.
4. Warm ghee in a medium saucepan over low heat. Add cloves, whole or dried and orange zest. Sauté 1 minute.
5. Add rhubarb and strawberries. Bring to boil and simmer, covered, until the rhubarb is soft and the strawberries have disintegrated, about 15 minutes. Stir occasionally.
6. Add the sultanas and soak water. Cook 5 minutes.
7. Add salt and serve with a garnish of orange rind threads.

Serves 4. European Influence.

Of this recipe,   To enjoy more,
Kapha, enjoy less .... change this to raw strawberries sprinkled with cloves and orange zest, a few grains of salt and a few sultanas
Pitta, enjoy less
Vata, enjoy some .... decrease sultanas; substitute palm sugar if you experience wind from dried fruit

STEWED INGREDIENTS, POWERFUL TASTE.

SEEDS, FIGS and APPLES

"Oh", said the waitress in the American diner. "Vegetarian, are you? You won't live any longer. It will just feel that way."

1/2 cup almonds
8 figs

4 firm apples
lemon juice

1 tbsp ghee
1 tsp cinnamon
1/4 cup linseed
1/4 cup sunflower seeds
a sprinkle of sea salt

1. Soak almonds and dried figs separately several hours or overnight.
2. Heat almonds in warm water until the skins swell. Cool, remove skins, chop coarsely.
3. Chop figs.
4. Peel and cut the apples into small chunks and mix in a squeeze of lemon juice.
5. Warm ghee in medium saucepan over medium low heat.
6. Sprinkle on the cinnamon and introduce the almonds and all seeds except for the linseed, toasting for up to 2 minutes. Add the linseed in the last half minute, they toast quickly.
7. Add the apple and cook about 5 minutes, stirring occasionally.
8. Incorporate the figs and salt and heat another 2 minutes.

Serves 6. North American Influence.

Of this recipe,	To improve for you,
Kapha, enjoy some	use less seeds and nuts
Pitta, enjoy some	use less seeds and nuts
Vata, enjoy some	make sure the apples are cooked and decrease the dried figs

SEEDS AND NUTS ADD CRUNCH AND ESSENCE.

STEAMED APPLES

What is the difference between a millet seed and a speck of rock that size?

a small handful of almonds

The Dressing
1/4 cup raisins
1 tbsp sesame seeds
1 tbsp palm or unrefined cane sugar
1/2 cup water
a sprinkle of sea salt
1 tsp ghee

4 large apples
lemon juice
nutmeg

1. Heat almonds in a small amount of warm water until skins swell. When cooler, remove skins. Cut into pieces and soak in fresh water while you proceed with the recipe.
2. Combine raisins, seeds, sugar and water in a small saucepan. Bring to boil and simmer, uncovered, until the water has evaporated, about 15 minutes. Stir occasionally. Add salt and ghee and keep warm.
3. Peel and dice apples and toss in a few drops of lemon juice.
4. Steam apples, covered, for 4 minutes, redistributing after 2 minutes.
5. Serve apples with the seed dressing, garnish with almonds, drained, and a light sprinkle of nutmeg.

Serves 6. European Influence, Germany.

Of this recipe,   Only if you,
Kapha, enjoy more .... steam the apples with some raisins, add a few grains of salt and sprinkle with nutmeg; most seeds and all nuts are to be used in very small amounts
Pitta, enjoy more .... decrease seeds, almonds and nutmeg
Vata, enjoy some .... cook apples well and decrease raisins; we trust that the cooked fruit will digest well with seeds and nuts; if it does not, delete them

LARGE ALMOND CRUNCH, SMALL SESAME CRUNCH AND APPLE DICE.

STONEFRUIT SPREAD

We stay well by balancing indulgence and repression; neither is helpful in excess.

500 gm = 1 lb plums, peaches or nectarines or a combination
1/3 cup palm or unrefined cane sugar
a sprinkle of earth or sea salt
a sprinkle of cinnamon or cardamom

1. Cut fruit into pieces into a heavy medium saucepan, removing stones.
2. Heat, covered, until fruit becomes pulp, about 20 minutes.
3. Remove skins if required (irritable bowels do not tolerate skins or seeds and peach skins may be too coarse).
4. Add sugar to the pulp and cook uncovered on low heat about 15 minutes, stirring occasionally. The volume condenses and the color becomes glossy rather than caramelized.
5. Add salt and spice and cool.

Yields about 1 cup. European and North American Influence.

Of this recipe,   Even better,
Kapka, enjoy less .... choose a less sour fruit and enjoy it raw with the spice(s)
Pitta, enjoy more .... in moderation
Vata, enjoy more .... in moderation

SMOOTH AND GLOSSY, SWEET AND SOUR.

NUTS AND SEEDS

CHESTNUT SAUCE

The reality brought to us by our senses presents one aspect of existence.

500 gm = 1 lb chestnuts in shell
1/8 tsp earth or sea salt
2 sprigs of celery leaves
2 tsp ghee
1/4 tsp celery seed
2 cups fresh stock or water
black peppercorns

1. Using a sharp knife carefully remove the attractively colored husk from the chestnuts.
2. Blanch the nuts in water to cover for two minutes. Remove the brown covering when the nuts are still hot. Hold each in a towel to protect the fingers that hold it. Cut nuts into small pieces.
3. Simmer chestnuts in the water, covered, with the celery leaves for 20 minutes, until soft. Mash occasionally. Remove celery leaves.
4. If the mass is still too coarse, press most of the chestnuts through a robust sieve. Some larger pieces of nut provide texture. Adjust to pouring consistency if desired by adding water or leave as a nut sauce.
5. Warm ghee in a small skillet over medium low heat. Add celery seeds and sauté for 1 minute.
6. Add skillet mix, salt and a few turns of the pepper grinder to the sauce.

Makes 2 cups. Scandinavian Influence, Denmark. In China and Japan sweet chestnut purée is a favorite.

Of this recipe,   To modify,
Kapha, enjoy less .... nuts are heavy; the celery seeds and pepper are the best part of this for you
Pitta, enjoy more
Vata, enjoy more

COOKED CHESTNUTS AND AN UNDERCURRENT OF CELERY.

FLAVORED ALMONDS

A contented heart makes all food delicious.

1 cup whole raw almonds
2 kaffir lime leaves, fresh
lemon grass stem, fresh
a sprinkle of ginger powder
sea salt

1. Heat almonds in a small amount of warm water until skins swell. When cooler, remove skins. Soak in water for up to 8 hours. The longer they soak the sweeter and more digestible they become.
2. Peel off outer lemon grass leaves and slice from the base of the stalk up in very thin rings. When the purple inner ring disappears, slice no further. Use the remaining stem to make stock or tea.
3. Roll the lime leaves into a cylinder and slice thinly.
4. Combine leaves and stalk and mince even finer.
5. Split almonds into halves. If they split on their own, great!
6. Toss all seasonings into almonds with no more salt than a pinch, bruising the seasonings and working them onto the almonds.

Makes 1 cup. Asian Influence, Thailand.

Of this recipe,	Because,
Kapha, enjoy less	nuts are heavy and oily, almonds are O.K.
occasionally	
Pitta, enjoy some	heavy is O.K., how oily do you feel?
Vata, enjoy more	

ALMONDS SUFFUSED WITH LIGHT CITRUS.

GREEN TOPPING

What one uses their life for and why is an exploration that
continues a lifetime.

2 dozen whole walnuts yielding 3/4 cup halves
1 1/2 cups fresh parsley, well packed
1/2 cup fresh basil, well packed
1/2 cup fresh sage, lightly packed
1/4 cup olive oil
barely 1/2 tsp earth or sea salt
2 tsp citrus juice
black peppercorns

1. Crush walnuts coarsely with pestle.
2. Remove herbs from stems and mince fine, each herb asserting its own fragrance. Combine with walnuts and oil.
3. Add salt just before serving together with the citrus juice and a few turns of the pepper grinder.

Use to garnish cooked vegetables, salad, flatbread, plain grains and legumes.

Of this recipe,   To adapt,

Kapha, enjoy less .... omit the nuts, decrease the oil, the herbs are great!

Pitta, enjoy less .... use less because all ingredients need to be reduced

Vata, enjoy more........... but not heaps! vata is the constitution most suited to oil dressings; add more citrus juice

CRUSHED WALNUTS AND FRESH HERBS.

HONEY SHAPES

Honey when unheated is the supreme nectar of the plant kingdom.

>1/2 cup sesame seeds
>1/2 cup + 2 tbsp sunflower seeds
>1/2 cup coconut
>a sprinkle of sea salt
>1 tsp ginger powder
>1/3 - 1/2 cup unprocessed honey
>
>carob powder, toasted coconut, toasted sesame seeds or all three

1. In a small skillet, dry roast the sesame, sunflower and coconut separately over medium low heat until a shade darker.
2. Blend all seeds into medium-fine meal.
3. Combine with the coconut, salt, ginger and honey. Begin with the lesser amount of honey.
4. Turn out the mix and oil your dry hands. Knead the mass until it sticks together. If it is too crumbly add additional honey.
5. Form into shapes. Dust with carob powder, coconut and/or seeds. Consider using different spices and coatings. If none of the ingredients are dry roasted the shapes are raw and can store for longer than a day, depending on local temperature.

Makes 2 cups, 24 bite-sized pieces. European/Asian Influence.

Of this recipe,	To explain,
Kapha, enjoy less	sesame and coconut are heavy
Pitta, enjoy less	sesame is oily and honey and ginger are heating
Vata, enjoy some	these are rich and filling

HONEY BINDS SEEDS AND COCONUT.

MACADAMIA PESTO

Taking care to prepare a dish increases the energy in it.

1 cup macadamia kernels
2 tbsp olive oil
2 tsp paprika
2 tsp cumin
1/2 cup coriander leaves
1/4 cup fresh parsley
1/4 tsp earth or sea salt
less than 1/2 tsp black pepper
2 tsp lemon juice

1. In a small skillet, toast the macadamias over medium low heat until parts are lightly browned.
2. Remove nuts to cool and add oil to pan. Using medium low heat warm oil and sprinkle in paprika and cumin. Remove from heat.
3. Mince the coriander and parsley.
4. Combine skillet spices, salt, freshly ground pepper, minced herbs and lemon juice.
5. Crush nuts in a mortar with a pestle or chop by hand. If you use a processor use the pulse option to retain some texture.
6. Combine all ingredients. Adjust to a sauce-like consistency with more oil or retain the more crumbly texture as desired.

Serves 6. Australian Influence.

Of this recipe,   To enjoy more,
Kapha, enjoy less .... replace macadamias with pumpkin or sunflower seeds and less of them; decrease oil; this will produce a crunchy spice-herb topping rather than a pesto
Pitta, enjoy less .... use seeds as above and decrease oil, paprika and pepper
Vata, enjoy more............ in moderation

TOASTED NUTS ARE COMBINED WITH SPICES AND FRESH HERBS.

NUT and SEED GARNISH

Although any one thing may work wonderfully for you, it doesn't automatically follow that everyone will benefit from it.

less than 1/4 tsp peppercorns
1 tsp coriander seeds
1 tsp cumin seeds
1 tbsp sesame seeds
less than 1/4 tsp sea salt
5 hazelnuts, shells removed

1. Warm a small skillet over medium low heat. Dry roast peppercorns for 1 minute. Adjust heat to prevent burning. That's the first perfume. Transfer to mortar and grind when cooled.
2. Dry roast coriander and cumin seeds 2 minutes and add to mortar. Crush the coriander.
3. Dry roast sesame seeds and salt until light brown. Add with mortar ingredients to a small serving bowl.
4. Dry roast hazelnuts 2 minutes and crush in mortar.
5. Add to the mix.
6. Sprinkle on vegetables, soup or staples.

Makes 3 tablespoons, serves 6-8. North African Influence, Egypt.

Of this recipe,   To modify,
Kapha, enjoy less .... decrease nuts and sesame seeds substantially
Pitta, enjoy less .... decrease nuts, sesame and pepper
Vata, enjoy more

DRY-ROASTED NUTS, SEEDS AND SPICES.

NUT CHUTNEY

To cook is to be an artist in mixed media.

1/4 cup whole almonds
1 tbsp lemon rind
2 tbsp lemon juice

The Spices
2 tsp ghee
2 tsp cinnamon
less than 1/2 tsp ground cardamom
1/4 tsp ground cloves
less than 1/2 tsp grated nutmeg

1 medium apple
2 tbsp pine nuts
2 tbsp palm or unrefined cane sugar
1/4 tsp earth or sea salt

1. Heat almonds in a small amount of warm water until skins swell. When cooler, remove skins. Cut into medium fine pieces. Soak those pieces in fresh water for 30 minutes.
2. Grate the lemon rind and collect the juice.
3. Warm the ghee in a small saucepan over low heat. Sauté the 4 spices for 1 minute.
4. During that time peel and then grate the apple onto the sautéing spices, adding 1 tablespoon lemon juice. Cook, stirring frequently until drier, about 5 minutes. Let cool, adding lemon rind.
5. In a small skillet dry roast the pine nuts over medium low heat for one minute. Keep watch that the pine nuts become light brown, not dark brown. Remove from heat.
6. Drain almonds and combine all ingredients.

A spoonful is a serving. Serves 6-8 people. Middle Eastern Influence, Israel.

To refine,
Kapha, use less lemon juice, far fewer nuts, more spices; use honey instead of sugar when cooled
Pitta, use less lemon juice, cloves, nutmeg and also decrease the nuts

APPLE AND SPICES ARE COOKED AND TOASTED NUTS ARE ADDED.

NUT PORRIDGE

The Yoga of Patañjali teaches that to make change, we apply effort, step by step.

3/4 cup almonds, cashews and/or Brazil nuts
2 1/2 cups water
2 tbsp arrowroot powder or other thickener
2 tsp ghee
1/4 tsp cinnamon, cardamom or ginger powder
sweetener such as palm sugar, unrefined cane sugar, honey or maple syrup
    to taste
a scant 1/4 tsp earth or sea salt
1 tbsp sesame seeds, optional

1. If using almonds soak overnight. Warm in fresh water to cover. When the skins swell, remove from heat. Remove skins.
2. Finely grate, crush or pulverize nuts, allowing some larger pieces as texture. An electric appliance is useful here.
3. Combine with water and arrowroot in a saucepan and bring to boil over medium low heat.
4. When the porridge thickens, dissolve the ghee on top. When it is molten, sprinkle on the spices. Too much spice detracts from the nutty flavor.
5. Stir in spices, sweetener and salt and remove from heat. If using honey, add when porridge has cooled.
6. Divide into 4 small bowls and garnish with another sprinkle of spice(s).
7. If wishing to garnish with sesame seeds, dry roast them in a small skillet over medium heat until golden. Let cool and sprinkle on.

Serves 4. Asian Influence, Hong Kong.

Of this recipe,   To fine-tune,
Kapha, enjoy less .... enjoy your serving with honey and more spice and still choose less
Pitta, enjoy less .... enjoy your serving with cane sugar, sugarcane juice or maple syrup, less spice and still choose less
Vata, enjoy more

SWEET NUT PURÉE, EASILY COOKED.

NUTS in MUNG FLOUR

Are you physically hungry or not? Only eat if you are.

1 1/2 cups raw cashews

The Spices

2 tsp ghee	1 tbsp tamarind purée or lemon juice
1 tsp cumin seed	1 1/2 cups mung flour
a sprinkle of asafoetida	1 cup water, more or less
1/2 tsp turmeric	
1/2 tsp earth or sea salt	lettuce leaves
1/2 tsp ground black pepper	

1. Have ready your steamer. See the Steamed Buns recipe for description.
2. Toss the cashews in a small skillet over medium heat until they are beginning to color. Remove and set aside.
3. Warm the ghee in the skillet, reducing heat to medium low. Add the cumin seed and asafoetida, sauté for 1 minute and turn off the heat. As the skillet begins to cool add the rest of the spices.
4. To make tamarind purée, pour about 2 tablespoons of hot water over 1 tablespoon dried tamarind. Let cool. Knead fruit off seeds and pass through a fine strainer. Collect 1 tablespoon of purée.
5. Combine all the ingredients except the lettuce. This is stiffer than a batter, it will make patties that hold their shape.
6. Place lettuce or other leaves onto the steamer rack and set tablespoon-size shapes onto the leaves, flattening to less than 1.5 cm = 3/4 inch. If using your hands, oil them first.
7. Steam for 15 minutes.
8. When removing steamed shapes, let steam dissipate from tops, then invert to remove leaves and dry the bottoms.
9. Serve warm with chutney or vegetables. Alternatively, you can boil them in soup as dumplings. Use rounded teaspoonfuls and low boil for 10 minutes.

Serves 3-4 as a meal with vegetables. Makes 24 tablespoon-size shapes as a snack. African-Indian Influence.

Of this recipe, To fine-tune,
Kapha, enjoy less ....it's only the cashews that need to be decreased substantially; use a few sunflower seeds for texture
Pitta, enjoy some ....use less nuts, omit the pepper
Vata, enjoy some ....the nuts are rich but the patties are dry; enjoy something unctuous as well

STEAMED CASHEW PATTIES.

PISTACHIO DRESSING

Prepare this recipe when the choicest ingredients have come your way.

1/4 cup shelled pistachios
1 tsp lemon zest
1/4 cup lemon juice
1/4 cup olive oil
a sprinkle of sea salt and pepper

1. Dry roast pistachios over medium heat for 5 minutes or toast in oven for15 minutes at 375°F (190°C, Gas 5). Cool. Rub off and discard as much skin as possible. Grind nuts with mortar and pestle, loosening them with some of the olive oil if needed. How green is that?
2. Grate 1 teaspoon of lemon peel, then juice the lemon.
3. Place the quarter cup of juice in a bowl, whisk in oil, and then the remaining ingredients.

Serves 6 over salad or cooked vegetables. Middle Eastern Influence, Lebanon.

Of this recipe,	To honor your dosha,
Kapha, enjoy less	a taste is enough
Pitta, enjoy some	remember that oily and/or sour is not ideal for pure pitta
Vata, enjoy more...........	vegetables are too "thin" without it

A CLASSIC DRESSING IS SWEETENED AND FORTIFIED WITH CRUSHED NUTS.

PUMPKIN SEEDS

If one does one's best, a fine meal results by divine grace.

1 cup raw pumpkin seeds
2 tsp ghee
1 tsp coriander powder
1/2 tsp cumin powder
1/4 tsp turmeric
a sprinkle of sea salt

1. Warm a medium skillet or saucepan over medium low heat.
2. Dry roast the pumpkin seeds for a few minutes, tossing occasionally.
3. Open a space in the middle of the skillet and dissolve the ghee.
4. Sprinkle on spices and warm the spice pool for half a minute. Toss the seeds into the spices, spices onto the seeds. Add salt.

Serve as a snack or garnish.

Makes 1 cup. Indian Influence.

Of this recipe,
Kapha, enjoy some
Pitta, enjoy some
Vata, enjoy some

SEEDS, SWELLED AND SPICED.

PUMPKIN SEED SAUCE

"It can't be the cheese", said the man with the stiff knees.
"I eat that everyday".

1/2 cup pumpkin seeds
1 generous tsp ghee
1/4 tsp mustard seed
1 tbsp fresh herb(s)
2 tsp arrowroot or kudzu

1/2 cup water
1/8 tsp sea salt
1 tsp lime juice

1. Add pumpkin seeds to a medium skillet and roast over medium heat, shaking the pan often. When the first few pop remove to another bowl.
2. Add the ghee to the skillet. Add mustard seeds and roast until the first one pops. Remove from heat and let the skillet cool.
3. Mince fresh herbs, varying those used each time if you wish.
4. Suspend arrowroot in the water. Add to the skillet and bring to boil, stirring constantly until the arrowroot mix becomes transparent and thicker.
5. Add herbs and salt and cook another minute.
6. Begin cooling, adding lime juice. Add pumpkin seeds and serve over grains, legumes, beans or vegetables.

Serves 6-8. Mesoamerican Influence, Mexico.

Of this recipe,   To enjoy more,
Kapha, enjoy some .... leave out the starchy thickener and the water
Pitta, enjoy some .... decrease the mustard seeds and choose less pungent herbs
Vata, enjoy more .... use more lime juice

TOASTED SEEDS SUSPENDED IN SAUCE.

SESAME, ALMONDS and DATES

Simsim is the Arabic word for sesame and is a term of endearment.

24 almonds
1 tbsp sesame seeds
12 medium or large dates
1/2 tsp cardamom
a sprinkle of sea salt

1. Soak almonds in water for 6-8 hours. Heat them in a small amount of warm water until skins swell. When cooler, remove skins. The soaking makes them more digestible, moister and sweeter which serves when they are eaten whole.
2. Toast sesame seeds and place on a small plate.
3. Combine cardamom and salt onto another small plate.
4. Slit each date into 2 halves and remove pit and cap.
5. Press each date portion flat onto the cardamom and salt mix and then the simsim. Place an almond on top. Mold date around the almond as far as it goes. When all dates have been prepared, sprinkle any remaining simsim and cardamom over them.

Serves 6. Middle Eastern Influence, Lebanon.

Be aware of how this dried fruit and nut combination works for you. If indigestion arises use only the dates and spices or only the nuts and seeds and spices.

Of this recipe,   Because,
Kapha, enjoy less .... sweet and heavy, enjoy one if you are hungry
Pitta, enjoy less .... decrease nuts and seeds
Vata, enjoy some .... these have good attributes for you if they don't produce wind, but don't make a meal of them

THESE DELECTABLES CAN BE MORNING OR AFTERNOON SNACK.

SWEET WALNUTS

We are not pursuing one specific taste because all ingredients have changes in taste place to place, year to year.

> **1 cup walnut pieces**
> **1/2 cup palm or unrefined cane sugar**
> **a sprinkle of sea salt**
> **1/2 tsp cinnamon**

1. Accept any size walnut pieces.
2. Mix with the remaining ingredients.
3. Warm a heavy pot or skillet over high heat.
4. Add mix and sauté until the sugar melts and coats the nuts, stirring constantly and lowering heat to prevent burning.
5. Remove onto a glass or glazed surface and separate pieces.
6. Cool before serving.

Makes 1 cup. Mesoamerican Influence, Mexico.

Of this recipe,	To fine-tune,
Kapha, enjoy less	have a stick of celery instead
Pitta, enjoy a few	use almonds, a less oily nut
Vata, enjoy some	sugar in this proportion can unsettle you

IN AYURVEDIC TERMS THIS IS CANDY.

TAMARIND CHUTNEY

At this time and in this place no one can cook a meal better than you.

1/4 cup dried lotus seeds, loosely packed, or sunflower seeds
1/4 cup tamarind pulp with seeds, slightly less without seeds
a generous 1 cup hot water
1/4 cup walnut pieces, loosely packed
3 tbsp palm or unrefined cane sugar or maple syrup
1 generous tsp ghee
1/8 tsp earth or sea salt
less than 1/4 tsp black pepper
several thin mandarin or orange peel threads

1. Soak lotus seeds 8 hours and simmer in a small saucepan, covered, for 30 minutes. Split seeds open and remove green germ if present. Chop the nuts fine and set aside.
2. Mash tamarind in hot water and let cool. Work tamarind off seeds and collect purée through a sieve. This yields about 1 cup.
3. Crush or chop walnuts with lotus seeds. If using sun seeds, add to crushed walnuts.
4. To prepare chutney, heat tamarind purée in the small saucepan and simmer to condense.
5. Add sweetener and continue cooking to a thicker glossy consistency, about 10 minutes.
6. Add ghee, nut blend and salt and combine ingredients with heat for 3 minutes. Cool.
7. Add pepper. Garnish with mandarin zest.

Serves 10. All servings are small. Chinese Influence.

Of this recipe,   To refine,
Kapha, enjoy less .... even with a small serving decrease seeds and nuts and use honey instead of sugar when cooled
Pitta, enjoy less .... even with a small serving decrease seeds, nuts and pepper and use the cane sugar or maple syrup
Vata, enjoy some .... use less lotus seeds

LOTUS AND WALNUTS IN A SWEET AND SOUR CONDIMENT.

TOASTED SUN SEEDS

Generally, we can sample a taste of any food.

1/4 tsp mustard seeds
1/4 tsp fenugreek seeds
1 cup sunflower seeds
2 tsp ghee
a sprinkle of sea salt

1. Warm a medium sized skillet or saucepan over medium heat and add mustard and fenugreek seeds. Heat 1 minute and transfer to mortar.
2. When cooler, grind seeds with pestle, especially the fenugreek.
3. Add the sun seeds to the same skillet, lowering heat and toast several minutes, flipping occasionally.
4. Open up a space in the center and dissolve the ghee. Add the mortar mix and warm through.
5. Combine all skillet participants and add salt.

Use as a snack, garnish, sauce ingredient or embed them in flatbread.

Serves 4-6. Russian/Indian Influence.

Of this recipe,   To fine-tune,
Kapha, enjoy some
Pitta, enjoy some .... decrease fenugreek and mustard seeds
Vata, enjoy some

AN APPETIZING AND HEALTHY SNACK.

SOUP

AVOCADO SOUP

Some creative food combinations, however innovative, create commotion for the digestion.

<u>The Sauté</u>
2 stalks celery
1/2 zucchini
1 tbsp olive oil
a sprinkle of asafoetida
1 1/2 tsp coriander powder
1/2 tsp earth or sea salt

2 avocados
4 cups water
2 tbsp fresh coriander, amply packed
2 tsp lime or lemon juice
black peppercorns

1. Cut the celery and zucchini into small dice.
2. Warm the oil in a medium soup pot over medium low heat. Add celery, asafoetida and coriander and sauté 3 minutes. Add zucchini and sauté 2 minutes. Add salt. Remove from heat.
3. Scoop the avocado out of its hard shell into a large bowl. Add the water and mash. Purée by guiding through a sieve into the soup pot.
4. Chop the fresh coriander, reserving a few leaves as garnish, then crush the leaves with a mortar and pestle, further releasing the fragrance. Add to the pot and warm to combine flavors. Remove from heat.
5. Add the lime juice.
6. Garnish with reserved leaves and pass the pepper grinder at the table.
7. Alternatively serve with all ingredients diced and uncooked (without the water) as a summer lunch salad. Still follow the recommendations below.

Serves 4. South American Influence, Peru.

Of this recipe,	To adjust,
Kapha, enjoy less	avocado is heavy; at most enjoy a small bowl
Pitta, enjoy some	avocado is oily so enjoy a small-medium bowl
Vata, enjoy some	decrease celery

A ROOM TEMPERATURE AVOCADO PURÉE WITH VEGETABLE DICE.

BARLEY and DILL SOUP

Barley is the grain of Mars.

4 cups water
1/2 cup whole barley

The Vegetables
1 medium potato
1/4 cup loosely packed fresh dill
1/4 cup loosely packed fresh
  parsley
1/2 lettuce
1 bunch New Zealand or
English spinach

The Seasonings
1/4 tsp caraway seeds
1/4 tsp nigella seeds
1/4 tsp fenugreek seeds
1 tbsp ghee
a sprinkle of asafoetida
1 tsp earth or sea salt
a few drops of lemon juice
4 nasturtium or other flowers, optional

1. Bring water to boil in a medium soup pot and then simmer.
2. Dry roast the barley in a small skillet until some of the seeds spin, swell and pop. Add barley to simmering water.
3. Cook the washed, unpeeled potato with the barley if it is organic. Otherwise cook it in a separate pot.
4. Chop the herbs, lettuce and spinach together.
5. After cooking the barley for 30 minutes, peel and mash the cooked potato and return to pot, discarding peel, making a smooth soup base. If too thick, add more water.
6. Add the greens and cook 2 minutes at a simmer, uncovered. Remove from heat and cover.
7. In the small skillet over medium low heat, dry roast the caraway, nigella and fenugreek seeds for two minutes. Let cool somewhat to crush coarsely. Meanwhile warm the ghee in the skillet and add asafoetida. Add the crushed seeds and sauté another minute.
8. To serve, stir salt and skillet mix into the soup. Cover and continue cooling 5 minutes. Add a few drops of lemon juice and float a flower on top of each bowl of soup.

Serves 4-6. European/Indian Influence.

Of this recipe,   To further customize,
Kapha, enjoy more
Pitta, enjoy more .... use only a petal from the peppery nasturtium
Vata, enjoy some .... barley, potato and cooked greens are O.K.
occasionally; add an extra teaspoon of ghee

A CLASSIC ETHNIC SOUP WITH FRESH HERBS.

BARLEY DUMPLING SOUP

Allow all changes to be gentle and gradual, creating the ever-evolving you.

1 small bitter melon
1 tbsp sea salt + 2 cups water

The Dumplings
3/4 cup whole barley or 1 cup barley flour
up to 1 cup water
2 tsp ghee
1 tsp paprika
1 tsp coriander
1/2 tsp earth or sea salt
1/4 cup barley sprouts, optional

The Soup
6 cups water
1 tbsp ghee
2 tsp paprika
a sprinkle of asafoetida
1 bunch rocket or nasturtium leaves or 1/2 daikon radish
6-8 quarter rounds of lemon

1. Trim the bitter melon's ends and cut in quarters lengthwise. Scoop out the central seed/ pith portion. Cut into 1 cm = 1/2 inch pieces and soak in a small saucepan in the salt water mix for 30-60 minutes. Next time omit the salting and decide if it is too bitter.
2. If you have a grain mill, toast whole barley in a medium skillet over medium low heat until the first grains swell and pop. Let cool and grind into flour. Set aside. Toasting any grain makes it more flavorful and more digestible.
3. To make the dumplings, set the 1 cup of water to boil.
4. Warm a small skillet over low heat. Add 2 teaspoons ghee. Add the 1 teaspoon of paprika and coriander and temper for 1 minute.
5. Combine flour, salt, sprouts if using and skillet mix. Slowly add enough boiling water to produce a warm soft dough. Form into many little spheres using 1/2 teaspoon per sphere.
6. To make the soup bring the 6 cups of water to boil in a medium pot. Add the barley spheres, cover and simmer for 15 minutes.
7. Meanwhile, warm the next portion of ghee in the same small skillet over medium low heat. Swirl in the next amount of paprika and asafoetida. This skillet mix is destined for the soup pot. Set aside and let cool.
8. Bring the bitter melon to boil in fresh water. Boil uncovered 3 minutes.Drain and rinse well with cold water. If using daikon radish as the pungent vegetable, cut into fine dice and cook with the bitter melon. If bit-

ter melon unavailable add dandelion or endive greens in the next step.

9. Add the bitter melon, the chopped greens and the skillet mix to the dumpling soup. Simmer uncovered for several minutes more.

10. Serve with a quarter round of lemon.

Serves 6-8. Tibetan/Indian Influence.

Of this recipe,   To fine-tune,
Kapha, enjoy more
Pitta, enjoy more
Vata, enjoy some .... enjoy the broth, a few dumplings and take less
of the bitter melon

WITH BITTER MELON AND PUNGENT GREENS.

BEAN HOTPOT

With this first morsel of food that I eat, may evil be destroyed.
With the second, may I remember to practice good deeds.
May the third help all to attain the path of enlightenment.

— Buddhist prayer

1/2 cup pinto beans
4 cups boiling water

Green
1/2 cup loosely packed fresh dill
1/4 cup loosely packed fresh parsley
4 sprigs fresh mint, each 15 cm = 6 in. long
1 bunch spinach, Swiss chard or other green

Yellow and Orange
4 tbsp lemon juice and 4 threads of zest
4 tbsp orange juice and 4 threads of zest

2 tbsp ghee
a sprinkle of asafoetida
2 tbsp coriander powder
3/4 teaspoon earth or sea salt
fresh ground black pepper

1. Inspect beans to remove debris and inferior beans. Soak 8 hours. Discard this water and bring to boil in fresh water in a medium saucepan. Discard this water as well, rinse the beans and cover again with 4 cups of fresh boiling water. Simmer, covered, at least one hour.
2. During this time, rinse and chop the chlorophyll-rich dill, parsley, mint and spinach together.
3. Combine the lemon and orange juices.
4. When the beans are well cooked, mash them, using the stock to make a soup base. How well mashed and how thick this is, is cook's choice. Add water if too thick or remove some stock before mashing, re-adding it if necessary.
5. In the final soup pot, warm the ghee over medium heat. Add the asafoetida and coriander and swirl. Add the beans and stock.
6. Heat this soup base to just under boil, add the greens. If you don't have fresh herbs, use a smaller amount of dried herbs. Cook 2 minutes, then add salt. Remove from heat and add pepper and juices.
7. If you love to decorate, serve with a thin spiral of orange and lemon peel intertwined.

Serves 4. Middle Eastern Influence, Iran.

Of this recipe,	To further adjust,
Kapha, enjoy more	decrease the citrus juices
Pitta, enjoy some	decrease the citrus and spinach
Vata, enjoy less..............	use more ghee and less beans

REMINISCENT OF DILL PICKLE.

BEET and CABBAGE SOUP

We consume food but if a large part of our thoughts are about food, it consumes us.

3 cups water
2 bay leaves
2 medium beetroot
2 medium carrots
3 medium potatoes
1/2 small cabbage

The Seasonings
1 tbsp ghee
1 tsp fennel seed
1 tsp mustard seed
1 tsp cumin powder
a sprinkle of asafoetida
1 tsp earth or sea salt
lemon wedges

1. In a large soup pot bring to boil 3 cups of water with the bay leaves.
2. Peel and dice the colors beetroot, carrot and potato. Add to the pot.
3. Cook just under boil, covered, about 20 minutes.
4. Slice cabbage into short, thin ribbons and place in a smaller pot with 1 cup of water. Bring to boil and simmer, uncovered, 5 minutes, covered for 10 minutes.
5. In a small skillet, warm the ghee over medium heat. Add all seeds and asafoetida and cook until the first seed pops. Take the skillet off the heat to cool, swirl in the cumin powder and salt.
6. Press the diced vegetables through a sieve back into the soup pot or mash them while they are in the pot. Add the cabbage and its cooking liquid. Add the skillet mix. Combine the ingredients with a little more heat.
7. Pass the pepper grinder and lemon wedges at the table.

Serves 6. Russian Influence.

Of this recipe,   To further customize,
Kapha, enjoy more .... increase the spices, decrease the lemon juice
Pitta, enjoy some .... decrease the beetroot and lemon juice
Vata, enjoy some .... decrease the cabbage and potato

SHREDDED CABBAGE IN A VEGETABLE STOCK.

BROAD BEAN SOUP

Cooking like everything else sits on a sliding scale; there are no absolutes.

1/4 cup almonds
1/4 tsp saffron, lightly measured
2 cups shelled fresh broad beans
2 tbsp fresh parsley
2 tbsp olive oil
1/2 tsp cinnamon
1/4 cup hazelnuts, shelled
1 tsp palm or unrefined cane sugar
1 tsp earth or sea salt

1. Heat almonds in a small amount of warm water until skins swell. When cooler, remove skins. Grate or process into fine meal.
2. Soak saffron threads in 1/2 cup warm water with the grated almonds. Swirl occasionally.
3. Shell fresh beans. Discard any inferior specimens.
4. Bring to boil 5 1/2 cups of water in a medium large soup pot and add beans. Cook, covered 10 minutes. Remove beans and remove loosened skins. Mash some, most or all and return to the pot.
5. Mince parsley leaves.
6. Warm the olive oil in a pool on top of the soup.
7. Add cinnamon to the pool and let infuse 1 minute.
8. Add the saffron-almond liquid. Add the parsley. Mix.
9. Simmer while you chop the hazelnuts and toast them. Fan away any chaff.
10. Add the salt, sugar and nuts.

Serves 4-6. European Influence, Spain.

Of this recipe,	To assist your dosha,
Kapha, enjoy some	decrease nuts substantially, use less oil
Pitta, enjoy some	decrease nuts and oil as well
Vata, enjoy some	prepare when beans are in season with more oil

A SAFFRON-ALMOND BROTH WITH FRESH BEANS.

BROWN LENTIL HOTPOT

The cook is the person preparing the offering for the fire of digestion.

1 cup lentils

1 leek
1/4 cup olive oil
a sprinkle of asafoetida
a sprinkle of ajowan seed or savory
3/4 tsp earth or sea salt

1/2 tsp aniseed
quarter lemon rounds
minced fennel or parsley

1. Inspect lentils to remove stones, debris and inferior ones. Soak for 1 hour.
2. Rinse lentils and bring to boil in a medium soup pot with 6 cups of water. If foam arises drain, rinse and add fresh boiling water. Or skim off all the foam and continue cooking in the same liquid. Simmer, covered, for 30 minutes.
3. Slice the root end of the leek.
4. Warm the oil in a small skillet over medium heat and sauté the leek until softer. Add asafoetida, and ajowan, warming for one minute.
5. Add skillet ingredients to lentils and continue cooking for another 30 minutes. Stir occasionally or mash to disintegrate the lentils. As cooking nears completion, adjust consistency, adding more water or leaving uncovered to condense.
6. Add salt.
7. Dry roast aniseed in the small skillet for 2 minutes on low heat. Add to soup.
8. Garnish with lemon and fennel.

Serves 4. European Influence, Spain.

Of this recipe,   To modify,
Kapha, enjoy more..........use less oil
Pitta, enjoy some............this could be heating, notice its effects
Vata, enjoy less...............use more oil

A FULL-BODIED SOUP WITH SUBTLE ANISE FLAVOR.

CHOKO, CELERIAC and BROCCOLI BROTH

Regularity of routine is calming to the nervous system.

The Vegetables
1 small choko
1 small celeriac
1/2 broccoli
4 cups water

The Seasonings
1 tbsp ghee
1 1/2 tsp fennel seeds
1 tsp grated fresh ginger
a sprinkle of asafoetida

2 tsp sumac
1 tsp dried tarragon
1 tsp earth or sea salt

1. Prepare vegetables: peel whole choko. Cut it along its seams to finish peeling and cut into even-sized pieces. You can include the young seed as well. Peel celeriac by cutting off outer layer with a knife. Cut into small pieces first longitudinally, then horizontally. Cut broccoli stems into pieces and cut the flowerets in half into a separate pile.
2. Bring water to boil in a small pot.
3. Warm ghee in a medium soup pot over medium low heat and sauté fennel seeds, then ginger, then asafoetida for a total of 2 minutes.
4. Add vegetables except for flowerets and sauté for several minutes.
5. Add the boiling water and simmer, covered, 10-15 minutes, depending on the size of your vegetable pieces.
6. Add the sumac (or lemon juice to taste at the end), tarragon and salt and stir through. Add the flowerets and keep at simmer for 5 minutes more, uncovered, waiting for them to be vibrant green.

Serves 4-6. European Influence.

Of this recipe,   To enjoy more,
Kapha, enjoy some .... favor broccoli over choko and increase the ginger; use less lemon juice
Pitta, enjoy more .... ginger, tarragon and lemon juice, if using, may be reduced
Vata, enjoy more .... broccoli in this amount is O.K.

VEGETABLES, INCLUDING GREEN BROCCOLI FLOWERETS, IN A PASTEL PINK BROTH.

COCONUT SOUP

The first time with a recipe, you could contemplate how you would do the steps as you read them.

In the Oven
1 coconut
1 small red pepper (capsicum)

2 tbsp dried tamarind

a sprinkle of asafoetida
1/2 tsp ginger powder
3/4 tsp earth or sea salt

The Vegetables
1 handful green beans
1 stalk celery
1 spring onion
1/2 yellow crookneck squash
1 cup assorted green leaves
1/2 cup mung bean sprouts

1. To prepare fresh coconut milk have 90 minutes up your sleeve.
2. Preheat oven to 400°F (200°C, Gas 6).
3. Drain coconut water. Its aroma tells you if the coconut is fresh and is a cooling drink. Bake coconut for 15 minutes along with the sweet pepper. When the coconut begins to crack, remove and hit it open. When the capsicum is charred, place in bag and cool briefly, then rub off skin and dice.
4. Work a butter knife between coconut and shell. Sections will pop out. Peel them and grate as fine as possible, which will help extract the maximum richness. This all works by hand or do the grating with a food processor.
5. Combine 3 cups of the coconut with 3 cups of water in a medium saucepan and bring to boil. Simmer, covered, 20 minutes.
6. Meanwhile, combine tamarind with 1/2 cup hot water. When cooler, squeeze fruit off the seeds and collect the thin purée through a sieve.
7. Cut the beans, celery and spring onion bottom into very small pieces.
8. Cut the yellow summer squash into its own pile of small pieces.
9. Chop the greens and spring onion top in both directions.
10. When the coconut has finished cooking, let cool. Collect the coconut liquid through a strainer into a medium soup pot. Put the drained coconut into the center of thin, clean cotton fabric and wring out into the soup pot.*
11. Heat coconut milk until just under the boil. Add the green bean pile and asafoetida. Simmer, uncovered, 5 minutes.
12. Add the yellow squash and greens and cook 2 minutes more.
13. Add the sprouts, red pepper and ginger. Cook 3 minutes. Mix in the salt and 3 tablespoons of tamarind purée to serve.
    *You can extract thinner coconut liquid by repeating the boiling water procedure a second time.

Serves 4. Philippine Influence.

Of this recipe,   To modify,
Kapha, enjoy less .... omit the coconut soup and enjoy the vegetables

using less squash; use spices of choice
Pitta, enjoy some .... decrease the tamarind, pungent greens, ginger
Vata, enjoy some .... the coconut provides the oily, grounding
component

A TROPICAL-TASTING VEGETABLE SOUP.

FLAVORPOT

The person who eats the food influences its nutritional outcome.

The Flavor
2.5 cm = 1 inch fresh ginger
4 spring onions
1 tbsp ghee or sesame oil
1/2 tsp aniseed
1 small cassia quill
2 shaves licorice root (each 7 cm = 3 in.) or 1/2 tsp powder
3 pods cardamom
6 cloves
1/2 tsp fennel seeds

4 cups water

The Finishing Tastes
1 tsp earth or sea salt
1 tsp palm or unrefined cane sugar
1/4 tsp Sichuan or black pepper

1. Grate ginger and slice spring onions.
2. Warm ghee in medium soup pot over medium low heat and add the ginger, spring onions, aniseed, cassia, licorice, cardamom removed from its pods, cloves and fennel seed.
3. When all are added, sauté for 5 minutes over low heat.
4. Add water to the soup pot, bring to boil and simmer, covered, 10 minutes.
5. Add salt, sugar and pepper and let cool several minutes.
6. Options include straining for a clear broth, stock or tea; using some to poach diced or sliced vegetables; cooking 2 cups of rice in the flavorpot. The cassia bark will still have lots of flavor. Place it in 1 cup boiling water and enjoy as a tea.

Serves 4. Chinese Influence.

Of this recipe,   To refine,
Kapha enjoy some .... the spice blend is good with less licorice and sugar; use it for vegetables or steamed millet
Pitta, enjoy some .... minimize the pungent tastes, using less ginger, spring onions, aniseed, clove and pepper
Vata, enjoy more .... being aware that pungent is also drying

AH, SO, THE ORIENTAL TASTE.

JERK BROTH

When the emotional gateway is open, new information is
allowed consideration.

1 spring onion
4 cups water

<u>The Seasonings</u>
2 tbsp ghee
1 tsp allspice
1 tsp cinnamon
1/2 tsp dried thyme or 1 tsp fresh
1/4 tsp nutmeg
2 tsp palm or unrefined cane sugar
2 tbsp lime juice
1/2 tsp earth or sea salt
1/4 tsp ground black pepper

coriander leaves

1. Chop fine the spring onion.
2. Bring the water to boil in its own kettle.
3. Warm the ghee in a medium soup pot over medium low heat. Add the onion
   and sauté for 2 minutes.
4. Add the ground allspice and cinnamon and rock for half a minute.
5. Add the boiling water and dried thyme if using. Stir, cover and remove from
   heat.
6. As the broth cools, add the fresh thyme, nutmeg, sugar, citrus juice, salt
   and pepper.
7. Serve topped with coriander leaves.

To make this a barbecue paste which reflects its origin, chop fine the spring
   onion and combine with all ingredients except the water and coriander in
   a mortar, using the pestle to produce a glossy paste. Rub onto food before
   barbecuing.

Serves 4. Caribbean/ Southern United States Influence.

Of this recipe,   To refine,
Kapha, enjoy some .... decrease the sugar, lime and ghee
Pitta, enjoy some .... decrease the spices, lime and ghee
Vata, enjoy more

SLIGHTLY SPICY HOT WATER.

KALE SOUP

The physical body is best nourished by food.

1/2 cup kidney beans
1 bay leaf

1 rutabaga, swede or turnip
8 kale leaves or collard greens
1 medium carrot

100 gm = 3 1/2 oz uncooked spaghetti

a sprinkle of asafoetida
1 tsp earth or sea salt
quartered lemon rounds
olive oil
black peppercorns

1. Inspect beans to remove anything foreign, soak them for 8 hours and then cook, using fresh water. When the water foams during boiling, rinse with fresh water and replace with 8 cups fresh boiling water. Cook with bay leaf in a large soup pot, covered, for 1 hour.
2. Finely dice the rutabaga and midribs of the kale leaves. Slice the carrot into thin sections.
3. Slice the curly edged greens into grass-width short slivers.
4. Crack spaghetti into short pieces.
5. When the beans are soft, mash 1 cup into a purée. Blend with some soup liquid and return to pot. You could mash all of the beans or none like this.
6. Add rutabaga, carrots, diced midribs and slivered kale. Add asafoetida.Cook uncovered.
7. After 5 minutes add the pasta and salt and cook uncovered at a low boil until al dente.
8. Garnish with lemon and pass the oil and pepper grinder at the table.

Serves 6-8. European Influence, Portugal.

Of this recipe,	To customize,
Kapha, enjoy some	use less oil and lemon juice and a different variety of bean
Pitta, enjoy more	use a little oil, less lemon and pepper
Vata, enjoy less..............	add more oil and lemon and still enjoy less

LIKE A MINESTRONE WITH KALE SLIVERED TO THE WIDTH OF GRASS.

LEEK and OAT SOUP

The cook unites food and sentient beings.

The Stock
4 cups water
2 bay leaves
2 cinnamon quills or 2 tsp ground cinnamon
1 tbsp grated fresh ginger
1 cup rolled oats

The Soup
4 generous cups sliced leeks
2 tbsp ghee

1 cup chopped spinach or other dark greens
1 tsp earth or sea salt
3 tbsp palm or unrefined cane sugar
3 tbsp lemon juice

1. Prepare stock by combining the water, bay leaves, cinnamon, ginger and oats in a medium soup pot. Bring to boil and simmer, covered. Stir occasionally.
2. As soon as that is going, chop the leeks. Using the lower portions, quarter them lengthwise almost down to the root so you can slice quarter rounds.
3. Warm ghee in a medium skillet over medium low heat and add leeks. Sauté for 15 minutes, turning the softening leeks occasionally.
4. Add the skillet ingredients to the stock and simmer 10 minutes. Stir occasionally.
5. Add the chopped greens to cook for the last few minutes, adding nutrition and visual dimension. Remove from heat. Adjust to desired consistency with water.
6. Season with salt, sugar and lemon juice.

Consider that this thick soup can be a sauce for vegetables or grains.

Serves 4-6. English Influence.

Of this recipe,	Better yet,
Kapha, enjoy some	use crushed millet instead of rolled oats; decrease sugar and lemon juice
Pitta, enjoy some	slow-cooked leeks are O.K. now and then; decrease lemon juice
Vata, enjoy more	

LEEKS SAUTÉED SWEET AND SOUR IN AN OAT BROTH.

MIXED VEGETABLE SOUP

It's about cultivating awareness.

1 large potato
a handful of Jerusalem artichokes
3 stalks celery
1 bulb fennel or aniseed
1 tbsp ghee
6 cups stock or water

The Seasonings
1 sprig rosemary
2 sprigs marjoram
2 sprigs thyme
2 bay leaves
1 tbsp lavender flowers
1 tsp earth or sea salt
juice from 1 lemon wedge
fresh ground black pepper

1. Cook the whole potato in boiling water to cover until soft, about 30-40 minutes. Add the sunchokes to this pot for 20 minutes of cooking time.
2. Meanwhile, cut the celery and fennel into even pieces. Warm ghee in a larger soup pot and sauté those vegetables a few minutes.
3. Heat the stock or water to boil and add to the celery and fennel in the large pot. Adjust heat to simmer.
4. Tie the herb sprigs together and add to the soup with the bay leaves. Place lavender in a tea ball or muslin bag and add as well. If you don't have the fresh herbs, use 1/2 - 1 teaspoon dried. Cook for 20 minutes, covered.
5. When the potato is cooked, peel, mash and thin with a little soup. Split the sunchokes and scoop out the vegetable. Add to the soup with the salt and lemon juice. Check for seasonings that would be a play of tastes on the palate. Remove the herb bouquet and lavender ball.
6. Garnish with fennel fronds or a mini-sprig of fresh herb. Pass the pepper grinder at the table.

Serves 6-8. European Influence, Belgium.

Of this recipe,	To further modify,
Kapha, enjoy some	decrease fennel
Pitta, enjoy some	decrease aniseed, rosemary, thyme and bay
Vata, enjoy some	decrease potato and celery and include an extra teaspoon of ghee

HERBS de PROVENCE COMPLIMENT THESE VEGETABLES.

MULTI-COLORED SOUPS

All thoughts unrelated to the activity at hand are suspended.

Prepare 2 soup colors separately. Using 2 ladles or pitchers, simultaneously introduce the 2 colors into each soup bowl, side by side. To make this more exciting, practice with another person who also has 1 or 2 colors. Or ladle one soup into the bowl and the next on the side or on the top. Join the visual together with a colored garnish which may also complete the 6 tastes.

Orange:
<u>Sweet Potato, Carrot or Winter Squash/Pumpkin</u>
Per person
> **1 cup orange vegetable(s), water, 1 tsp ghee, 1/2 tsp coriander powder, 1/2 tsp ginger powder, 1/4 tsp earth or sea salt**

1. Peel and cube or grate orange vegetable(s) and place in saucepan with water to cover. Bring to boil, cover and simmer until done. Or bake/roast for a sweeter flavor.
2. Meanwhile, warm the ghee in a small skillet over medium heat. Swirl in coriander and ginger powders, turning heat off as you add them.
3. Drain and mash cooked vegetables, re-adding cooking liquid to make a ladlesome consistency as needed. Add skillet mix and salt.

Green:
<u>American Greens, Mediterranean Greens, Asian Greens, Antipodean Greens, European Greens, African Greens, Indian Greens in Split Pea Broth</u>
Per person
> **100 gm = 4 oz greens, 1 tsp ghee, a handful of fresh or dry green herbs, eg parsley, dill, coriander, rosemary, oregano, basil, thyme, sage, chives, tarragon, spring onion tops**

1. Prepare Split Pea Broth below. Make a thicker version as the greens will thin it.
2. Finely chop the greens and wash well, using the stems in another way.
3. Place greens and ghee into broth and let simmer just at boiling, uncovered, for 2 minutes.
4. Taste the soup before adding the herbs; it may be to taste already.
Try different herbs on different occasions.

<u>Split Green Pea</u>
Per person
> **1/2 cup green split peas, 1 1/2 cups water, 1 small bay leaf, 1 tsp ghee, 1/4 tsp mustard seed, 1/4 tsp cumin powder, a sprinkle of asafoetida, 1/4 tsp earth or sea salt, 1/4 tsp ground pepper**

1. Pick through peas to remove debris and inferior ones. Soak in water for several hours and rinse. Bring to boil, rinse off the foam, and simmer in 1

1/2 cups boiling water with the bay leaf, covered, for 1 hour.

2. Warm the ghee in a small skillet over medium heat. Add the mustard seeds and when the first one pops, remove from heat and swirl in the cumin, asafoetida and salt.

3. When the split peas are well cooked and soft, remove the bay leaf and press the peas through a sieve. Return to the soup pot with the spicy ghee and pepper. Heat to serving temperature to blend the flavors.

Magenta:
Beetroot
Per person
1 small beetroot, water, 1 tsp ghee, 1/4 tsp earth or sea salt

1. Wash the whole beets well and cook in water until very soft, about 45 minutes or bake, whole, in a moderate oven for 1 hour.

2. Mash with water or stock, press through medium sieve and add ghee and salt. You would like about 1 cup of puréed beetroot 'sauce' per person. Beetroot does not get as smooth as other vegetables.

Yellow:
Dal
Per person
1/2 cup yellow split peas, 1 1/2 cups water, 1 tsp ghee, 1/4 tsp fenugreek seeds, 1/4 tsp cumin powder, 1/4 tsp turmeric, a sprinkle of asafoetida, 1/4 tsp earth or sea salt, 1/2 tsp amchoor or a few drops of lemon juice

1. Pick out unwanted matter and inferior specimens from the split peas. Soak in water several hours. Drain, rinse and bring to boil in fresh water. Discard this water, rinse and add the 1 1/2 cups boiling water. Simmer for 1 hour, covered.

2. In small skillet over medium heat, warm the ghee. Add the fenugreek and sauté 1 minute. Add the cumin, turmeric and asafoetida, swirl and remove from heat. Add salt and amchoor.

3. When peas have disintegrated and become homogeneous by your mixing and mashing, add the spice blend. Heat another 5 minutes.

Turmeric or Saffron
Per person
1/4 tsp turmeric may be added to any white soup below or use 1/8 tsp lightly measured saffron threads per person soaked in 2 tbsp warm water for 30 minutes

White:
Rice
Per person
1/8 cup white rice, 2 cups water, several slices of fresh ginger, 1/4 tsp earth or sea salt, 1/8 tsp pepper, 1 tsp ghee

1. Rinse rice and bring to boil in the water. Add the ginger.
2. Cover and cook over very, very low heat for 2 hours, stirring every 15 minutes to create a congee consistency. Add water if the volume is less than 1 cup or the congee is too thick. Congee is when most of the whole rice converts to rice cream. It is very digestible.
3. Add salt, pepper and ghee and remove ginger slices.

Potato
Per person

1 small potato, 1 cup water, 1 small bouquet garni of fresh herbs which usually includes thyme and bay and often parsley, rosemary and marjoram tied together, 1/4 tsp earth or sea salt, 1/8 tsp pepper, 1 tsp ghee, 1 tbsp chopped white of spring onions or leek

1. Place peeled potato cut in pieces in the water with the bouquet garni. Bring to boil and simmer, covered.
2. Warm ghee in a small skillet over medium low heat and sauté spring onion whites.
3. When the potato is soft, remove bouquet garni and mash the potato in the soup pot. Add the skillet ingredients.
4. Add salt and cook a few minutes more. Add pepper.

Parsnip
Per person

1 small parsnip, 1/4 cup rolled oats, 1 cup water, 1 tsp ghee, 1 tbsp white sesame seeds, 1/4 tsp earth or sea salt, 1/8 tsp pepper

1. Bake the whole, unpeeled parsnips in a moderate-slow oven for 30-40 minutes until sweet and soft. Alternatively, peel and grate the parsnip and place in soup pot with water. Bring to boil and simmer, covered, for 20 minutes. This water can be used in the next step.
2. Bring 1 1/2 cups water to boil, combine with the cooked parsnip and oats. Simmer, stirring occasionally for 15 minutes, until it is a smooth consistency.
3. In a small skillet, warm the ghee and add the seeds, sautéing until a shade darker. Add to soup with the salt and pepper.

Each serving with 2 colors can be enough for a whole meal with flatbread or crackers. Global Influence.

Kapha, choose any, minimizing sweet potato, winter squash/pumpkin, parsnip and rice
Pitta, choose any, minimizing carrot, beetroot and pungent greens
Vata, choose any, minimizing split peas, greens, potato; and winter squash/pumpkin unless your appetite and digestion feel robust

COLORS AND TASTES BEGIN SEPARATE UPON SERVING AND THEN INTERMINGLE. ANY COLOR CAN STAND ALONE.

NOODLE SOUP

Cook's choice how many dishes comprise a meal.

The Seasonings
3 lemon grass stalks or 3 tsp dried
1 Kaffir lime leaf
2 cm = 1 inch fresh galangal or 1 tsp dry
2 cm = 1 inch fresh turmeric or 1 tsp dry
2 cm = 1 inch fresh ginger or 1 tsp dry

The Vegetables
125 gm = 4 oz yard long or green beans
125 gm = 4 oz asparagus or fiddlehead ferns
1 bunch spinach
1 sweet pepper (capsicum) color of choice
1 cup snow pea or other sprouts

6 cups water
100 gm = 3 1/2 oz thin wheat noodles, uncooked
1 1/2 tsp earth or sea salt

More Seasonings
1 tbsp sesame oil
1 tbsp ghee
6 curry leaves
1 1/2 tsp aniseed, crushed
3 tsp coriander powder
1 1/2 tsp cumin powder
1 tsp amchoor or 2 of lime juice at the end

1/4 cup coconut, optional

1. Slit the lemon grass stems and crush. Crush the lime leaf.
2. Grate the three rhizomes: galangal, turmeric and ginger.
3. Trim the beans and asparagus and cut into small pieces.
4. Cut the spinach into small ribbons and wash well.
5. Peel the sweet pepper if necessary and cut into small pieces.
6. Chop the snow pea sprouts, reserving the top quarters as garnish.
7. In a large covered soup pot bring the water to boil.
8. Add the noodles, beans, asparagus, lemon grass, lime leaves and salt. Return to boil and boil uncovered for 5 minutes.
9. Meanwhile, in a small skillet over medium low heat warm the oil and ghee. Add grated roots or root powders, curry leaves, aniseed, coriander, cumin and amchoor at a rhythmic rate rocking the pan to produce an even color and a wonderful aroma. Heat for 2 minutes.
10. When the noodles have cooked halfway, add the spinach, sprouts and

sweet pepper.

11. When the noodles are fully cooked add the skillet mix, lime juice if using and let cool.

12. Toast the coconut in the small skillet over low heat until golden.

13. Garnish the soup with the rest of the sprouts and the toasted coconut. The lemon grass, lime and curry leaves are not eaten.

Serves 4-6. Asian Influence, Singapore.

Of this recipe,   To enjoy more,
Kapha, enjoy some .... use buckwheat noodles and less coconut
Pitta, enjoy some .... enjoy cooked spinach and capsicum
occasionally and decrease galangal and ginger
Vata, enjoy more............ use less spinach and sprouts

VEGETABLES AND NOODLES IN A FLAVOR BROTH, A ONE COURSE MEAL.

POMEGRANATE LENTIL SOUP

Because energy is dynamic, so are we. Change is accommodated easily in a healthy person.

> a generous 1/4 cup brown lentils
> 2 -3 pomegranates
> 1/4 cup dried apricots
> 1 small carrot
> 1 bunch spinach
> 2 tbsp olive oil
> 1 tsp cumin seed
> a sprinkle of asafoetida
> 1/2 tsp earth or sea salt
> fresh parsley or coriander
> black peppercorns

1. Inspect lentils to remove debris and inferior specimens and soak for several hours.
2. Halve the pomegranates crosswise and squeeze and sieve juice to the amount of about 1 cup. Squeeze out the seeds by hand if necessary. Chop apricots into small pieces and soak in this juice while lentils are cooking.
3. Rinse lentils and add 4 cups fresh water. Bring to boil in saucepan with water to cover. If the water foams replace with more fresh boiling water. Cover and cook for 45 minutes, until lentils are soft, mashing periodically.
4. Cut the carrot into small dice and add for the last 15 minutes of lentil cooking.
5. Slice the spinach into short ribbons and wash well.
6. Warm the olive oil in a medium skillet or saucepan over medium low heat. Sprinkle in the cumin and asafoetida and sauté 1 minute. Add the spinach and cook until wilted.
7. When the lentils are soft and the liquid has decreased and condensed to about 3 cups, add the spinach sauté and salt. Stir and let cool. Add the pomegranate juice and apricots.
8. Garnish with minced parsley or coriander leaf. Pass the pepper grinder at the table.

Serves 4. Middle Eastern Influence.

Of this recipe,	To improve for your dosha,
Kapha, enjoy more	use less apricots
Pitta, enjoy some	several of these ingredients are not your best but their amounts are not large
Vata, enjoy some	with extra olive oil

LENTIL VEGETABLE BROTH WITH THE DELICACY OF POMEGRANATE JUICE.

POTATO SOUP

Would you rather eat a meal prepared in ease or prepared in haste?

Soup Base
a generous 1/4 cup brown rice
a generous 1/4 cup hulled millet
2 bay leaves
4 cups water

The Vegetables
3 medium potatoes
2 stalks celery
1 cup diced parsnip
1/2 cup diced turnip

The Seasonings
1 tbsp ghee
1/4 tsp whole cloves
a generous 1 1/2 tbsp fresh or 2 tsp dried parsley
3 tsp fresh or 1 1/2 tsp dried marjoram
1 tsp earth or sea salt
black pepper
lemon

1. Place grains, water and bay in large soup pot. Bring to boil and simmer, covered, 40 minutes.
2. Cut vegetables into medium dice and add after 20 minutes.
3. If using dried herbs soak in a small amount of broth, rocking occasionally.
4. Warm ghee in a small skillet over medium low heat, crush cloves and add. Swirl and remove from heat. Let cool.
5. Add a generous tablespoon chopped fresh parsley, chopped fresh marjoram (or soaked herbs), skillet mix and salt to soup.
6. Simmer a few minutes more. Stir the grains up from the bottom for each serving.
7. Add a turn of the black pepper grinder, a squeeze of lemon and garnish with the remaining parsley.

Serves 4 as a meal in itself. Antipodean Influence, New Zealand.

Of this recipe,   Even better,
Kapha, enjoy some .... decrease parsnip
Pitta, enjoy some .... decrease turnip, cloves, marjoram and pepper
Vata, enjoy some .... decrease celery and potato

A HEARTY GRAIN-VEGETABLE SOUP.

PUMPKIN SOUP

The meal is ready when the cook is satisfied.

700 gm = 24 oz pumpkin/winter squash
1/4 cup loosely packed fresh dill or 1 tsp dried

The Skillet Mix
1 tbsp pumpkin seeds
1 tsp ghee
1/2 tsp caraway, ground
a sprinkle of asafoetida
1/2 tsp earth or sea salt

sunflower oil

1. Cut pumpkin into pieces and steam or poach, covered, in a medium-large soup pot until soft, about 20 minutes.
2. When pumpkin is cooked combine pumpkin cooking liquid with water to the quantity of 2 cups and return this stock to the soup pot. Warm over medium low heat.
3. Scoop pumpkin out of shell, mash and return to soup pot through a sieve. Add dill and simmer, covered, for 10 minutes.
4. Meanwhile warm a small skillet over medium low heat and add pumpkin seeds. Toss occasionally and when the first one pops empty seeds into a small dish and cool.
5. While the skillet is still warm liquefy the ghee and add ground caraway and asafoetida, lowering heat. Swirl for 2 minutes and add to the soup.
6. Add the salt and cook another several minutes.
7. To serve, remove the fresh dill and design the top with the seeds and oil.

Serves 4. European Influence, Austria.

Of this recipe,   To enjoy more,
Kapha, enjoy less .... decrease the pumpkin itself in the soup
Pitta, enjoy more .... use less caraway
Vata, enjoy more .... we need strong digestive fire for pumpkin;
decrease caraway

VIBRANT ORANGE WITH EASTERN EUROPEAN TASTE.

RED BROTH

When the outer appearance of an event is not investigated to reveal its inner truth, mental indigestion occurs.

4 cups water
1 bay leaf
2 tsp ghee
1 tsp caraway
2 tsp coriander powder
2 tsp mild paprika
1 tsp dry marjoram, or 1 tbsp fresh
1 tsp dry basil, or 1 tbsp fresh
1/2 tsp earth or sea salt
black peppercorns

1. Bring water and bay leaf to boil in a kettle or medium pot with the lid on and simmer.
2. When the water has simmered 10 minutes, warm ghee in a medium soup pot over medium low heat. Add caraway and sauté 2 minutes. Add coriander and paprika. Paprika scorches quickly, so proceed with the next step.
3. Add simmering water with dried marjoram and basil. Cook 2 minutes, then remove from heat and allow flavors to infuse.
4. Add salt. Chop and add fresh herbs and freshly ground black pepper as the broth cools.
5. Try this as a tea sipped from a small bowl, with crackers or flatbread, as stock for cooking rice or as you wish.

Serves 4. European Influence, Hungary.

Of this recipe,   To modify for your dosha,
Kapha, enjoy more
Pitta, enjoy some ....decrease all seasonings except coriander
Vata, enjoy some ....decrease caraway

PURE WATER IS THE VEHICLE FOR HERBS AND SPICES.

RED LENTIL SOUP

*The caliber of energy that is given to this work is immediately
the caliber of energy you receive.*

1 cup red or other lentils	**The Seasonings**
5 cups water	1 tbsp ghee
1 quill cinnamon	1 tsp paprika
2 carrots	1 tsp turmeric
1/4 tsp loosely measured saffron threads	1 tsp ginger
	1 tsp sumac
1 tsp sesame seeds	a sprinkle of asafoetida
	1 tsp earth or sea salt

1. Inspect the lentils for small stones, inferior ones, etc. and remove.
2. Soak for several hours.
3. Bring the lentils and water to boil and if foam arises, drain, rinse and change with another 4 cups of fresh boiling water. Or skim off all the foam and continue cooking in the same liquid. Simmer for 45 minutes with the cinnamon. Add the carrots, sliced, and cook 15 minutes more.
4. Meanwhile scoop out 1/4 cup soup and float saffron on top. Swirl occasionally to develop color, aroma, taste and attributes.
5. Warm the ghee in a small skillet over low heat. Sprinkle in the paprika, turmeric, ginger, sumac, asafoetida and swirl. Heat for one minute and let cool. If cinnamon quills are unavailable add 1 teaspoon ground cinnamon.
6. When the lentils are well cooked, mash if desired, adding the saffron water, salt and skillet mix. Heat another 5 minutes while dry-roasting the sesame seeds over medium low heat.
7. Ladle soup into bowls with a small squeeze of lemon if no sumac powder is available and garnish with the seeds.

Serves 4. North African/Mediterranean Influence.

Of this recipe,	To enjoy more,
Kapha, enjoy more	
Pitta, enjoy some	decrease lentils, paprika and ginger
Vata, enjoy less	use more ghee; enjoy lentils on occasion

LENTILS FORM THE STOCK, SPICES FORM THE INTRIGUE.

SUNCHOKE SOUP

Thus every step is equally important.

750 gm = 1 1/2 lb Jerusalem artichokes
3 sticks of celery
1 small turnip
1 tbsp ghee
4 cups water
1 tsp earth or sea salt
lemon rounds

1. Immerse whole sunchokes in boiling water, cover and simmer for 20 minutes or until soft.
2. Meanwhile, cut celery and turnip into small pieces.
3. Warm ghee in a medium soup pot and sauté those vegetables for 10 minutes.
4. Bring water to boil, add to vegetables and simmer, covered, 15 minutes.
5. Scoop sunchokes from their peels, mashing their yield.
6. Add to the soup along with salt. Heat a few more minutes.
7. Garnish each bowl of soup with lemon.

Serves 4-6. Eastern European Influence, Bulgaria.

Of this recipe,	If only for you,
Kapha, enjoy more	
Pitta, enjoy some ....decrease turnip	
Vata, enjoy some............decrease turnip and celery	

CELERY AND TURNIP DICE FLOATING IN A BASE OF SWEET MASHED SUNCHOKES.

SWEET MUNG SOUP

The objective is to not create leftovers. If a dish needs time to mellow let it do so in a few hours, not a few days.

The Stock
1 cup split mung beans
5 cups water
4 tbsp palm or unrefined cane sugar
a sprinkle of earth or sea salt
a sprinkle of asafoetida

The Seasonings
1 tbsp ghee
1 tsp fennel seed
1 tbsp fresh mint
4 thin citrus rounds
1/2 tbsp fresh Thai basil, optional

1. Inspect beans to remove stones, inferior ones, etc. and rinse.
2. In a medium saucepan combine mung and enough water to cover. Bring to boil and simmer, covered, 5 minutes.
3. In a separate kettle bring to boil the 5 cups water.
4. Drain and rinse the mung beans and restore liquid with the boiling water. Bring up to boil and skim off any foam that arises. Cover and simmer 30 minutes, stirring occasionally.
5. Add the sugar, salt and asafoetida and simmer another 20 minutes. During this time use a potato masher to help disintegrate the mung. Replenish water if becoming too thick.
6. Warm the ghee in a small skillet over medium low heat and sauté the fennel seeds until the aroma is fragrant. Add to the soup.
7. Let cool. Chop the fresh mint and use as garnish with the citrus.

Serves 4. Asian Influence, Vietnam, Thailand, China, Philippines.

Of this recipe,   To modify,
Kapha, enjoy less .... use minimal ghee, scant sugar and add 1/2 tsp ginger powder
Pitta, enjoy more
Vata, enjoy some .... this is a cooling dish so add 1/4 tsp ginger to aid your digestive fire

A LIGHT SUMMER SOUP, MUNG IS COOKED SMOOTH, SWEET AND SPICED.

TARO and SORREL HOTPOT

The time in which a cooked dish relaxes and cools before serving helps to further mingle its components.

1 small taro root, about
   1 kg = 2 lbs
3 cups water

The Green Vegetables
100 gm = 4 oz yard long or green beans, about 1 cup when chopped
1 bunch fresh coriander
1 bunch sorrel or other greens plus lemon juice or tamarind
a sprinkle of nutmeg

2 tsp sesame oil
a sprinkle of asafoetida
1 tbsp sesame seeds
1 tsp earth or sea salt
black peppercorns

1. Peel and dice the taro into 1 cm = 1/2 inch cubes. Taro must be cooked.
2. Place half the cubes in a medium soup pot with the water. Bring to boil and simmer, covered, for 20 minutes.
3. Meanwhile, trim the beans and cut into bite-sized pieces.
4. Chop the coriander stems. Set the leaves on hold.
5. In a medium skillet, warm the oil over medium heat. Add the taro cubes, green beans and coriander stems and sauté several minutes, turning them on to several sides.
6. Lower heat, add the asafoetida and sauté until the taro and beans are soft through, about 15 minutes. Add water if vegetables are sticking. Add the sesame seeds in the last few minutes.
7. With the taro in the soup pot cooked, remove from heat and mash it in the pot.
8. Cut the sorrel into small ribbons. If you can't find sorrel, use any mild green with lemon juice or tamarind added before serving.
9. Add the skillet sauté, sorrel and salt. Stir and cover the pot for a few minutes.
10. Add pepper and nutmeg and garnish with chopped coriander leaves.

Serves 3-4. South American Influence, Brazil.

Of this recipe,   To customize,
Kapha, enjoy less .... use potato instead of taro and bitter or pungent greens instead of some of the sorrel; use less oil and sesame seeds
Pitta, enjoy more .... decrease the sorrel somewhat and use bitter greens as well
Vata, enjoy more

TARO, SAUTÉED AND BOILED, WITH GREEN VEGETABLES.
SIMPLIFY BY CHOOSING EITHER METHOD NEXT TIME.

THICK VEGETABLE SOUP

Eventually we use experience and intuition for all quantity measurements.

Mixed Vegetables
2 carrots
1 leek
2 parsnip
3 stalks celery
3 potatoes

4 cups water, perhaps more
1 tsp earth or sea salt
1 1/2 tbsp ghee
fresh parsley
black peppercorns

1. Wash, peel if necessary and chop vegetables, the leek and celery quite small.
2. Bring water to boil in a medium-large soup pot. Add vegetables and simmer, covered, until soft enough to press through a sieve. The amount of time this takes depends on the size of the vegetable pieces.
3. Mash and/or press through sieve back into the stock and add water if necessary to make a thick purée.
4. Apply another few minutes of heat, adding salt.
5. Dissolve 1 teaspoon ghee on top of each serving, sprinkle with chopped parsley and pass the pepper grinder at the table.

Serves 6. Scandinavian Influence, Finland.

Of this recipe,   If you can,
Kapha, enjoy more .... decrease parsnip and ghee on your serving
Pitta, enjoy more .... decrease black pepper
Vata, enjoy more .... decrease celery and potatoes

VEGETABLES PROVIDE FLAVOR AND TEXTURE.

VAL VEGETABLE SOUP

A garnish includes the serving dish and other visuals.

Soup Base
1 cup whole or split val or
    other beans
1 cup split mung beans
1 carrot
2 stalks celery
1 potato
1/2 turnip
1/2 zucchini
4 leaves of bok choi
1 handful rocket leaves

Skillet Mix
1 tbsp ghee
1/2 tsp nigella seeds
1 tsp cumin powder
1 tsp coriander powder
1 tsp turmeric
1 tsp ginger powder
1 tsp tarragon
1 tsp oregano
1 tsp amchoor (or 1 tbsp
    lemon juice)
a sprinkle of asafoetida

1 tsp earth or
    sea salt
black
    peppercorns
coriander
    leaves

1. Inspect the val to remove anything foreign or any inferior beans. Soak 8 hours, rinse and cook using 6 cups water. If the water foams during boiling, rinse with fresh water and replace with 6 cups boiling water. Or skim off all the foam and continue cooking in the same liquid. Cook in a large soup pot, covered, 1 hour.
2. Inspect the mung. Rinse and add to the beans to cook for 45 minutes. In the first 15 minutes remove any foam that collects on the top with a spoon.
3. Mix soup contents from time to time to help disintegrate mung.
4. Within the last half hour medium dice carrot, celery, potato and turnip. Add the diced vegetables to the soup.
5. Dice zucchini, sliver bok choi and chop rocket leaves.
6. Warm the ghee in a medium skillet over medium heat. Add the spices and herbs an aroma at a time and swirl, turning heat down. Add the chopped zucchini, bok choi and greens. Cook for 5 minutes.
7. Add skillet ingredients to soup along with salt, pepper and lemon juice if using. Adjust to ladlesome consistency with water if necessary. Cook another few minutes, then begin cooling.
8. Garnish with chopped coriander leaf.

Serves 4 as a meal in itself. Global Synthesis.

This is an example of using vegetables that are handy and creating your own spice blend.

Of this recipe,   If you can,
Kapha, enjoy more .... minimize amchoor (or lemon) and zucchini
Pitta, enjoy more .... minimize the pungent rocket, nigella, ginger, oregano and pepper and the amchoor or lemon
Vata, enjoy some .... the bean base could be mostly mung, less val; use less potato and celery

VAL BEANS, VEGETABLES AND SPICES IN A SMOOTH MUNG
STOCK.

STAPLES

A CUSTOMABLE PLATTER

The wisdom of ayurveda is infinite and becomes fine-tuned to the individual.

1 cup chickpeas

The Seasonings	The Vegetables	1 tbsp olive oil
3 tbsp olive oil	1 small eggplant	1 tbsp parsley,
1 tsp cumin seed	1 large carrot	finely
a sprinkle of asafoetida	300 gm = 10 oz okra	chopped
1/2 tsp cinnamon	300 gm = 10 oz snow	black pepper
2 tsp paprika	peas	lemon wedges
2 tsp sumac or 1 lemon in wedges		
3/4 tsp earth or sea salt		

1. Pick through the chickpeas to remove anything inedible or inferior and soak in water for 8 hours.
2. Using fresh water, bring to boil, drain and rinse off the foam and add fresh boiling water to cover. Or skim off all the foam and continue cooking in the same liquid. Simmer, covered, 1 hour.
3. Meanwhile, warm olive oil in a small skillet over medium heat. Add cumin seed and asafoetida for 1 minute and remove from heat. When the skillet is just warm, add cinnamon, paprika and sumac. Add salt. Transfer to small jar with 1/2 cup bean cooking liquid and shake.
4. Preheat oven to 400°F (200°C, Gas 6). Add the 1 tablespoon of olive oil to the bottom of a large, flat, covered casserole dish and warm it in the oven.
5. Prepare vegetables individually by peeling and cubing eggplant, slicing carrots thinly, leaving okra whole and trimming snow peas and leaving whole.
6. When chickpeas are soft, drain, reserving liquid and mash half a cup with enough of that liquid to make a dip-like consistency. Mix the rest of the drained chickpeas into this dip.
7. Place the chickpeas in the center of the warmed casserole dish. Arrange the vegetables in areas around them.
8. Drizzle the liquid spice dressing over everything.
9. Cover and bake for 20 minutes, making sure eggplant is well cooked.
10. Garnish with parsley, pass the black pepper and lemon wedges at the table.

Serves 4-6. Mediterranean Influence, Turkey.

Of this platter,
Kapha, enjoy more of everything except okra and lemon; if only for kapha, use ghee, mustard or sunflower oil and less of it
Pitta, choose less carrot; if only for pitta, use less paprika, lemon and black pepper
Vata, choose less chickpeas and eggplant

CHICKPEAS ARE THE HUB OF A BAKED VEGETABLE WHEEL.

ADAPTABLE FLATBREAD

Wheat is the grain of the sun.

> 3 cups soft wheat flour such as atta
> 1 tsp earth or sea salt
> 2 tbsp ghee
> 1/4 tsp cumin seed
> 1/2 tsp ginger powder
> 1 cup water

1. Combine the flour and salt on a table top or in a bowl.
2. Warm the ghee in a small skillet on medium heat. Add the cumin seed and sauté until the seeds sizzle. Remove from heat and cool 1 minute. Swirl in ginger powder. With a fork stir the melted ghee into the flour mix and then add the water, not all at once. With your hands create pliable dough.
3. Knead for 5 minutes and let rest for 30-180, covered with a film of ghee. The longer it rests, the more elastic it becomes. Prepare your vegetables, soup or staples now.
4. Lightly flour a surface if necessary and roll portions of the dough out to about 10mm = 1/4 inch thickness or less, making rounds with a circular motion or other shapes.
5. Warm a large unoiled skillet over medium high heat. When hot, start cooking the flatbreads one by one, adjusting the heat to prevent burning. After 1-2 minutes turn the bread to the other side. The first side would be golden with darker brown spots. Cook the second side until it colors like the first side. As a traditional option, hold the flatbread with 1 or 2 tongs over direct flame to puff it up.
6. Pile on a plate and cover. If using ghee on the cooked breads, spread a little now. The breads will keep warm unless your cooking space is very cold.

Serves 4-6. Every grain-growing country offers flatbread recipes.

Of this recipe,	To refine,
Kapha, enjoy less	Buckwheat or Rye Flatbread recipe is preferred
Pitta, enjoy more	you needn't use the ginger and can brush the cooked flatbread with a small amount of ghee
Vata, enjoy more	brush the cooked flatbread with a small amount of ghee

SOFT RICH FLATBREAD CAN ACCOMPANY SOUP, VEGETABLES OR STAPLES.

BAKED RICE and VINE LEAVES

Earth energy rises into leaves and flowers in the morning.

2 cups long grain rice
24 young vine leaves or other greens

2 tbsp olive oil
2 tbsp pine nuts
1/2 cup raisins or currants
1 lemon

The Broth
2 tbsp olive oil
1 1/2 tsp paprika
4 cups water
1/2 tbsp fresh tarragon or 1 tsp dried
2 tsp minced rosemary or 1 tsp dried
1 tbsp fresh basil or 1 tsp dried
1 1/2 tsp earth or sea salt

1. Rinse rice and soak in water until needed.
2. Remove stems from the leaves, cut leaves in thirds along their lines of growth and leave in three piles. Reserve 3 leaves with stems removed and uncut. In China they'd use mulberry leaves.
3. Prepare the broth by warming 2 tablespoons oil in a medium saucepan over low heat.
4. Add the paprika and sauté 1 minute.
5. Add the water, cover and bring to boil; add tarragon, rosemary, basil, salt and simmer on low heat, covered.
6. Meanwhile preheat the oven to 400°F (200°C, Gas 6).
7. Coat the bottom of a lidded casserole with remaining oil and place in the oven to warm.
8. Drain the rice.
9. To prepare, remove baking dish from oven and separate one pile of leaves over the bottom. Cover with one third of the rice (about 2/3 cup) in a single layer. Distribute one third of the nuts and one third of the raisins. Repeat leaves, rice, nuts and raisins twice more and top with the 3 whole leaves.
10. Ladle the simmering broth over the top, cover and place in oven.
11. Bake 30 minutes. Remove from oven and begin to cool, covered.
12. Garnish with lemon wedges or rounds.

Serves 4. Mediterranean Influence. This is a spring dish. Others leaves can be substituted, however the taste would change.

Of this recipe,   To accommodate your dosha,
Kapha, enjoy less .... use quinoa instead of rice and half the oil; use less nuts and a small squeeze of lemon
Pitta, enjoy more .... use less oil, less nuts and a small squeeze of lemon
Vata, enjoy more

THE CLASSIC COMBINATION IN EASY-TO PREPARE LAYERS.

BARLEY-MILLET PORRIDGE

In Japanese Temple cooking there are at least two people in the kitchen. One chants prayers, the other cooks.

> 4 cups water
> 1/2 cup whole barley
> 1/2 cup whole, hulled millet
> 1/4 tsp saffron, lightly measured
> 1/2 cup raisins or other dried fruit
> 1 tbsp ghee
> 1/4 cup whole seeds, see below
> a sprinkle of sea salt
> honey or maple syrup, optional

1. Set the water to boil in a medium saucepan, covered, and simmer until needed.
2. Inspect grains and remove unwanted and inferior material. Dry roast barley in a medium saucepan shaking the grains over medium heat for 2 minutes. Add to simmering water. Dry roast the millet, rolling the grains around for 1 minute and add to water.
3. Cook for 40 minutes, until millet is disintegrated and barley is chewy, adding water if needed.
4. Meanwhile soak saffron in 1 tablespoon warm water.
5. Add the raisins or other dried fruit to the porridge in the last 10 minutes. If using fruit larger than raisins, cut into small pieces and soak in its own water.
6. Warm the ghee over medium heat in a small skillet. Toss in the seeds and sauté until slightly darker in color.
7. When the porridge is cooked add the salt, saffron and its liquid.
8. Serve the porridge garnished with the ghee and seeds. Use honey or syrup if needed.

Serves 4. Whole Grain Cooking

Of this recipe,   To further refine,
Kapha, enjoy more .... decrease ghee and use pumpkin or sunflower seeds; sweeten with honey when cool
Pitta, enjoy some .... use less millet, more barley and choose pumpkin or sunflower seeds and maple syrup
Vata, enjoy some .... millet and barley are both drying, substitute rice for half of each; decrease or delete dried fruit and use honey(warming); use nuts, they are more unctuous

ROASTED BARLEY AND MILLET SWEETENED WITH DRIED FRUIT, GARNISHED WITH SEEDS.

BEAN and RYE PATTIES

Listen to the ingredients respond to the heat that is applied.

The Seasonings
1 tbsp ghee
1 tsp caraway seed
1 tsp cumin seed
a sprinkle of asafoetida
1 tsp paprika
1 tsp cumin
1 tsp coriander
1 tsp cinnamon
1/2 tsp turmeric
3/4 tsp earth or sea salt
1/2 tsp black pepper

1 cup lima or other beans

1 tbsp lemon juice
1 cup rye flour
3 coriander plants
1 tbsp pistachio nuts

1. Inspect beans to remove anything foreign or inferior, soak them for 8 hours and then cook, using fresh water. When the water foams during boiling, rinse and replace with more fresh boiling water. Or skim off all the foam and continue cooking in the same liquid. Simmer, covered, for 1 hour.
2. Warm the ghee in a small skillet over medium heat. Add the seeds and asafoetida, swirl and lower heat. When the skillet is just warm add the ground spices and sauté for 1 minute. Remove from heat and add salt and pepper.
3. Mince the coriander plants from roots to leaves, saving some leaves as garnish.
4. When the beans are soft, drain, saving stock, and mash. Combine with coriander, skillet mix, lemon juice and flour. Use stock if the beans and flour are too dry to hold together.
5. Chop the pistachios and add.
6. Warm a thin layer of ghee in a medium skillet over medium heat. Form the mix into thin, flat shapes, wide or narrow, and sauté the first side for 5 minutes, until golden dark. Listen to the sound and adjust the heat accordingly. Flip and cook the other side for about 5 minutes.
7. Serve with coriander leaf garnish along with chutney or vegetables.

Serves 3-4. Middle Eastern/North African Influence, Tunisia.

Of this recipe,   To modify,
Kapha, enjoy more .... baking without additional ghee would be better than pan frying: shape 16 patties, flatten and bake at 350°F (180°C, Gas 4) for 20 minutes for an even drier result
Pitta, enjoy some .... use wheat instead of rye flour
Vata, enjoy less .... use wheat flour, more ghee for cooking and still enjoy less

A BEAN DIP TURNED INTO PATTIES.

BEAN and VEGETABLE CASSEROLE

Our skin is an organ of consumption. We put on it only those substances that we would take by mouth.

3/4 cup kidney or other beans

1 medium potato
2 large carrots
1 small cauliflower
2 tbsp olive oil

The Seasonings
2 tsp ghee
1/2 tsp cumin seed
a sprinkle of asafoetida
1 tsp cinnamon
1 tsp cumin powder
1/2 tsp earth or sea salt
1/2 tsp black pepper
1 lemon
a sprig of fresh green herb

1. Inspect beans to remove debris and inferior specimens and soak in water for 8 hours.
2. Drain, rinse and bring to boil in fresh water. As foam arises, drain, rinse and replenish with fresh boiling water to cover. Or skim off all the foam and continue cooking in the same liquid. Simmer, covered, 1 hour.
3. Meanwhile, chunk into medium size the potato, carrots and cauliflower.
4. Heat the olive oil in a large pot over medium heat and sauté the vegetables for 10 minutes. Add 1/4 cup water (bean liquid if available), cover and simmer 20 minutes, stirring occasionally. Replenish liquid to keep vegetables moist.
5. Warm the ghee in a small skillet over medium heat. Add cumin seed and asafoetida. Lower heat. As the skillet temperature lowers swirl in spices, salt and pepper.
6. Add the cooked drained beans to the vegetables, the tempered seasonings and about 1 tablespoon of lemon juice. Add the remaining bean liquid if serving over rice.
7. Chop the herb(s) you are using and garnish.

Serves 4. Mediterranean Influence, Greece.

Of this recipe,   To customize,
Kapha, enjoy some .... although beans are good for kapha, kidney is not your best bean; also halve the olive oil and use sunflower, decrease lemon
Pitta, enjoy more .... use less lemon
Vata, enjoy less .... increase the oil and lemon and still enjoy less

BEANS, CHUNKY VEGETABLES AND SPICES COOKED ON THE STOVE TOP.

BLACK BEANS

The blends of seasonings and proportions create infinite tastes.

1 cup black beans

The Seasonings
3 cm = 1 inch fresh ginger
1 tbsp tamarind or lemon juice
1 tsp mustard seed
1/2 tsp whole cloves
1/2 tsp black peppercorns
1 tbsp ghee
1 tsp cinnamon
a sprinkle of asafoetida
1 tsp earth or sea salt
1/4 cup palm or dark brown sugar

1. Inspect beans and remove debris and inferior ones. Soak for 8 hours. Rinse and bring to boil with fresh water. If water foams rinse and replace with fresh boiling water. Or skim off all the foam and continue cooking in the same liquid. Simmer, covered, 1 hour. Keep beans as whole as possible.
2. Prepare ginger by grating finely and prepare tamarind by soaking 2 table-spoons in 3 tablespoons hot water. Work the tamarind off the seeds and collect the purée through a strainer.
3. Warm a small saucepan over medium heat. Dry roast the mustard seeds until the first ones pop and remove from heat. Add the cloves and peppercorns. After one minute transfer to a mortar and grind the spices.
4. Warm the ghee over low heat in the same saucepan. Add all spices, stirring for 1 minute, then the sugar, tamarind juice and about 1/2 cup of bean liquid. Continue cooking to create a spice syrup.
5. When the beans are cooked drain the cooking liquid and add the syrup. Cook uncovered at a simmer until the syrup has thickened and coats the beans.

Serves 4. Serves 6 over cooked grain. Caribbean Influence.

Of this recipe,   To enjoy more,
Kapha, enjoy some .... use less sugar and tamarind
Pitta, enjoy some .... use less mustard, cloves, pepper, ginger and tamarind
Vata, enjoy less .... use more ghee; use aduki beans

BEANS IN A SWEET-SOUR-PUNGENT SAUCE.

BLACK-EYED PEA SALAD-EAST

The pace that we eat at can affect the pace of digestion.

1 1/2 cups black-eyed peas
2 cups diced cucumber

Seasoning
2 tsp palm or unrefined cane sugar
1 tbsp tamarind purée
1/2 tsp earth or sea salt
a sprinkle of asafoetida

1 cup coconut, finely grated and fresh is ideal
1 tbsp fresh mint

1. Inspect peas to remove inedibles and inferior specimens. Soak in water for 6 hours. Rinse and bring to boil in a medium saucepan with water to cover. Cook covered for 45 minutes, replenishing water if necessary. When cooked let cool on a serving platter.
2. Peel if necessary and dice cucumber.
3. Combine seasoning ingredients and toss through cucumber. Use light brown sugar if palm or jaggery sugar is not available.
4. Toss in coconut and distribute everything over the peas.
5. Garnish with finely chopped mint leaves.

Serves 4. Indonesian Influence, Bali. Using this as a summer meal, increase raw ingredients so that they are a majority over the cooked beans.

Of this recipe,   To fine-tune,
Kapha, enjoy some .... use celery and carrot instead of cucumber and decrease dressing ingredients
Pitta, enjoy more
Vata, enjoy less .... decrease beans

WITH DICED CUCUMBER AND COCONUT.

BLACK-EYED PEA SALAD-WEST

Ayurveda promotes pro-action to maintain wellness.

1 1/2 cups black-eyed peas
1 sweet red pepper (capsicum)

The Dressing
1/2 cup olive oil
1 tsp cumin
a sprinkle of asafoetida
1/2 cup lemon juice
1 tsp ground mustard
1 tsp dried thyme or 2 tsp fresh, lightly filled
1/2 tsp earth or sea salt

1. Inspect and remove debris and inferior peas and soak for 6 hours. Rinse and bring to boil with water to cover. Simmer covered for 45 minutes, then drain and let cool.
2. Bake pepper in a hot oven until the skin is charred. Place in bag to just cool, then rub off skin, rinse, pat dry and slice into strips.
3. Heat olive oil in a small skillet over medium heat. Add cumin and asafoetida and begin to cool.
4. Combine dressing ingredients and shake or whisk together. Let stand for 15 minutes.
5. Mix dressing again and toss through peas. Place on serving platter.
6. Arrange red pepper strips on top and garnish with thyme or parsley.

Serves 4. North American Influence, Southern U.S.

Of this recipe,   To enjoy more,
Kapha, enjoy some .... decrease oil and lemon juice
Pitta, enjoy some .... decrease dressing
Vata, enjoy less............. decrease peas, substitute rice

GRILLED SWEET RED PEPPER OVER DRESSED BEANS.

BORLOTTI BEANS

Perhaps we need to acclimate to food that looks different than we are used to.

1 cup Borlotti or pinto beans

Kapha Churna
1/2 tsp black peppercorns
3/4 tsp coriander seed
1/2 tbsp ghee
1/2 tsp ginger powder
1/2 tsp cinnamon
1/2 tsp turmeric

1/4 tsp earth salt
1/2 tsp unfired honey

1. Inspect beans to remove debris and inferior specimens and soak in water for 8 hours.
2. Drain, rinse and bring to boil in fresh water. As foam arises, drain and replenish with fresh boiling water to cover. Or skim off all the foam and continue cooking in the same liquid. Simmer, covered, 1 hour.
3. In a small skillet dry roast the peppercorns and coriander seeds over medium low heat for 2 minutes. Transfer to mortar and grind.
4. In the same skillet at low heat, add the ghee. Introduce all spices heightening their essences by infusing in the ghee for 2 minutes.
5. When the beans are soft, drain them. Add skillet ingredients and salt. Reserve cooking liquid for that day if useful.
6. When cool add honey.

Serves two as main dish, 4 as side dish.

This is a kapha-specific dish. The spice blend is tailored to supply the warming, stimulating effect and proper tastes on the palate. It can be purchased as Kapha Churna with the difference that it will have cane sugar instead of honey. Kapha constitutions can use this spice blend often.

THE DEFINITIVE KAPHA-FRIENDLY SPICE BLEND WITH LEGUMES.

BUCKWHEAT BESAN CREPES

A bird called to include its song in my cooking.

The Seasonings

1/2 tsp fenugreek seed
2 tsp ghee
2 tsp fresh grated ginger
a sprinkle of asafoetida
1 tsp cumin powder
1 tsp coriander powder
1/2 tsp turmeric powder
1 tsp earth or sea salt

2 cups of water
1 tbsp fresh or 1 tsp dried mint
1 cup buckwheat flour
1/2 cup besan (chickpea flour)
ghee or sunflower oil

1. Warm a small skillet or saucepan over medium heat. Add the fenugreek seeds and roast for half a minute. Remove and crush seeds as fine as they allow.
2. Warm the ghee in the same skillet over medium heat.
3. Add the ginger and asafoetida, turning heat down, sautéing for 1 minute. Infuse the rest of the spices and fenugreek powder into the ghee for 1 minute. There are more spices than ghee.
4. Add 1 1/2 cups of the water carefully into the skillet. Mince the mint leaves and add. Stir the potion. Remove from heat and allow to cool.
5. Warm a large griddle or skillet over medium heat and dissolve 1/4 teaspoon of ghee or oil into a film that covers the surface.
6. Meanwhile, combine the flours in a bowl and whisk in the skillet liquid.
7. Continue whisking the batter, adding the last half cup of water as needed.
8. Start making the crepes right off, using very small amounts of ghee or sunflower oil on the griddle between crepes.
9. Cook until the top starts to look dry and the bottom is not burnt, then flip and cook the other side until done. Adjust heat accordingly.
10. Keep warm with a tea towel cover until all are ready.
11. Serve with vegetables.

Makes about 8 crepes, can serve 2-4 people. Indian Influence with buckwheat, the staple of the Russian army.

Of this recipe,   To refine,
Kapha, enjoy more .... minimise the ghee
Pitta, enjoy less .... use more besan, less buckwheat and less ginger
Vata, enjoy less.............. neither flour is ideal

THE BATTER RECIPE FOR KAPHA.

BUCKWHEAT FLATBREAD or PASTA

Once a sense of familiarity is felt in preparing this recipe, experiment with variations.

3 cups finely ground buckwheat flour
1 tsp ginger powder
a few grains of earth or sea salt
1 tsp melted ghee
1 cup of water, maybe more

1. Make a ring of the flour, ginger, salt and oil on a flat surface or in a bowl.
2. Add water into the center, gradually incorporating the flour into the water. Knead for several minutes to homogenize. Let the dough rest if possible.
3. For flatbread, divide into 12 pieces and roll each out on a buckwheat or cornmeal-dusted surface to a 15 cm = 6 inch round or equivalent.
4. Warm a medium skillet over medium high heat. Cook the flatbread for several minutes on each side, adjusting heat down if necessary.
5. Cool each separately to crisp and then stack them together.
6. For pasta, roll out even thinner sections than for flatbread on the surface as above and cut into noodles. Toss each section with a little extra flour only if they are sticky.
7. Heat a large covered pot of water to boil. Add the noodles carefully and bring to boil again. Cook 7-10 minutes at a low boil, uncovered.
8. Drain and serve.

Makes 12 flatbreads or 4 servings of pasta. Eastern European/Korean Influence.

Of this recipe,   To explain,
Kapha, enjoy more .... this is one of your flatbread and pasta recipes and you can add more spices and herbs
Pitta, enjoy less .... use the Adaptable Flatbread recipe
Vata, enjoy less.............. use the Adaptable Flatbread recipe

BUCKWHEAT, SIMPLE AND ADJUSTABLE.

BUCKWHEAT-GRAIN PANCAKES

In some cooking traditions the food is not tasted until offered to its source.

The Dry

1/4 tsp earth or sea salt	1 1/2 cups water
1/4 tsp nutmeg	2 tsp grated orange rind
1/2 tsp ground ginger	1 tsp melted ghee
3/4 cup buckwheat flour	additional ghee
1/4 cup millet flour	
1/4 cup barley flour	

1. Warm a griddle or large skillet over medium heat.
2. Combine the dry ingredients.
3. Add them to the water with the orange rind. Add the ghee. The batter will thicken on standing which gives options to the density of the cakes.
4. Coat the griddle with a thin film of ghee.
5. Cook pancakes, size of choice, until the top side has formed craters and is drier, then flip to cook second side. Use minimal ghee on this side as well.
6. When cool and serving with fruit use honey; with soup or vegetables use no sweetener.

Serves 2. North American/European Influence.

Of this recipe,   To substitute,

Kapha, enjoy more .... honey is the best sweetener for kapha but maple syrup and buckwheat pancakes are a classic so ask your intuitive body to guide you

Pitta, enjoy some .... decrease buckwheat and millet by half and substitute wheat flour; use maple syrup to sweeten

Vata, enjoy less .... decrease all three flours by three quarters and substitute wheat flour; use more ghee and use maple syrup or honey if sweetening

THESE PANCAKES GO WITH SOUP, VEGETABLES OR COOKED FRUIT.

CHEF'S KICHURI

To make any change, a small amount of consistent, concerted effort is needed.

1 cup basmati rice
1/2 cup split mung beans
4 cups water

1 bunch fresh coriander
2.5 cm = 1 inch fresh ginger
1 tsp earth salt
lemon wedges

The Seasonings
1 tbsp ghee
1/2 tsp mustard seed
1/2 tsp cumin seed
1 tsp ground cumin
1 tsp ground coriander
1 tsp ground turmeric
a sprinkle of asafoetida

1. Pick over mung beans, discarding unwanted material and inferior specimens. Wash rice and mung and add water to cover in a medium-large pot. Soak for 1 hour if possible.
2. Bring to boil in the 4 cups of water. Skim off all the foam as it arises. Cover and simmer 20-30 minutes.
3. Cut fine the coriander stems and add to the cooking kichuri. Set aside the leaves.
4. Grate the ginger and add to the cooking kichuri. Continue stirring, creating a creamy consistency. Add water if necessary.
5. Warm the ghee in a small skillet over medium heat. Add the mustard and cumin seed. When the seeds start to pop, remove from heat. When slightly cooler add the powders and swirl them evenly into the ghee.
6. Add the skillet ingredients to the kichuri in the last 5 minutes. Stir in the salt. Begin to cool, still stirring now and then.
7. Chop the coriander leaves and garnish.
8. Provide the lemon wedges for a few drops of juice.

Serves 4. Indian Influence. Everyone, enjoy more!

A SAVORY RICE AND SPLIT MUNG PORRIDGE.

<u>Variations on a theme</u>
2 medium potatoes, 2 medium carrots, 2 stalks celery, 1 bunch spinach

While the rice and mung are coming to boil cut the vegetables into medium
pieces.

When the rice and mung are de-foamed add all the vegetables except for the
spinach. The vegetables and staples will cook together.

Cut the spinach into short ribbons and wash well. Use a medium skillet to
prepare the spices. Then add the spinach and cook until wilted. Proceed as
above from step 6. This addition will then feed 6 people as an entire meal
and is balanced for all constitutions.

<u>Further variations</u>

Use any combination of vegetables, fossicking the refrigerator or taking free
rein in the market. If you are curious, look up the affinity of each vegetable
for your dosha, keeping in mind that a little bit of anything is generally acceptable. You could add these vegetables at different times depending on
how long they need to cook to become digestible. You could cut them into
different shapes and sizes or grate one or all. You could steam them and
serve them over the top or mixed into the kichuri. You could sauté them
with the ghee and spices and add to the kichuri. You could discover that
vegetables sautéed in ghee with spices is something you want to eat often.
The greens can vary or be a combination.

The fresh ginger could be added to the kichuri pot when all the foam has been
removed or could be sautéed in the skillet along with the spices. The kichuri
ingredients can simply be mixed together and baked, 350°F (180°C, Gas 4)
for 30-40 minutes, covered, until the liquid is absorbed. The spices will infuse the ghee as it bakes. To do this, rinse the rice and mung, dry roast the
seeds and use boiling water. Add a few drops of lemon juice when done.

To make this a one pot camp meal, begin with the ghee, add the spices and
sauté. Add the unwashed, unsoaked rice and mung (still inspect for little
rocks) and water. As it comes to boil add vegetables and later on, spinach.
Use more water if cooking over a fire, where even a soup usually turns into
a stew.

To create a less creamy texture add the seasoned ghee and grated ginger after
the mung has been de-foamed. Stir once only. When cooked, cool in the
pot until firmer.

THE BASIC RECIPE IS THE PREMIER AYURVEDIC MEAL. SIMPLE
TO PREPARE, SHORT IN COOKING TIME, IT IS EASILY DIGESTED,
BALANCING TO ALL DOSHA-S, PROVIDING PROPER BULK IN THE
COLON. A TRUE COMFORT FOOD.

CHICKPEA FLOUR SAUCE

It is the rajasic mind that breathes down our necks, not time.

The Seasonings

1 tbsp ghee
1 tsp cumin seed
1 tsp mustard seed
1/2 tsp nigella seed
a sprinkle of asafoetida
1 tsp coriander powder
1/2 tsp turmeric powder
1/2 tsp cinnamon powder

1/4 cup chickpea flour
1 1/2 cups water
1/2 tsp earth or sea salt

1. Warm the ghee in a medium saucepan over medium heat.
2. Add seeds and asafoetida and heat until the first seed pops. Remove from heat and swirl in the remaining spices. Let cool.
3. In a small mixing bowl add the water a little at a time to the chickpea flour, using a whisk to keep it smooth. When all the water has been incorporated add the batter to the spices in the saucepan.
4. Using medium heat whisk continuously until the sauce thickens and boils. Turn down heat and whisk in the salt and cook for another minute.
5. Remove from heat and whisk another minute.
6. Thin with water if too thick.

Makes 1 1/2 cups, serves 6. Pakistani Influence.

Of this recipe,   To further accommodate,
Kapha, enjoy more .... use less ghee
Pitta, enjoy more .... decrease mustard and nigella seeds
Vata, enjoy less .... prepare your sauce with rice or wheat flour

A SAVORY STOVE-TOP SAUCE.

CHICKPEAS DUKKAH

The difference between taking care and hurrying does not amount to that much time.

The Seasonings
2 tbsp sesame or olive oil
1/4 cup ground coriander
1 1/2 tbsp cumin powder
1 tsp cinnamon
a sprinkle of asafoetida
2 tsp sumac or 2 tbsp lemon juice added later

1 tsp dried thyme or 2 tsp fresh, lightly packed
barely 1 tsp earth or sea salt
1/2 tsp black pepper
1/4 cup walnut pieces
fresh thyme or parsley

1 1/2 cups chickpeas
1/2 cup sesame seeds

1. Inspect chickpeas to remove anything foreign or inferior, soak them for 8 hours and then rinse and cook, using fresh water. When the water foams during boiling, rinse and replace with more fresh boiling water. Or skim off all the foam and continue cooking in the same liquid. Simmer, covered, for 1 hour.
2. In a small skillet over medium heat, dry roast the sesame seeds until lightly colored. Set aside in a bowl.
3. Add oil to skillet. Reduce heat and add coriander, cumin, cinnamon, asafoetida and sumac. Infuse for 2 minutes. There is less oil than spice powders here. Remove from heat.
4. Mash the chickpeas, using liquid as needed, or leave whole. If using dried thyme, rehydrate for 10 minutes in a small amount of hot chickpea stock. Add the skillet ingredients along with the thyme, salt and pepper. If using lemon juice, add now. Add the seeds and walnuts.
5. Garnish with fresh thyme if available or fresh parsley. Use as a dip, spread or base for vegetables.

Serves 6. North African Influence, Egypt.

Of this recipe,   To further customize,
Kapha, enjoy some .... decrease the sesame, walnuts, and lemon and keep the texture drier
Pitta, enjoy some .... decrease the sesame, walnuts, thyme and pepper
Vata, enjoy less .... chickpeas are drying, the nuts and seeds are oily; add extra sesame or olive oil and still enjoy less

A SPICE VARIATION OF HOOMUS.

CHICKPEAS KEBSA

It is an honor to serve by preparing this food.

1 cup chickpeas

The Seasonings
1 tbsp ghee
1 tsp ground cardamom
1 1/2 tsp ground cinnamon
1 1/2 tsp ground cumin
1 tsp grated nutmeg
1 tsp ground coriander
1 tsp ground cloves
a sprinkle of asafoetida

1/2 tsp earth or sea salt
1/2 tsp black pepper
a squeeze of lemon
coriander leaves

1. Remove any inedibles or inferior specimens from the chickpeas and soak in water 8 hours.
2. Rinse and using fresh water, bring them to boil. If foam arises rinse and add fresh boiling water. Or skim off all the foam and continue cooking in the same liquid. Simmer, covered, for 60 minutes.
3. Meanwhile, warm ghee in a small skillet over low heat.
4. Sprinkle on the delicate spices, either singly or combined. Infuse for one minute and remove from heat.
5. When the skillet mix has cooled, add to the drained, cooked chickpeas with the salt and pepper. There will be 4 cups worth. Mash if desired, using cooking liquid if necessary.
6. Sprinkle with a few drops of lemon juice and color with coriander leaves and thin ribbons of lemon zest.

Serves 4. Middle Eastern Influence, Syria.

Of this recipe,   Even better,
Kapha, enjoy more
Pitta, enjoy some ....lessen the amount of spice blend
Vata, enjoy less..............chickpeas are drying; use more ghee, use more lemon juice, still enjoy less

EXOTIC FLAVOR WITH COOKED CHICKPEAS.

CREAM of RICE

Resistance to change is part of the process.

> 3/4 cup ground rice flour, brown or white
> 6 cups water
>
> 1/4 cup raw pistachios or other nuts
>
> <u>The Spices</u>
> 1 tsp aniseed
> 1/2 tsp caraway
> 1 tbsp ghee
> 1 tsp cinnamon
> 1/4 tsp ginger
> 1/2 tsp rock or sea salt
> 1/2 cup palm or unrefined cane sugar, honey or maple syrup to
>   taste

1. Combine the rice flour with 1 cup of water. Bring to boil the other 5 cups.
2. Whisk the rice flour mix into the boiling water, whisking until it comes to boil again. Cover and simmer on lowest heat while you prepare the spices. If you can, add a quill of cinnamon here instead of the teaspoon of powder later.
3. Toast the pistachios in a small skillet over medium low heat. Remove.
4. Use the same skillet to dry roast the caraway and aniseed. Cool and grind. If you can't grind them, using them whole will be intriguing as well.
5. Warm the ghee in the skillet over low heat. Add all the spices and swirl for a minute, remove from heat and cool.
6. When the cream of rice is desired consistency, add the spices, salt and sugar. Let cook a few minutes more to blend.
7. Garnish with toasted pistachios.
8. If you are using honey, let cool to body temperature before adding.

Serves 6. Middle Eastern Influence.

Of this recipe,   Better yet,
Kapha, enjoy less .... use millet flour instead of rice flour and choose honey and sunflower or pumpkin seeds
Pitta, enjoy more .... use less aniseed, caraway and nuts and use sugar or maple syrup
Vata, enjoy more .... use any sweetener and decrease caraway

THE WAY IT MIGHT HAVE TASTED BEFORE IT CAME OUT OF A BOX.

DARK RICE and SWEET POTATO

Traditionally we use our hands for preparing and eating food.

The First Saucepan
3/4 cup black glutinous rice
2 1/2 cups water
5 jujubes (Asian or other dates)

1 sweet potato

The Seasonings
1 tbsp ghee
1/2 tsp ginger powder
1/2 tsp amchoor powder or lemon juice
1/2 tsp earth or sea salt
3 tsp palm or unrefined cane sugar
3 tbsp coconut, fresh and finely grated is ideal

1. Rinse rice and combine with the water and jujubes in a medium saucepan.
2. Bring to boil, stir, cover and simmer, stirring occasionally, condensing the liquid and cooking the rice.
3. Peel and cube the sweet potato to about 2 cups. Cook in its own saucepan in simmering water until soft, about 15 minutes. Drain (saving stock to use this day) and return to its cooking pot. Cover, set aside and keep warm.
4. Check that the rice is cooked at 40 minutes and that the water has been absorbed. If so, open a space in the bottom of the saucepan and warm the ghee. Add the ginger and amchoor. Cook another few minutes. Add the salt, sugar, and mix.
5. Toast the coconut in a small skillet. At first sign of color, remove from heat and cool.
6. Serve the dark pudding with the sweet potato cubes on top and the coconut garnish.

Serves 4 as main course. Southeast Asian Influence, Indonesia.

Of this recipe,   To accommodate,
Kapha, enjoy less .... use a lighter grain like millet, a more astringent vegetable like spinach and very little coconut so leave the recipe as is and enjoy less
Pitta, enjoy more
Vata, enjoy more .... add more ginger

LIKE THE COLORS OF TIBETAN BUDDHIST ROBES, A CHEWABLE RICE AND SOFT SWEET POTATO.

DARK YELLOW RICE

In traditional medicines, stagnation is considered something to be avoided.

2 cups basmati rice
4 cups water
4 lemon grass stems

Dry Roast
4 macadamia or candlenuts, grated
2 tsp cumin seed
2 cardamom pods
1 tbsp coriander seed
2 cloves
1/2 tsp black peppercorns

Skillet Mix
2 tbsp ghee
2 tsp turmeric
1 tbsp grated fresh galangal or
   ginger
1 tsp cinnamon

Additional Flavors
1/2 cup tamarind juice or 1/4
   cup lime juice
1 1/2 tsp earth or sea salt
1/2 tsp nutmeg
4 sprigs coriander leaves

1. Inspect rice to remove debris and rinse. Combine with water in a medium saucepan. Using the lower parts of the lemon grass stems, crush with a pestle and add.
2. Bring to boil, stir and simmer, covered, 15 minutes.
3. In a small skillet over medium low heat dry roast the nuts, cumin, cardamom pods, coriander seeds, cloves and peppercorns 1-2 minutes.
4. Grind cardamom in mortar first, discarding pods and then grind the rest of the dry roasted ingredients.
5. Warm ghee in the skillet over medium low heat. Add the mortar mix, turmeric, galangal and cinnamon powder. Sauté 2 minutes and remove from heat.
6. Combine 2 tablespoons dried tamarind with 1/2 cup hot water. Mash the fruit mass off the seeds. Collect 1/2 cup fruit liquid through a strainer. Add to skillet.
7. When the rice is cooked, let it rest 5 minutes.
8. Remove lemon grass stems from the rice. Add the skillet mix, salt and nutmeg, tossing through gently with a fork.
9. Serve as a cone, hemisphere or other shape with a coriander cap.

Serves 4. Indonesian Influence, Bali.

Of this recipe,   To customize,
Kapha, enjoy less .... enjoy the spices without the nuts; use less ghee, salt and tamarind/lime juice and use millet instead of rice
Pitta, enjoy more .... use less pepper, salt, nutmeg and galangal
Vata, enjoy more

YELLOW, ONE OF FOUR SACRED COLORS; PREPARE THE SPICES WHILE THE RICE STEAMS.

DONUTS in ROSE SYRUP

A cook endeavors to bestow a beneficial influence on others.

24 almonds and/or raisins

The Syrup	**The Donuts**
13 aromatic roses	2 cups flour, see below
1 cup water	a sprinkle of sea salt
3/4 cup palm or unrefined cane sugar	2 tbsp ghee
1 lemon round	1/2 tsp ginger powder
a sprinkle of sea salt	water

1. Heat almonds in warm water until the skins swell. Remove skins when cool enough to handle. Soak in fresh water until needed.
2. To prepare the syrup collect the roses, harvest the petals and snip off a majority of the white found at their bases. Wash the petals.
3. Combine water and sugar in a small saucepan and bring to boil.
4. Add lemon and after 1 minute add the petals. Cook down, stirring every 5 minutes. Simmer until a light and pink syrup is obtained, then stir in the salt. Let cool, then strain and collect the syrup. Squeeze out the petal mass as well.
5. Bring a pot of water to boil or prepare your steaming apparatus. Keep at a simmer.
6. Place flour and salt in mixing bowl, rub in ghee and add ginger.
7. Add water to make smooth pliable dough.
8. Pinching off 1 teaspoon amounts of dough, wrap it around 1/2 of an almond cut horizontally and/or a raisin. When all are ready, bring the pot of water up to boil again and add donuts. Low boil for 10 minutes or steam for 20.
9. Drain and transfer to serving dish. Pour on the rose syrup and mix through. Stir occasionally for 15 minutes to saturate the shapes. Pat dry, chop and toast if desired the remaining almonds and use with raisins as garnish.

Serves 4-6. European Influence, Bosnia.

Of this recipe,   To modify,
Kapha, enjoy less .... your usual rye, millet and barley flour blend would be too crumbly so enjoy this recipe only on occasion
Pitta, enjoy more .... use wheat flour and smaller pieces of almond; taste the sweetness and astringency of the rose syrup, that combination is good for pitta
Vata, enjoy more .... use wheat flour; use rose petal syrup on occasion

FILLED DOUGH SPHERES BOILED AND SATURATED WITH ROSE ESSENCE.

FESTIVE RICE

Translating the written recipe to an actual event is magic already.

1/4 cup dried apricots	**The Seasoning**	fresh coriander
1/4 cup dried currant	2 tbsp ghee	lemon wedges
	1 tsp cumin seed	
2 cups basmati rice	1 tsp mustard seed	
3 3/4 cups water	a sprinkle of asafoetida	
1 quill cassia or cinnamon or	1 1/2 tsp cumin powder	
1 tsp powder	2 tsp coriander powder	
	1 tsp turmeric	
1/4 cup raw pistachios	6 curry leaves	
1/4 cup raw cashews	1 1/2 tsp earth or sea salt	

1. Cut non-sulfured apricots into small pieces and soak in a small amount of water. Soak currants separately. Stir now and then.
2. Inspect rice and remove debris. Rinse off the surface starch, drain and spread to air dry.
3. Bring the 3 3/4 cups of water and cinnamon quill to boil, covered, and then simmer, to be added to the rice.
4. To prepare the seasoning, warm ghee in a medium saucepan (large enough to cook the rice) over medium heat.
5. Add cumin and mustard seeds and asafoetida and heat until it sizzles gently. Turn heat to low and add the rest of the seasonings, enriching the ghee.
6. Add rice to ghee and sauté until coated. Add simmering water carefully. Mix well, bring to boil, cover and simmer for 15 minutes.
7. Take the saucepan off the heat and let rest, covered, 5 minutes.
8. Chop the nuts into various sizes and toast in a small skillet.
9. To serve, garnish the rice with the dried fruit, toasted nuts, chopped coriander and lemon.
10. Authentic festive rice would also have small amounts of gold or silver foil as garnish for health and opulence.

Take note if your digestion is comfortable with fruit, nuts and carbohydrate combined.

Serves 4-6. Indian/Middle Eastern Influence.

Of this recipe,   To fine tune,

Kapha, enjoy some .... rice is an occasional dish, use millet or quinoa instead; use less nuts and lemon juice; use gold foil

Pitta, enjoy more .... decrease nuts and lemon juice; use silver foil

Vata, enjoy more .... use less or no dried fruit; use gold and sometimes silver foil

Pitta and Vata, use the fruit soaking water to flavor drinking water

A HANDFUL OF NUTS AND DRIED FRUIT EMBELLISH CURRIED RICE.

GREEN SPLIT PEAS and AUBERGINE

Courage is supported by glucose, determination is supported by oxygen.

1 cup green split peas
1 medium aubergine (eggplant)

3-5 coriander plants
1 tbsp nuts or seeds of choice

The Seasonings
1/4 cup olive oil
1 tsp cumin seed
a sprinkle of asafoetida
1/2 tsp ginger powder
1 1/2 tbsp sweet paprika
3/4 tsp earth or sea salt
1 lemon, juiced

1. Inspect peas and remove anything foreign or inferior, soak them for 4 hours and then rinse and cook, using fresh water. When the water foams during boiling, rinse and replace with more fresh boiling water. Or skim off all the foam and continue cooking in the same liquid. Simmer, covered, for 1 hour, until very soft and the liquid is mostly evaporated.
2. Peel the aubergine, cut into cubes and steam for 15 minutes, until soft and translucent.
3. Warm olive oil in a small skillet over medium low heat. Add cumin and asafoetida and sauté 2 minutes. Remove skillet from heat and add ginger. Cool further and add paprika and salt, developing the rich red color of the paprika.
4. Collect 2 tablespoons of lemon juice. Add it to the skillet mix.
5. Chop very fine the coriander stalks and leaves or just leaves to the amount of one cup. Toss half through the peas, the other half through the aubergine.
6. To serve place peas down first, aubergine on top, skillet dressing over that. Garnish with a few nuts or seeds, toasted if desired.

Serves 2 or 4 with rice. North African-Middle Eastern Influence.

Of this recipe,   To improve for your dosha,
Kapha, enjoy some .... use less oil and lemon juice and millet instead of rice; use sunflower seeds
Pitta, enjoy some .... decrease aubergine, paprika, oil and juice; use seeds
Vata, enjoy less .... enjoy on occasion with oily nuts

CORIANDER TOSSED THROUGH PEAS AND AUBERGINE WITH A TRANSLUCENT RED PAPRIKA DRESSING.

GRIDDLECAKES, SWEET and SAVORY

Herbs can help remind the body mind of its own natural energy patterns.

The Batter
1 cup millet or barley flour
1 cup wheat flour
1/2 tsp earth or sea salt
2 cups water
1 tsp melted ghee

Sweet
1/2 tsp cardamom
1 tsp cinnamon

Savory
1/2 tsp turmeric
cumin seed

1. Combine batter ingredients and stir, without over-mixing, until the consistency of heavy cream.
2. Divide batter into halves, about 1 1/2 cups each, and add sweet spices to one half, turmeric to the other.
3. Warm a griddle with a thin film of ghee over medium heat. Cook cakes, adjusting heat if necessary, until both top and bottom are dry and golden. Sprinkle the upper side of the savory cakes with some cumin before flipping. If the batter is thickening, add some more water.
4. Serve with honey (best sweetener for kapha), maple syrup, marmalade and chutneys.

Yields 6 of each variety, 10 cm = 3 1/2 inch diameter. Serves 2-3 as a main meal. World Influence.

Of this recipe, everyone enjoy some on occasion. Politically correct, it neither helps nor hinders anyone in particular.
Pitta and vata constitutional people can use more ghee on the griddle.

ONE BATTER PROVIDES THE BASE FOR VARIOUS TASTES.

HANDMADE PASTA

People connect around food.

Per person
3/4 cup wheat flour(s)
a grind of black pepper
1 tsp melted ghee
1/4 cup water
earth or sea salt

Have ready either ample counter space to roll out and leave the pasta for a few
   minutes or the classic broom handles to hang spaghetti lengths over.

1. Mix flour, pepper and ghee together on a bench top or in a bowl.
2. Make a well in the middle and add the water with a sprinkle of salt.
3. Combine into dough and knead for 5 minutes. Let rest 30 minutes, covered
   with a damp cloth.
4. Roll out to a 25 x 35 cm = 10 x 14 inch rectangle, quite thin but not emaci-
   ated.
5. Dust the top lightly with flour and turn over.
6. Cut into strips, shapes, squares, depending on how it will be served.
7. Let rest while you bring 5 cups of lightly sea-salted water to boil.
8. Dust off excess flour and add pasta. Stir until water resumes a boil. Cook
   uncovered until al dente, a few minutes only.

For European-American-type recipes you could add 1/4 tsp dried or fresh
   herbs.
For Indian-type recipes you could add 1/4 tsp cumin and turmeric powder.
For Southeast Asian recipes you could use a lemon grass/Kaffir lime leaf tea as
   the dough-making liquid.

Most countries have a boiled dough recipe.

Of this recipe,   To refine,
Kapha, enjoy less .... use the buckwheat or rye flatbread recipe
Pitta, enjoy more .... decrease black pepper
Vata, enjoy more

A BASIC DOUGH RECIPE THAT CAN BE FLAVORED IN ESSENCE WITH THE REST OF THE MEAL.

KAFFIR NOODLES

A small amount of spicing enkindles the digestive fire, a large amount inflames the body and mind.

1 tbsp tamarind or lemon juice
250 gm = 9 oz broccoli stems
24 basil leaves (1 tsp dried)
4 Kaffir lime leaves or lime rind
400 grams = 14 oz wheat noodles (4 servings)
1/4 cup finely grated coconut, fresh is ideal
1 tbsp ghee
250 gm = 9 oz mung bean sprouts
1 tsp earth or sea salt

1. To make tamarind juice, pour about 1/4 cup hot water over 2 tablespoons dried tamarind. Let cool. Knead fruit off seeds and pass through fine strainer. Collect 1 tablespoon of purée. If using dried basil soak in the purée.
2. Slice broccoli stems into julienne strips.
3. Cut basil leaves into short ribbons.
4. Mince Kaffir lime leaves or grate 1 teaspoon lime zest.
5. Begin cooking noodles according to directions.
6. In medium skillet over low heat toast dessicated coconut, if using, until beginning to color. Remove from skillet.
7. Return skillet to burner and warm ghee over medium heat. Add broccoli and cook about 5 minutes, moving it around the skillet occasionally. Adjust heat. Add coconut.
8. Add bean sprouts and cook a few minutes more.
9. Turn heat off, add salt and tamarind. As it cools add lime and basil leaves and toss to mix.
10. Serve over noodles.

Serves 4. Southeast Asian Influence, Thailand.

Of this recipe,	To enjoy more,
Kapha, enjoy some	use buckwheat noodles, less ghee, less coconut and less tamarind juice
Pitta, enjoy more	decrease tamarind juice somewhat
Vata, enjoy some	decrease sprouts

TOSSED WITH SPROUTS, BROCCOLI AND FRESH BASIL.

KASHA FLATBREAD

Ghee flame is to candle flame as incandescent light is to fluorescent light.

1 1/2 cups water
1/2 cup buckwheat groats for kapha; 1/4 cup for pitta and vata
1 tsp sunflower oil for kapha; 2 tsp ghee for pitta; 2 tsp ghee for vata
3 cups flour: rye for kapha; wheat, any variety, for pitta and vata
1/4 tsp earth or sea salt for kapha and pitta; 1/2 tsp for vata
additional water

1. Heat the 1 1/2 cups water to boiling.
2. In a small saucepan dry roast the groats circulating them for a few minutes.
3. Add boiling water to the groats carefully, cover and simmer over low heat for 15 minutes.
4. Remove from heat, add oil, and let cool, covered.
5. Combine flour and salt on a flat surface or in a bowl.
6. Add cooked groats to flour with any liquid still in the pot.
7. Add additional water to make soft dough and knead several minutes. Traditionally, some poppy seeds would be added. These increase heaviness and drowsiness. Use them if that is not an issue.
8. Separate into 15 pieces. Roll each out on floured surface to round or other shape.
9. Heat an ungreased griddle over medium high heat. Kapha: brush a thin film of ghee on it. Pitta and Vata: warm 1/4 teaspoon ghee on it for each flatbread.
10. Cook 2 minutes on the first side. Adjust heat to prevent burning or smoking. When you flip the flatbread darker brown spots should be visible. Cook several minutes on the second side.
11. Kapha and pitta, stack singly to cool and crisp; vata, stack them in a covered pile to keep them softer.

Makes 15 flatbreads. Russian Influence.
Instructions for each dosha are built into this recipe.

COOKED BUCKWHEAT IN A GRAIN FLATBREAD.

LEMON MINT RICE

Rice is the grain of the moon.

1 3/4 cups water
1 tsp lemon rind
1 tbsp olive oil
1 cup long grain rice
1/2 tsp turmeric
1/2 tsp earth or sea salt
1/4 cup lemon juice
3 tbsp fresh mint

1. Bring the water to boil and grate the lemon rind.
2. Inspect rice to remove debris and rinse. Drain and air-dry.
3. Heat the oil in a medium saucepan.
4. Add the rice and sauté a few minutes, watching it become translucent. Add the turmeric, watching it become yellow.
5. Add water, salt and rind to rice. Stir, cover and cook over low heat 20 minutes. Let cool undisturbed for 10 minutes.
6. Remove lid and pour lemon juice evenly on top. Toss lightly with fork and replace lid for another 5 minutes.
7. Chop the mint and garnish.

Serves 3-4. Mediterranean Influence, Greece.

Of this recipe,   To modify,
Kapha, enjoy less .... enjoy rice on occasion, using instead millet, quinoa or amaranth and decrease lemon juice to just a squeeze
Pitta, enjoy more .... with less lemon juice
Vata, enjoy more

SIMPLE, SAVORY, COLORFUL.

LENTILS and NOODLES

Your ingredients communicate to you via their aromas.

3/4 cup brown lentils
2 bunches spinach or similar greens
1/2 tsp earth or sea salt

500 gm = 1 lb fettuccine noodles
1 cup minced coriander leaves
  and stems
black peppercorns

a generous 1/4 cup olive oil
2 tbsp sumac powder (or lemon juice at the end)
a sprinkle of asafoetida
1/2 tsp earth or sea salt

1. Inspect and remove debris and inferior specimens from lentils and soak for a few hours if possible.
2. Rinse lentils and bring to boil in a medium saucepan. Discard water if it foams and cook covered in fresh boiling water for 30 minutes or until soft. Or skim off all the foam and continue cooking in the same liquid.
3. Cut spinach into ribbons and wash well.
4. When lentils have disintegrated add spinach and cook several minutes adjusting liquid until a sauce-like consistency is obtained. Remove from heat, add salt and set aside.
5. In a large covered pot bring noodle-cooking water to boil.
6. Meanwhile warm the oil in a small skillet over medium heat.
7. Add the sweet, slightly tangy sumac and pungent asafoetida to the skillet and swirl. Remove from heat and add salt.
8. When the noodle water is boiling add noodles and cook al dente.
9. Mince coriander.
10. When the noodles are cooked, drain and return to pot.
11. Stir up and add skillet ingredients and most of the coriander to coat noodles. Lift noodles upward with 2 forks rather than stirring. Transfer to serving dish. Top with lentil-spinach sauce and remaining coriander. Squeeze on lemon juice if using.
12. Serve with fresh ground black pepper available.

Serves 6. Middle Eastern Influence, Jordan.

Of this recipe,	To improve for your dosha,
Kapha, enjoy less	use buckwheat noodles, more lentil sauce, less skillet mix
Pitta, enjoy some	increase noodles relative to lentil sauce; decrease skillet mix
Vata, enjoy some	increase noodles relative to lentil sauce

GREEN CORIANDER AND PINK SUMAC CONTRIBUTE FLAVOR AND COLOR .

MATH BEANS, BEETS and KUMQUATS

Giving your teeth something to chew stimulates the natural movements of digestion.

1 1/4 cup math or aduki beans
  (math is slightly larger than barley)
1 bay leaf
1 medium beetroot

1/4 tsp saffron stigmas, lightly measured
10 kumquats

2 tsp ghee
2.5 cm = 1 inch fresh ginger
a sprinkle of asafoetida
1 tsp cinnamon
1/2 tsp earth or sea salt

2 tsp unprocessed honey

1 tbsp coriander leaves
1/4 cup pistachio nuts or 1 tbsp sesame seeds

1. Sort through the beans to remove stones, inferior specimens, etc. and soak for 8 hours. Rinse and using fresh water, bring to boil. As they foam, drain, rinse and replace with fresh, boiling water. Or skim off all the foam and continue cooking in the same liquid. Simmer, covered, for at least 1 hour, with the bay leaf, until beans are soft and well cooked. If you have an organic beetroot cook it whole with the beans until soft to the center. Or cook whole beetroot in simmering water to cover.
2. During this time soak saffron in 1 tablespoon of warm water. Swirl occasionally.
3. Cut the kumquats into quarters and remove seeds.
4. Chop the coriander.
5. Toast the pistachios or sesame in a small skillet or under the grill.
6. When the beans are cooked, drain and set aside. Set the beetroot aside. Warm the ghee in a medium saucepan over medium low heat.
7. Grate the ginger into the saucepan, add the asafoetida and sauté for a minute. Add cinnamon.
8. Mix in the beans and kumquats. Add the saffron and its liquid. Cook for another 5 minutes.
9. Mix in the salt and let cool. Add the coriander.
10. Peel and cube the beetroot.
11. To serve, add honey to the cooled bean-kumquat mix. Top with beet cubes and garnish with nuts/seeds.

Serves 4 as a side dish. North African Influence, Algeria.

Of this recipe,	To customize,
Kapha, enjoy more	less kumquats, nuts/seeds
Pitta, enjoy some	less kumquats, beetroot, ginger, nuts/ seeds
Vata, enjoy some	less beans, another teaspoon ghee

MAGENTA ROOT AND ORANGE FRUIT, A BED OF SPICED BEANS.

MILLET and RICE

Poor quality food causes us to eat more in seeking nourishment.

The Fresh Herbs, lightly packed
1/2 cup coriander leaves
1/2 cup chives
1/4 cup mint
1/4 cup tarragon
1/4 cup watercress
1/4 cup parsley
2 tbsp fenugreek leaves

1/2 cup millet
1/2 cup brown rice
1 tbsp ghee
1/2 cup basmati rice
1/2 cup sesame seeds
1 tsp earth or sea salt

1. Finely mince all herbs. If any are unavailable fresh add between 1 teaspoon and 1 tablespoon dried, depending on the herbs' strength. Watercress can be substituted by 1/2 teaspoon black pepper; fenugreek with fenugreek sprouts or 1 teaspoon dry roasted and crushed seeds.
2. Inspect grains and remove debris such as small stones. Your teeth will appreciate it.
3. Combine millet, brown rice and ghee in a medium saucepan with 3 cups of water. Bring to boil and simmer, covered, for 30 minutes.
4. Add basmati rice and another cup of water to the millet-rice for another 15 minutes. Add water so it is not bone-dry or cook off excess water so it is not soup-like. You can stir the pot.
5. Toast the sesame seeds until golden.
6. When the grains are cooked, mash them. If using dried herbs add now. Let cool and add the salt and minced fresh herbs. The pâté would be aromatic, dry and somewhat sticky.
7. Oil your hands and shape like burgers, finger food or anything in between. Sprinkle with sesame seeds and press in.

As a substantial part of a meal serves 4. Makes 48 tablespoon-sized patties. Whole grain cooking with an Iranian herb blend.

Of this recipe,   To fine-tune,
Kapha, enjoy some .... increase the millet, decrease the rices and sesame seeds
Pitta, enjoy some .... decrease the sesame and herbs
Vata, enjoy some .... decrease the millet, increase the basmati rice; press in raw sesame seeds and sauté your patties in a small amount of ghee over low heat

GRAIN PATTIES WITH FRESH HERBS AND SESAME SEEDS.

MILLET BERBERE

Millet is the grain of Mercury.

1 1/2 cups hulled millet	**Seeds, Pods. Whole Spices**
3 cups water	8 cardamom pods
1/2 tsp earth or sea salt	1 tsp cumin seed
2 + 2 tsp ghee	1 tsp coriander seed
	1/4 tsp ajowan seed
1 tsp ginger powder	1/2 tsp fenugreek seed
1/2 tsp grated nutmeg	6 cloves
	1 tsp black peppercorns
2 tbsp raw pistachios	
1 tsp earth or sea salt	fresh coriander
	lemon sections

1. Inspect the millet and remove extraneous debris, especially small stones.
2. Put the 3 cups of water and 1/2 teaspoon salt on to boil in its own pot.
3. In a medium saucepan warm the 2 teaspoons ghee over medium heat. Roast the millet for 1-2 minutes. Carefully add the boiling water, stir, cover and simmer for 30 minutes. Millet cooks like rice, best left to its own devices. If you stir often, it will become sticky. That works in some recipes.
4. Meanwhile, in a small skillet over medium low heat, dry roast the seeds, pods and whole spices for a few minutes. Grind the cardamom first, discarding the pods. Then add the other spices and continue grinding. There can be some coarseness to the blend.
5. Toast the pistachios in the same skillet and transfer to a small dish.
6. Warm the next two teaspoons of ghee in the skillet over low heat. Add the ground spices and ginger and infuse for 1 - 2 minutes. Remove from heat and add nutmeg and salt. Keep warm.
7. When the millet is cooked, let rest 10 minutes.
8. When firmer, toss the skillet mix through gently, thus keeping the millet firm.
9. Garnish with coriander leaf and small sections of lemon.
10. Alternatively, mix vigorously so that the grains cohere, pat this into a flat base and serve mild vegetables on top.

Serves 4. African Influence, Ethiopia.

Of this recipe,	To enjoy more,
Kapha, enjoy more	with only a few drops of lemon
Pitta, enjoy less	use mostly rice, some millet and decrease the spice blend substantially, it is very pungent, too pungent to really be ayurveda-approved; use a few drops of lemon
Vata, enjoy less	substitute mostly rice, using less millet and less spice blend

MILLET IS STEAMED AND MIXED WITH AN AFRICAN SPICE BLEND.

MUNG DAL

We receive energy in part from our environment. We return it through our desire and attachment to that which we received. What is the energy balance at the end of the day?

1 cup split mung beans
4 cups water

The Seasoning	The Seasoning (cont'd)
1 tbsp ghee	1 tsp coriander powder
1 tsp fenugreek seed	1 tsp turmeric
1 tsp nigella seed	1 tsp aniseed
1 tsp cumin seed	1 tsp earth or sea salt
1 tsp mustard seed	coriander leaves
a sprinkle of asafoetida	lemon wedges

1. Pick over mung beans, discarding unwanted material and inferior specimens. Wash and soak in water for 1 hour. Rinse and bring to boil in a medium saucepan with water to cover.
2. Bring the 4 cups of water to boil. When the mung foams, rinse and replace with the boiling water. Remove any additional foam. Simmer for 30-40 minutes until very soft.
3. Warm the ghee in a small skillet over medium heat. Add the fenugreek, nigella, cumin and mustard seeds. Amplify their essence for 2 minutes and then remove from heat. Add the asafoetida, coriander, turmeric and aniseed to the ghee.
4. Mash the mung to a purée consistency adding water or cooking longer as needed.
5. Add the skillet mix within the last 15 minutes of cooking. When cooked add the salt. When cooler garnish with coriander leaves or omit the aniseed and garnish with Thai basil.
6. Serve with the offer of lemon wedges.

Serves 4 as a side dish. Indian Influence.

Of this recipe,	To improve for your dosha,
Mung is a tridoshic bean	
Kapha, enjoy more	use a smaller squeeze of lemon and less salt
Pitta, enjoy less	mung is good but the seasonings are too pungent
Vata, enjoy some	a moderate serving with these spices will not be too drying

A VARIETY OF SMALL SEEDS IN A RICH YELLOW AND SMOOTH BASE.

MUNG and OKRA

The basic inclination of the body mind is to be healthy.

The Vegetables
12 okra or 15 snow peas
water
1/2 tsp earth or sea salt
1 sweet red pepper (capsicum)

1 lime or other citrus juice

The Custard
1/4 cup coconut, fresh and finely
  grated is ideal
1 tbsp linseed
1 tsp ghee
1/2 tsp turmeric
a sprinkle of asafoetida
1 cup mung bean flour

1. Combine the whole okra, salt and water to cover in a medium saucepan. Bring to boil and simmer uncovered 10 minutes. If using mange tout, steam for 5 minutes.
2. Blacken the entire skin of the whole red pepper in a very hot oven. Wrap in a towel or bag to cool a short time, rub off charred skin and slice the red into strips, short or long. Transfer strips to a holding dish and keep warm.
3. When the okra is cooked, drain and collect the liquid. Trim okra stems and tips and cut each ladyfinger into rounds. You will appreciate a sharp knife. Keep okra warm.
4. To prepare the custard, toast the coconut and linseed in a large skillet or saucepan over medium low heat. Stay with this process so as not to char either ingredient. Transfer to holding dish.
5. Warm the ghee in the same skillet over low heat. Add turmeric and asafoetida.
6. To prepare the custard combine the okra cooking liquid with additional water if necessary to make 2 cups. Whisk in the mung flour. If you have not cooked the okra in water, whisk 2 cups fresh water, 1/2 teaspoon salt and the mung flour.
7. Continue whisking while adding the batter to the skillet or saucepan and now bring to boil. Lower heat and whisk often for 5 minutes. Does it remind you of a sulfur hot spring? Add coconut-linseed in the last 2 minutes.
8. Stripe this base onto the middle of a serving platter, okra and pepper on either side. Squeeze a small amount of lime or other citrus juice on top and serve.

Serves 2 as main meal, 4 as side dish. Caribbean/Indian Influence.

Of this recipe,   To further accommodate,
Kapha, enjoy some .... decrease coconut and linseed; you may not like
the custard texture
Pitta, enjoy more .... sweet red pepper in this amount is O.K.
Vata, enjoy more
As a one-pot option, sauté the okra and pepper in 2 teaspoons of ghee. When cooked, keep warm and prepare the custard in the same skillet.

MUNG AS A CUSTARD AND ALSO RED PEPPER.

MUNG DAL TOO

The wisdom of ayurveda grows roots firm, deep and supportive.

1 cup split mung beans

1 tbsp milk
a sprinkle of saffron stigmas

<u>The Skillet Mix</u>
4 tbsp grated coconut, fresh is best
1 tbsp ghee
1 tsp turmeric
2 tsp cumin
a sprinkle of asafoetida
1 tsp earth or sea salt
fresh coriander leaves

1. Remove debris and inferior beans from the mung and soak for 1 hour if possible.
2. While the mung is soaking, warm the milk and float the saffron on. Swirl periodically.
3. Rinse the mung and bring to boil in a small saucepan with fresh water. When it foams rinse and cover with more boiling water. Or skim off all the foam and continue cooking in the same liquid. Simmer for 30-40 minutes, covered, stirring more towards the end to help disintegrate the dal.
4. Warm a small skillet over medium low heat. Add coconut and toast until golden. Remove coconut.
5. Add the ghee to the skillet. Add the turmeric, cumin and asafoetida. Ghee has the ability to take the properties of what is infused in it to all cells without losing its own properties. Remove from heat.
6. When the mung is cooked to a thicker creamy consistency, add the saffron and liquid, the skillet mix and the salt. Mix well. Let cool a few minutes.
7. Chop the coriander leaves.
8. Garnish with the toasted coconut and coriander leaves.

Serves 4 as a side dish. African Influence, Kenya.

Of this recipe,   To modify,
Kapha, enjoy some .... decrease ghee and coconut and sauté some fresh grated ginger in the skillet mix
Pitta, enjoy more
Vata, enjoy some .... include some fresh grated ginger in the skillet mix

BOTH SAFFRON AND TURMERIC ADD COLOR.

PANCAKE-WRAPPED VEGETABLES

What at first seems foreign to the mind soon becomes familiar.

The Pancakes
1 cup water
2 1/2 cups wheat flour
1 tsp earth or sea salt
3 tbsp sesame oil

The Seasonings
2 tsp coriander seed
1 tsp cumin seed
4 tbsp sesame oil
1 tbsp galangal or
  ginger root
2 lemon grass stalks
3 Kaffir lime leaves
4 coriander roots
1 tsp turmeric
1/2 tsp cinnamon
1 tsp earth or sea salt
black pepper

The Vegetables
1/2 daikon (Oriental
  radish)
1 medium carrot
125 gm = 4 oz green
  beans
1 stalk celery
coriander leaves

1. To make pancake dough, bring water to boil.
2. Combine flour, salt and oil in bowl.
3. Add up to the one cup of boiling water to make soft, pliable dough.
4. Knead for several minutes and set aside, covered.
5. To make seasoning, dry roast coriander and cumin seeds, cool and grind in mortar with pestle. Add sesame oil to the mortar.
6. Grate fine the galangal and add to mortar. Peel off outer lemon grass leaves and slice from the base of the stalk up in very thin rings. When the purple inner ring disappears, slice no further. Add rings to the mortar. Use the remaining stem to make stock or tea.
7. Mince and add the lime leaves or 1 tsp lime or lemon zest and coriander roots.
8. Add the turmeric, cinnamon and salt. Further mash the seasonings with the pestle to release their flavors. Set aside.
9. Prepare the vegetables by peeling and trimming if required and cutting into at least 24 sticks of each vegetable, 8 x 1 x 1 cm = 3 1/2 x 3/8 x 3/8 inches.
10. Warm a medium skillet over medium heat and add the spice mix from the mortar and the vegetables.
11. Sauté for 10 minutes, uncovered, rotating occasionally. Add water if necessary to prevent vegetables from sticking.
12. Meanwhile, prepare the pancakes. Divide the dough into 12 sections. Divide each section in half and roll each half out on a lightly floured surface to a 15 cm = 6 inch round. Brush the surface of one circle with sesame oil and cover with the other pancake. Do this with the other 11 pairs. It is possible to start cooking the pancake pairs before you make all twelve.
13. When the vegetables are cooked, firm but not raw, remove skillet from heat and add black pepper. Set aside.
14. Back to the pancakes: Heat the largest griddle/skillet you have over medium low heat with a thin film of sesame oil. Place as many pancake pairs on

it as fit. Cook 2 minutes and turn over. The cooked side would be just starting to show golden patches. Cook the other side another 2 minutes. Remove
pancake pairs and separate the halves, allowing each to cool separately.
Notice that you have only cooked one side of each pancake. Make sure that
side is indeed cooked.

15. When all pancakes are cooked and separated and not necessarily cool,
place one stick of each of the four vegetables on one edge and roll it up.
Create a sculpture of rolls on the serving platter. Garnish with coriander
leaves.

Makes 24 rolls. Asian Influence, Burma and China.

Of this recipe,   To enjoy more,
Kapha, enjoy less .... enjoy the vegetable sauté without the pancakes
Pitta, enjoy more .... decrease the galangal/ginger; use mild daikon
Vata, enjoy more

COOKED VEGETABLE STICKS ARE ROLLED IN ORIENTAL
PANCAKES.

PAN-COOKED CHICKPEA SNACK

That which is ingested frequently has the bigger impact on our health.

1 cup chickpea flour
3/4 tsp earth or sea salt
2 cups water

The Seasonings
1 tbsp ghee
1 tsp cumin seed
a sprinkle of asafoetida
2 tsp grated fresh ginger
6 curry leaves
2 tsp sumac powder

1. Whisk flour, salt and water together, working away any lumps.
2. In a medium skillet, warm the ghee over medium low heat.
3. Sauté the cumin seeds and asafoetida for 1 minute; add ginger and curry leaves, then sumac for 2 minutes without scorching.
4. Add the besan batter and stir constantly over medium-low heat until the ingredients homogenize and leave the sides of the pan.
5. Continue cooking the dough for another 5 minutes, first one side, then the other.
6. Let cool. Cut and serve as a snack with chutney, as soup dumplings or a base for vegetables.

Serves 4-6. Indian Influence.

Of this recipe,   Even better
Kapha, enjoy more .... use less salt and sumac
Pitta, enjoy more .... use less ginger, salt and sumac
Vata, enjoy less .... use more ghee and enjoy only on occasion; use rice flour and then enjoy more

CHICKPEA CURRY PANCAKE.

PESTO PASTA

What channel is the mind tuned to?

500 g = 1 lb pasta, handmade is best
a generous 1/4 cup olive oil
4 tbsp packed chopped, torn or snipped basil leaves
3/4 tsp earth or sea salt
1/2 tsp fresh ground black pepper
1/2 cup pine nuts

1. Cook pasta as is your custom.
2. Mix basil, salt and pepper into the oil.
3. In a small skillet over low heat roast the pine nuts until golden.
4. When pasta is ready, add olive oil mix and blend through gently.
5. Garnish with the nuts.

Serves 5. Mediterranean Influence, Italy.

Of this recipe,   Better yet,
Kapha, enjoy less .... use barley, millet or buckwheat pasta, less oil and salt and fewer nuts
Pitta, enjoy some..............don't overuse the salt or pepper, decrease the nuts
Vata, enjoy more

DELIGHTFUL TASTE IN A TEXTURED VERSION.

PIGEON PEAS

Genetically engineered products do not have access to the original lineage of plants.

1 cup pigeon peas or other lentils
2 cm = 3/4 inch fresh ginger
1 black cardamom pod
1 cinnamon quill

12 vegetable drumsticks or 20 green
    beans

1/4 tsp grated nutmeg
1/4 tsp ground black pepper
3/4 tsp earth or sea salt
fresh sacred basil or coriander leaf

More Seasonings
1 tbsp ghee
2 tsp coriander seed, crushed or
    2 tsp powder
4 green cardamom pods
1/2 tsp fenugreek seed
1/2 tsp ajowan seed
1/2 tsp aniseed
1 tsp cumin seed
4 cloves
a sprinkle of asafoetida

1. Inspect peas and remove inedibles and inferiors. Soak for 2 hours.
2. Rinse and bring to boil in a medium saucepan with water to cover. If water foams, rinse and cover with fresh boiling water. Or skim off all the foam and continue cooking in the same liquid. Cover and simmer.
3. While cooking the peas grate the ginger and add. Add the black cardamom pod and the cinnamon.
4. Cook for 40 minutes.
5. Meanwhile, warm the ghee in a small skillet over medium low heat.
6. Add all the seeds, a shape at a time, first removing the cardamom seeds from their pods. Add the whole cloves and asafoetida. Rock the infusion for 2 minutes.
7. Check that the peas have disintegrated. If so, add the skillet masala and the drumsticks, cutting them into lengths to fit the pot if necessary.
8. Adjust liquid to create a dal consistency, either adding water or uncovering the pot. Cook another 10 minutes.
9. Let the dal cool. Add the nutmeg, black pepper and salt.
10. Garnish with chopped herbs. To eat drumsticks, split and draw them through your teeth, harvesting the inner vegetable or split and scoop with a spoon.

Serves 4. Indian Influence.

Of this recipe,   To modify for your dosha,
Kapha, enjoy more
Pitta, enjoy some .... decrease all seasonings
Vata, enjoy less .... as with all legumes, increase oil and still enjoy less

A PROVOCATIVE ARRAY OF WHOLE SPICES AND THE FRUIT PODS
OF THE MORINGA TREE.

PINE NUT and RICE PORRIDGE

The difference between people who live in accordance with nature and those who do not, is reflected as accord or discord with life.

4 Chinese dates

2 tsp ghee
1/2 cup pine nuts
3/4 tsp ginger powder
1/2 tsp cardamom

1/4 cup rice flour
water
1/4 tsp earth or sea salt

1. Cut dates into water to cover and soak.
2. Warm ghee in a small saucepan over medium low heat. Add nuts, ginger and cardamom. Warm without browning the nuts. Remove from heat.
3. Meanwhile add the rice flour to 1 1/2 cups water. Stir and let stand.
4. Transfer nuts and spices to a mortar or blender and crush together. (Whatever ghee remains in the saucepan will be used.)
5. Add 1 cup of water, a little at a time, to loosen the nuts. You are aiming for a mostly smooth nut sauce with some character pieces. Set aside.
6. Stir the rice flour in water just before pouring into the same small saucepan. Warm over medium low heat and whisk constantly until bubbles form.
7. Add the nut blend and bring to boil. Simmer 2 minutes, adding salt and date-soaking water. Adjust consistency with additional water or condensing.
8. Garnish with dates.

Serves 2. Korean Influence.

Of this recipe,   To refine,
Kapha, enjoy less .... you can use barley, millet, rye or buckwheat instead of rice flour but nothing can replace the oily pine nuts
Pitta, enjoy some .... decrease the nuts and ginger
Vata, enjoy more

THE TASTE OF PINENUTS AND THE FORTIFYING EFFECT OF JUJUBES.

PUY LENTILS

There are a lot of psychological issues around food.

3/4 cup Puy or other lentils
1 1/2 tbsp sesame seeds

The Seasonings
1 tbsp olive oil
1 tsp cumin powder
a sprinkle of asafoetida
a sprinkle of ajowan seeds or savory herb

1 lemon
fresh parsley
fresh oregano or 1 1/2 tsp dried
1/2 tsp earth or sea salt
black peppercorns

1. Remove debris and any inferior specimens from these small speckled pulses grown on French volcanic soil and soak for several hours.
2. Rinse lentils and bring to boil in fresh water. Discard that water and cover with fresh boiling water. Or skim off all the foam and continue cooking in the same liquid. Cover and simmer 30-40 minutes.
3. During that time warm a small skillet on medium heat. Add sesame. When the seeds are golden brown remove from skillet and transfer to holding dish.
4. Add oil to skillet and add cumin, asafoetida and ajowan, sautéing on medium low heat for 1 minute. Let cool.
5. Grate the lemon rind to the amount of one teaspoon.
6. Mince the fresh herbs to the amount of one tablespoon each and combine. If your herbs are strong in taste, use less.
7. When the lentils are soft, drain and add skillet mix. If using dried herbs add to lentils now. Add salt.
8. Mix in lemon rind and a squeeze of lemon juice.
9. When cooler add fresh herbs.
10. Garnish with the sesame seeds and pass the pepper grinder à la table.

Serves 4. European Influence, France

Of this recipe,   Even better,
Kapha, enjoy more .... decrease sesame seeds
Pitta, enjoy some .... decrease herbs, spices and sesame
Vata, enjoy less .... increase oil and be prepared to have none if you experience flatulence; you may prefer to mash the lentils with cooking liquid to make it moister

A LENTIL SALAD GARNISHED WITH SESAME SEEDS.

QUINOA
Is your body relaxed while you cook?

2 cups water
1 orange
1 cup quinoa
1/2 tbsp ghee
1 tsp fennel seed

1 tbsp fresh oregano, lightly packed, or 1 1/2 tsp dried
1 tbsp minced fresh basil or 1 1/2 tsp dried
1/2 tbsp minced fresh mint or 1/2 tsp dried
1/2 tsp earth or sea salt
black peppercorns

1. Bring the water to boil in whatever vessel you would like to use.
2. Cut the orange into segments. Unpeel rind from one section and mince 2 teaspoons of rind if the orange is organic. Set the segments aside for later.
3. Inspect quinoa to remove small stones, etc. Rinse well and drain.
4. Warm ghee in a medium saucepan over medium low heat and add the fennel seeds and orange rind. Sauté one minute. Add the quinoa, boiling water carefully, stir, cover and simmer 15 minutes.
5. While the cooked quinoa is cooling for at least 5 minutes, mince the herbs if you are using them fresh. Remove the rest of the orange sections and cut into bite-size pieces as a garnish.
6. Add salt and dried herbs, if using, to quinoa without over-mixing. If using dried herbs replace saucepan lid and let sit another 5 minutes.
7. Place quinoa on serving platter and garnish with fresh herbs and orange sections. Pass the pepper grinder at the table.

Serves 2 as a main dish with vegetables. Greek Influence with South American quinoa.

Of this recipe,   To make it better,
Kapha, enjoy more
Pitta and Vata, enjoy less ....add another teaspoon of ghee to your servings; pitta, minimize pepper and oregano and use sweet oranges; eat something dense as well with this grain

A STEAMED GRAIN, LIGHT IN COLOR, LIGHT IN TEXTURE, WITH DARK ACCENTS OF FRESH HERBS.

RED LENTILS

A small amount of good quality oil used in cooking aids metabolism.

1 cup red lentils
2 cups water
1/4 tsp earth or sea salt

2 medium potatoes
1 tbsp ghee
a sprinkle of asafoetida
1 small red pepper (capsicum)

The Seasonings
1 tbsp parsley
1/4 tsp earth or sea salt
black pepper
1 tbsp pumpkin seeds
1 lemon, cut into wedges

1. Inspect lentils and remove debris and inferior ones. Soak in water to cover for 1 hour.
2. Rinse, drain and simmer in the 2 cups of water in a small saucepan for 45-50 minutes. If any foam arises, drain, rinse and cover with more boiling water. Or skim off all the foam and continue cooking in the same liquid. When the lentils are soft, drain any excess water and enhance the flavor with the salt.
3. Cube the potatoes, warm the ghee and brown them. Add the asafoetida and a small amount of water, cover and cook until firm and done, about 10 minutes.
4. Peel the red pepper if necessary and dice. Add to the potatoes for the last 2 minutes. Mix in the salt.
5. Chop fine the parsley.
6. Shake the pumpkin seeds in a small pan over medium low heat until the first few pop.
7. Place the lentil mix on a serving platter and the vegetables on top.
8. Garnish with black pepper, parsley and pumpkin seeds.
9. Serve with lemon wedges.

Serves 4. North American Influence, United States and Canada.

Of this recipe,   To refine,
Kapha, enjoy more .... use minimal lemon juice and less ghee
Pitta, enjoy some .... red lentils are O.K. occasionally, use less lemon juice and peppers
Vata, enjoy some .... enjoy the red lentils with sweet potato instead of potato; you may wish to mash the lentils with cooking liquid to make them creamier

A BED OF LENTILS, VEGETABLES ON TOP AND PUMPKIN SEED GARNISH.

RICE

If your job does not allow you enough space to take care of
yourself, it is part of the imbalance.

2 cup basmati rice
4 cups water

Pitta Churna
3/4 tsp coriander seed
1/2 tsp fennel seed
1/2 tsp cumin seed
1 tsp green cardamom pods
2 tbsp ghee
1 tsp turmeric
1/2 tsp cinnamon
1/4 tsp earth salt

fresh coriander and/or mint

1. Rinse rice and bring to boil in the water. Cover and simmer on low heat 15
   minutes. Let cool completely.
2. Meanwhile, dry roast seeds and pods in a small skillet over medium low heat
   for 1 minute. Transfer cardamom to mortar, discarding husks, and grind.
   Add the other seeds and grind them as well.
3. Warm ghee in the same skillet over medium low heat. Add all spices, sam-
   pling this aroma. Warm for 2 minutes, remove from heat and add salt.
4. Mince coriander and/or mint.
5. Toss skillet blend through rice and serve with leaf garnish.

Serves 4. Indian Influence.

This is a pitta-specific dish. The spice blend is tailored to supply the
cooling effect and proper tastes on the palate. You can buy it as Pitta
Churna, which would also have cane sugar in it. Pitta constitutional
people can use this spice blend often. You can use coriander, fennel, cumin
and cardamom powders instead of dry roasting and grinding the seeds,
adding them to the ghee in addition to the other spices, but using seeds is
fresher and more flavorful.

THE DEFINITIVE PITTA-FRIENDLY SPICE BLEND WITH PITTA-
FRIENDLY GRAIN.

RICE and SWEET ADUKI BEANS

There is more success in changing diet using the mentality of abundance than the mentality of deprivation.

The Beans
1 1/2 cups aduki beans
1/2 cup palm or unrefined cane sugar
1/4 tsp earth or sea salt
a sprinkle of asafoetida

2 tsp ghee
3/4 cup Arborio or short grain rice

1/2 tsp earth or sea salt
1/2 tsp aniseed
12 whole + 1 tbsp chopped pistachio nuts

The Risotto Stock
3 cups water
1 tsp ghee
3 cloves
1 cinnamon quill
1 tsp dried ginger or several thin
    slices fresh
1/2 tsp turmeric

1. Inspect beans to remove debris and soak in water for 8 hours. Drain, rinse and bring to boil in fresh water. If foam arises, drain again, rinse and replenish with fresh boiling water to cover. Aduki beans tend not to foam. Cook thoroughly, covered, about 75 minutes.
2. Meanwhile, bring the 3 cups of risotto water to boil.
3. Warm 1 teaspoon ghee in a medium saucepan over medium low heat. Add cloves, cinnamon, ginger and turmeric and sauté 1 minute.
4. Add the boiling water. Simmer, covered, 5 minutes and keep at a simmer.
5. In a medium large pot warm the 2 teaspoon of ghee and after inspecting the rice for debris, sauté it for 2 minutes.
6. Begin to add the simmering spice liquid, first to coat the bottom of the pot and then 3 tablespoons at a time. Cook over medium low heat stirring until each amount of liquid is absorbed and continue adding the liquid in this manner until the rice is soft to the center. Any stock left is a spice tea! Add aniseed and salt, cover and let cool.
7. Drain the beans and return to their cooking pot with sugar, salt and asafoetida. Over low heat mash until the consistency is that of mashed potato. Let cool.
8. To assemble, oil palms and shape 12 spheres of rice with a pistachio in the center. Or wash hands between spheres to prevent the rice from sticking.
9. Place one twelfth of the bean mix on a piece of thin damp cotton fabric and spread it out to 5 mm = 1/4 inch thick. Place a rice ball in the center of the bean mix and using the cloth, mold the bean mix around the rice ball. Finish sculpting by hand. Proceed with the rest.
10. Garnish with toasted chopped nuts.

A simpler serving suggestion is to layer the sweet beans - rice - sweet beans alternately in a ramekin per person and chop all the nuts for garnish.

Makes 12 spheres. Serves 4 - 6. Japanese Influence.

Of this recipe,   To customize,
Kapha, enjoy some .... use millet instead of rice and much less sugar
Pitta, enjoy more .... decrease cloves, ginger and aniseed
Vata, enjoy some .... aduki is a good bean for all

RICE IS COOKED AS A PALE YELLOW RISOTTO AND DEEP
MAROON BEAN PURÉE IS WRAPPED AROUND IT.

RICE and URAD DAL PATTIES

Our bodies have become accustomed to what we were fed as children. It is nourishing because it is familiar. Is it nourishing to all levels?

1 cup basmati rice	1 tsp earth or sea salt
2 cups water	1 cup urad dal flour
	a generous 1/2 cup water
1 tbsp ghee	
1/2 tsp mustard seed	ghee
1 tsp cumin seed	coriander leaves
a sprinkle of asafoetida	

1. Rinse and inspect the rice to remove debris. If you can, soak it in water for about an hour.
2. In a saucepan, combine the rice and 2 cups water, bring to boil and simmer, covered, for 15 minutes. Let cool for 30 minutes.
3. Warm the tablespoon of ghee over medium heat and add the seeds and asafoetida. Temper for 1 minute.
4. Combine the rice, skillet mix, salt, flour and water, the flour making it firm, the water making it coherent and the spices making it tasty and digestible.
5. Divide the mix into about 20 portions and form into shapes of your choice. Allow them to be 1.5 cm = 3/8 inch high.
6. Warm a teaspoon of ghee in a large skillet over medium high heat and spread it into a thin film.
7. Sauté the rice-urad patties on the first side until golden brown, about 5 minutes, and turn over to cook to the same color on the second side. Adjust heat down as the skillet warms up. If the skillet has become dry, add another quarter teaspoon of ghee. Continue cooking until all the shapes are cooked.
8. Garnish with coriander leaf and serve with chutney.

Serves 4. Indian Influence.

Of this recipe,	To refine,
Kapha, enjoy less	there is no substitute that tastes the same
Pitta, enjoy some	decrease the urad dal and substitute mung flour
Vata, enjoy more	

COOKED RICE AND DAL FLOUR PROVIDE THE TASTE OF DOSA-S WITHOUT FERMENTATION.

RICE RAS el HANOUT

Spice seeds collect an extraordinary amount of sun in their oils.

Per Serving
1/2 cup basmati rice
1 cup water
1 tsp ghee

1. Inspect and rinse rice. Drain and toss occasionally to air dry.
2. Begin to heat cooking water, covered, in a separate pot. When boiling, lower to simmer.
3. Warm ghee over low heat in a saucepan large enough to accommodate the number of servings of rice being cooked.
4. Chose the spices and herbs that follow in such a way that the salty, sour, bitter and pungent tastes will be present (sweet and astringent will be present in the rice). Add the salty and sour tastes at the end. Beginning with not more than 6 ingredients and using not more than 1/4 teaspoon of each, heighten their profile in the warm ghee. If using dried herbs they release their flavor more readily into a small amount of warm water. If using fresh herbs chop the delicate-leaf varieties and add before serving. Chop coarser herbs such as rosemary and add with the simmering water.
5. Sauté spices 1-2 minutes and add the rice. Add the simmering water. Stir once and simmer, covered, for 15 minutes.
6. Let cool without disturbing for 5 minutes. Add salty and sour tastes.
7. Sample the aroma and flavor of your blend. You could note and adjust it on an ongoing basis. It could take years to develop an original, mysterious, satisfying blend. Some spices will not taste good if cooked too long.

BASIC STEAMED RICE WITH YOUR OWN SPICE BLEND AS "HEAD OF THE SHOP".

Since we never eat a plateful of pure spice, a small amount will not imbalance anyone. The best tastes for Kapha are bitter, pungent and astringent; for Pitta, sweet, bitter and astringent and for Vata, salty, sweet and sour. Choose to have ready from any of the following spices:

Ingredient	Kapha	Pitta	Vata
Ajowan	use more	use less	use more
Allspice	use more	use less	use some
Amchoor	use less	use less	use more
Aniseed	use more	use less	use more
Asafoetida	use some	use less	use some
Basil, dried	use more	use less	use more
Bay leaf	use more	use less	use more
Black pepper	use more	use less	use some
Caraway	use more	use less	use some
Cardamom, black	use more	use less	use some
Cardamom, green	use more	use more	use more
Cayenne	use some	use less	use less
Celery seeds	use more	use less	use some
Cinnamon/Cassia	use more	use some	use more
Citrus peel	use more	use more	use some
Cloves	use more	use some	use some
Coriander leaf	use more	use more	use more
Coriander seeds	use more	use more	use more
Cubeb	use more	use less	use less
Cumin	use more	use more	use more
Curry leaf	use more	use more	use more
Dill	use more	use more	use some
Earth salt	use less	use less	use some
Fennel	on occasion	use more	use more
Fenugreek	use more	use less	use more
Galangal	use more	use less	use some
Ginger	use more	use less	use some
Juniper berries	use more	use some	use some
Kaffir lime leaf	use less	use some	use more
Lemon grass	use some	use some	use more
Lemon verbena	use some	use some	use some
Licorice root	use less	use more	use more
Lotus seeds	use some	use more	use less
Mace	use more	use less	use less
Mahleb	use less	use less	use more
Marjoram	use more	use less	use some
Mint	on occasion	use more	use some
Mustard seed	use more	use less	use some
Neem leaves	use more	use more	use less

Nigella seed	use more	use less	use some
Nutmeg	use more	use less	use some
Oregano	use more	use less	use some
Papaya seed	use more	use less	use some
Paprika	use more	use less	use some
Parsley	use more	use some	use some
Pomegranate seed	use more	use more	use some
Poppy seed	use less	use less	use some
Rosemary	use more	use some	use some
Rose water	on occasion	use more	use less
Saffron	use some	use some	use some
Sage	use more	use less	use some
Sansho pepper leaf	use more	use less	use less
Savory	use more	use some	use more
Sea salt	use less	use less	use some
Sesame seeds	use less	use less	use more
Sichuan pepper	use more	use less	use less
Star anise	use more	use less	use some
Sumac	use less	use less	use more
Tamarind	use less	use some	use more
Tarragon	use more	use less	use more
Thyme	use more	use less	use some
Turmeric	use more	use more	use some
Vanilla bean	on occasion	use some	use some

RYE FLATBREAD

Rye is the grain of Jupiter.

2 tsp coriander seed
1 tsp black peppercorns
3 cups rye flour
1/2 tsp caraway seed
1/4 tsp earth or sea salt
1 tsp ghee
1 cup water

1. Grind coriander and pepper with mortar and pestle to a medium-fine texture.
2. Toss with flour, caraway, salt and ghee on a flat surface or in a bowl.
3. Add water a little at a time to a hollow in the center of the flour. Work the flour in.
4. When you have pliable dough knead for 5 minutes, then let it rest for 15-60 under a slightly damp tea towel.
5. Roll portions of the dough out to about 5 mm = 1/8 inch thickness, about 12 cm = 5 inch diameters. Fashion about 15 rounds or shapes.
6. Heat a large unoiled skillet over medium high heat. When hot, start cooking the flatbreads, adjusting the heat to prevent burning. After about 1-2 minutes turn the bread to the other side. The first side is cooked with golden to darker brown spots. Cook the second side like the first.
7. Allow to cool individually, then pile up and serve.

Makes 15 flatbreads. North African Spice Blend.

Of this recipe,   To adapt,
Kapha, enjoy more .... the chewy-crunchy texture needs to be well-chewed and helps stimulate digestion
Pitta, enjoy less .... enjoy one with ghee
Vata, enjoy less.............. enjoy one with ghee
-or-
Pitta and Vata, use wheat instead of rye flour and decrease caraway and pepper

A CRISP FLATBREAD APPROPRIATE FOR KAPHA.

SAUTÉED CELERY PANCAKES

Assess what is happening as reflective of the five elements.

The Skillet Mix
1 tsp ghee
3/4 tsp caraway
1 tsp cumin seed
 a sprinkle of asafoetida
1 tsp celery seed
1/4 tsp black pepper
3/4 tsp earth or sea salt

6 stalks celery
1 tsp oregano

1 1/2 cups chickpea flour

1. In a large skillet warm ghee over medium low heat. Add caraway, cumin and asafoetida and sauté 1 minute. Begin to cool and add the celery seeds, freshly ground pepper and salt.
2. Finely grate celery with its juice into a mixing bowl. Add oregano.
3. Add skillet mix to grated celery and bring skillet to medium heat.
4. Add chickpea flour to celery and mix to sticky dough.
5. Warm a small amount of extra ghee on the skillet and add tablespoon portions of mix, pushed off with another spoon.
6. Sauté until golden, add a film of ghee to the skillet, flatten the pancakes and sauté other side until golden.
7. Serve with lemon rind chutney or coriander-mint dressing.

Makes about 30, serves 6 as appetizer. Indian Influence.

Of this recipe,	To make it better,
Kapha, enjoy more	use minimal ghee or mustard oil when cooking the patties
Pitta, enjoy more	minimize spices
Vata, enjoy less	use wheat flour and less caraway; use carrot in place of most of the celery

CELERY AND SPICES FIRMED UP WITH CHICKPEA FLOUR.

SCULPTED ADUKI BEANS

It is suggested that to glue beans and seeds to a board and call it art is dishonoring food. With this recipe we can be artistic and honorable.

1 cup aduki beans
1/2 cup walnut pieces
3 tbsp packed fresh parsley
2 tbsp olive oil
2 tsp coriander powder
a sprinkle of asafoetida
3/4 tsp earth or sea salt
1 tbsp lemon juice

1. Sort through the beans to remove stones, inferior specimens, etc. and soak for 6 hours. Rinse with fresh water, bring to boil. Rinse and change with fresh, boiling water if foam arises. Aduki beans tend not to foam. Simmer, covered, for at least 1 hour, until beans are soft and well cooked.
2. Grind walnuts with mortar and pestle and mince parsley.
3. When beans are cooked, drain, reserving stock for use later on in the day if desired.
4. Warm olive oil in small skillet over medium low heat. Add coriander and asafoetida and infuse for 1 minute.
5. Mash beans with all ingredients.
6. With damp or oiled hands, depending on what this will be served with, create spheres of all sizes or slabs or rings or...
7. Brush with olive oil. Garnish with parsley if desired.

Serves 4-6. Middle Eastern Influence, Armenia.

Of this recipe,   Better yet,
Kapha, enjoy some .... decrease the walnuts, lemon juice and oil
Pitta, enjoy some .... decrease the walnuts and lemon juice; use a
light hand with the oil
Vata, enjoy some .... increase the nuts relative to the beans; you'll
notice how dry beans are when you shape them

MASHED ADUKIS WITH EMBEDDED WALNUTS.

SEMOLINA DUMPLINGS

Choose this recipe when you want to enjoy the manual art and therapy of kneading dough.

1/4 cup water
a sprinkle of saffron threads
2 cups fine semolina
1 cup whole wheat flour
2 tsp ghee
1/2 tsp earth or sea salt
3/4-1 cup water

1. Heat the quarter cup of water until warm. Remove from heat.
2. Float the saffron on top and swirl. Swirl occasionally for about 30 minutes.
3. Combine semolina, flour, ghee and salt in a large bowl or on the counter. Open a space in the center and add the saffron water and the rest of the water in several increments, using your hands to mix. The dough should be pliable and not dry. Knead for 5 minutes and let rest for 30, covered.
4. Set a large covered pot of lightly sea-salted water to boil.
5. Pinch off rounded teaspoon pieces and make spheres.
6. When the water is boiling, slip dumplings in and stir. Bring to boil and continue boiling for 10-15 minutes, uncovered. The dumplings will be firm and cooked to the center.
7. Serve with a sauce or dressing. Or include different herbs and spices into the dumplings and then serve with a light dressing of oil or ghee. Or cook them in a soup.

Serves 4-5. Mediterranean Influence, Italy.

Of this recipe,   To modify,
Kapha, enjoy less .... enjoy a large raw or cooked salad with a
dumpling cut up as garnish if you wish to taste one
Pitta, enjoy more
Vata, enjoy more

GLUTINOUS SAFFRON SPHERES.

SOYBEAN SALAD

Eating before the previous meal is digested is like throwing raw beans into cooked beans and expecting an edible result.

The Salad
3/4 cup soybeans
100 gm = 4 oz yard long or green beans
100 gm = 4 oz snow peas
1/2 choko

The Dressing
1/2 cup olive oil
1 tbsp fresh chives
a generous 1/4 cup lime or lemon juice
1/2 tsp earth or sea salt

4 sprigs fresh thyme, 2 tsp dried

1. Inspect beans and remove unwanted material and inferior specimens. Soak them overnight, then change the water and soak during the day.
2. In a large soup pot, bring 6 cups of water to boil and add soybeans. Cover and cook 90 minutes. Skim off all the foam.
3. Trim beans and snow peas and cut into lengths of choice.
4. Peel and dice choko, including young seed.
5. When the soy is almost done drain excess water. Add green beans and choko and cook uncovered 5 minutes.
6. Add snow peas, cook another 5 minutes uncovered.
7. Remove from heat and begin cooling. Add dried thyme if using.
8. Meanwhile combine the oil, chives, lime juice and salt into a dressing.
9. Serve warm or at room temperature adding fresh thyme leaves on top and pass the dressing at the table.

Serves 4. Caribbean Influence.

Of this recipe,   To enjoy more,
Kapha, enjoy less .... soybeans are heavy, use another dried bean; use less dressing and use sunflower or mustard oil instead of olive oil
Pitta, enjoy some .... use less dressing
Vata, enjoy less .... use whole mung instead of soy; they soak and cook in less time and are more easily digested

A DRESSED SOYBEAN AND VEGETABLE DISH, THE SOY HOLDING ITS SHAPE BEAUTIFULLY.

SPICE and NUT FLATBREAD

Work with these ayurvedic principles with a light mind so as not to limit the scope of links with other teachings.

2 cups wheat flour, any variety	**Skillet Mix**
1/2 tsp earth or sea salt	2 tbsp ghee
3/4 tsp ground black pepper	1 tsp cumin seed
	3 tbsp sesame seeds
3/4 cup water	3/4 tsp aniseed
	1/2 tsp ginger powder
	1 tbsp chopped pistachios

1. Combine flour, salt and black pepper on a large surface or bowl.
2. In a small skillet warm the ghee over medium low heat.
3. Add the rest of the skillet mix. Sauté for 2 minutes until fragrant and re-move from heat. Let cool a few minutes.
4. Drizzle the textured ghee on top of the flour and rub it in with your fingers.
5. Make a well in the center and add the water.
6. Knead relaxedly for 5 minutes. Expect the nuts and seeds to keep escaping. Let rest 30-180 minutes, covered with a damp cloth.
7. Preheat oven, if using, to 400°F (200°C, Gas 6).
8. Divide into 12 pieces and roll each to a 15 cm = 6 inch diameter circle or equivalent. The thinner you roll the dough, the more cracker-like it will be.
9. Heat a griddle over medium high heat. Cook both sides of the flatbread until golden with darker patches. This takes about 1-2 minutes each side. Adjust heat to prevent burning.
10. Alternatively place on baking trays and bake for 10-12 minutes or until golden around the edges.
11. Pile the cooked breads on a plate and cover with a tea towel until you are ready to serve them.

All grain-growing regions have their own flatbreads. The spices here are of Middle Eastern Influence.

Of this recipe, To further refine,
Kapha, enjoy less .... roll thin and cook or bake dry; use less nuts, sesame seeds, ghee; more other spice seeds and ginger; less salt; better yet, use the Buckwheat or Rye Flatbread recipe
Pitta, enjoy more .... use less skillet mix and black pepper; coat with a little ghee after cooking
Vata, enjoy more .... favor thicker flatbreads as they are less dry; coat with ghee after cooking

NUTS AND SEEDS DECORATE THIS STAPLE.

STEAMED BUNS

A goal can change based on the outcome of the steps preceding it.

The Wrappers
2 cups wheat flour
a small amount of earth or sea salt
1/2 tsp fennel seed
2 tsp ghee
1/2 cup water, maybe more

lettuce leaves or baking paper
1 tbsp sunflower seeds

sunflower oil or ghee

The Filling
1 1/2 cups water
1/2 cup buckwheat groats
1 kiwi fruit
1 apricot or star fruit
1/4 tsp ginger powder
1/4 tsp sea salt
1/2 tsp coriander powder
a generous 1/4 cup palm or
unrefined cane sugar

1. For the wrappers combine flour, fennel and salt on a flat surface or in a bowl and rub in ghee. Open a space in the center and add water to form soft, pliable dough. Knead for 5 minutes, cover with a dampened tea towel and set aside.
2. To make the filling heat water to boiling.
3. In a small saucepan dry roast the groats moving them for a few minutes. Add boiling water slowly, stir, cover and simmer over low heat 15 minutes.
4. Peel and dice the fruit to the amount of one-half cup. Other fruit can be substituted.
5. Assemble a steaming apparatus. A bamboo steamer is traditional. Or sit a perforated rack over water in a large pot. Add water to the pot, making sure its level is 35 mm = 1 1/2 inches below the rack. Therefore it may be necessary to raise the rack. Be ingeneous. Heat the water and maintain at a simmer.
6. Mix groats with remaining filling ingredients and set aside.
7. Apportion dough into 12 pieces. Roll each out into a 15 cm = 5 inch circle. Place 1 tablespoon filling on the circle and seal dough into half moon or envelop shapes. The envelopes only have to be sealed at the edges. Trim off the excess dough, which will be enough to make two more buns.
8. Cut out 14 small sections of lettuce and place in the steamer. Sit a bun on each. This prevents the buns from sticking to the steamer and possibly tearing when they are removed.
9. If using a metal steamer place a tea towel over the top of the pot to catch the condensation, then the lid, then drape the towel over the lid and away from the heat source.
10. Adjust heat to produce uniform steam and cook for 30 minutes, replenishing with more boiling water if needed.
11. Toast or dry roast sunflower seeds and chop medium fine.
12. Brush cooked buns with oil or ghee and sprinkle with sun seeds. Try filling

with something savory next time.

Makes 14 buns. Russian-Asian Influence

Of this recipe, To fine-tune,
Kapha, enjoy less .... decrease sugar; use apple, rye, barley and/or
millet flour and sunflower oil; you might rather bake the buns, moderate
oven about 20 minutes
Pitta, enjoy some .... enjoy kiwi and star fruit rarely, otherwise enjoy
more
Vata, enjoy some .... buckwheat in this amount on occasion is O.K.;
delete the fruit if these buns cause flatulence several hours on

FRUIT AND SWEET BUCKWHEAT FILLING IN CHEWY POUCHES.

STEAMED RICE in MUGS

The steamer is to the east as the oven is to the west.

12 almonds	**The Saucepan Mix**	**The Vegetables**
2 cups water	1 tbsp sesame oil	1 medium carrot
1/4 tsp earth or	1 tsp mustard seed	16 snow peas
sea salt	1 cup basmati or long	1/2 turnip
	grain rice	
	a sprinkle of asafoetida	

4 large coffee mugs or equivalent

Check that you have a steamer large enough to hold the 4 coffee mugs. If not, do you have one large enough for two? If not, you can bake this or serve it from the cook top. It is always possible to adapt.

1. Heat almonds in a small amount of warm water until skins swell. When cooler, remove skins. Chop into medium pieces and leave to soak in fresh water.
2. Bring the water and salt to boil, then simmer, covered, waiting to cook the rice.
3. Warm the oil in a medium saucepan over medium heat.
4. Add mustard seeds. When the first pops add debris-free rice and asafoetida.
5. Sauté until rice becomes glossy and more translucent.
6. Add the salted water carefully, stir once and cook, covered, over low flame, 15 minutes. Let cool undisturbed for 5 minutes.
7. Cut the carrot into matchstick lengths, not too thin. Cut the snow peas into smaller pieces, removing stems and tips. Grate the turnip.
8. Steam carrots and turnip for 5 minutes each in its own section of the steamer; add snow peas into its own pile and steam everything for two minutes more.
9. To combine in mugs, divide most of the vegetables onto the bottom, then the cooked rice, then arrange the remaining vegetables on top.
10. Check the water level in the steamer and position mugs. Cover and steam 10 minutes with low steam flow. Refer to Steamed Buns recipe for more information on steamers.
11. Drain almonds, pat dry and toast if desired.
12. Remove mugs carefully. They will be hot. Garnish with almonds.

Serves 4 as a light meal. Japanese Influence.

Of this recipe,   To refine,
Kapha, enjoy less .... use millet instead of rice (see Millet Berbere)
and bake instead of steam; use fewer almonds and decrease oil
Pitta, enjoy more .... use less oil, mustard, turnip and almonds
Vata, enjoy more

RICE AND VEGETABLES ALREADY COOKED, STEAMED AND SERVED IN MUGS.

STEAMED YAM CAKE

There is a shift in taste happening.

1 cup mashed yam
1 3/4 cups coconut milk (see Coconut Soup)
1 cup rice flour
1/2 cup palm or unrefined cane sugar
1 1/2 tsp ginger powder
1/4 tsp earth or sea salt

1/4 cup grated coconut

1. Have a steamer ready or set up a steaming apparatus including a round casserole dish that will sit on an elevated rack inside a covered pot. The casserole dish would hold 3 cups of batter. Oil the casserole dish.
2. Cook whole yam in simmering water, covered, until soft, about 20 minutes. Drain and mash.
3. Set steamer water to boil. Refer to Steamed Buns recipe for more information on steaming.
4. Combine the yam with the rest of the ingredients except coconut and place in the casserole dish. Fresh coconut milk is nectar in itself but if not an option right now, use water and 1 tablespoon of coconut or other mild-tasting oil.
5. Place casserole dish on rack in steamer and cover with steamer lid. Steam for 40 minutes. Make sure there is no condensation forming and raining on your cake.
6. Let cool for one hour.
7. Toast coconut and garnish the cake before serving.

Serves 8-16. Philippine Influence.

Of this recipe,	To enjoy more,
Kapha, enjoy next to none	it can't be done
Pitta, enjoy some	decrease the ginger
Vata, enjoy more.....................	within the ability of your digestion

STEAMING GIVES TEXTURE TO THIS RICH CAKE.

STICKY RICE BALLS

Let the mind be occupied with coordinating all the parts into a whole.

The Rice
2 cups Arborio rice (short grain)
3 1/2 cups water
1/2 tsp earth or sea salt
1 tsp ghee

The Coatings
1 tbsp sesame seeds + 1/2 tsp sea salt
1 tbsp black sesame seeds + 1/2 tsp sea salt
1 tbsp minced parsley
1 tbsp sumac powder

1. Inspect rice to remove inedibles and combine with water, salt and ghee in medium saucepan. Bring to boil, stir, cover, steam over low heat 20 minutes, stirring every five. Let cool. Stir occasionally.
2. Dry roast each color of sesame seed and salt separately and place each in a small plate. Note the time it takes the beige sesame seeds to become golden and apply just less than that to the black.
3. Place minced parsley in another, sumac in a fourth. Substitute if you don't have these colors.
4. When the rice is cool, dampen or oil your hands. Scoop out rounded teaspoonfuls and shape into spheres. If the rice doesn't stick together, mashing it will help. If it is sticking to your hands, wash or re-oil them.
5. Roll each in, or cap with one garnish or a combination. Place on decorated serving tray.

Makes 75 spheres. Asian Influence, Japan.

Of this recipe,   To accommodate your dosha,
Kapha, enjoy less .... a true kapha does not like sticky food
Pitta, enjoy more .... use less sesame seeds
Vata, enjoy more

WHITE RICE SPHERES WITH COLORED GARNISH.

STOVE-TOP COOKED GRAIN

Oats are the grain of Venus.

Overnight
1 cup whole or cracked oats
1/2 cup whole hulled millet
1/4 cup raisins

Saucepan Mix
1/2 tbsp ghee
1/4 cup coconut
1 tsp cinnamon
a sprinkle of earth or sea salt

Seeds
1 tbsp linseed
1/4 cup sunflower seeds
1/4 cup pumpkin seeds

1. Inspect grains and remove debris. Soak grains and raisins together overnight in water to cover.
2. To prepare, warm ghee in medium saucepan over medium-low heat and add coconut, stirring and observing as coconut is toasted. If using fresh coconut, add in the next step. Add cinnamon and mix through.
3. Add the grains, raisins and soak water.
4. Bring to boil and simmer 20 minutes until water has evaporated and grains are cooked, adding salt towards the end. Add more water if necessary.
5. Dry roast linseed in a small skillet over medium low heat. As soon as the first seeds pop, add to grains. Toast the sunflower and pumpkin seeds together until a pumpkin seed pops. Remove from heat.
6. To serve, sprinkle seeds on top of grains.

Serves 4. European Influence, Switzerland.

Of this recipe,   Better yet,
Kapha, enjoy some .... use more millet than oats, less coconut, seeds and ghee; use additional spices such as cloves and ginger
Pitta, enjoy some .... use mostly oats with a sprinkle of millet and a teaspoon more of ghee
Vata, enjoy some .... use mostly oats, a sprinkle of millet and a teaspoon more ghee; it may be necessary to decrease or delete the raisins

COOKED GRAINS ARE EASIER TO DIGEST THAN RAW ONES.
RAISINS ADD SWEETNESS, SEEDS PROVIDE TEXTURE.

SWEET RICE DUMPLINGS

How do J cook rice? Let me count the ways.

The Nut Mix
a generous cup of walnut pieces
2 tbsp palm or unrefined cane sugar
1 1/2 tsp cinnamon
1/4 tsp sea salt

The Dough
1 cup fine white rice flour
1/4 tsp earth or sea salt
1 tsp ghee
1/3 cup boiling water

The Glaze
2 tbsp unprocessed honey
2 tbsp lemon juice
aniseed
walnuts

1. Set a medium pot of water to boil.
2. Finely crush the walnuts, there can still be some small intact pieces, and mix with the next three ingredients.
3. Combine the flour, salt, ghee and nut mixture. Add water to create a soft dough, moist and cohesive.
4. Scoop out about 36 rounded teaspoon-size sections, round each into a sphere, then place all of them into the boiling water.
5. Boil gently, uncovered, moving the shapes around and off the bottom now and then until they rise to the surface, about 5 minutes. Cook 1 minute more.
6. Drain. Let cool and dry separately to firm the surfaces.
7. Combine the honey and lemon juice and baste the dumplings. Do this for 10 minutes, so that the dumplings absorb some of the glaze.
8. To serve, mix again in the glaze, sprinkle with aniseed and a few chopped walnuts. Balance the colors to the eyes' satisfaction.

Makes 36 snack spheres. Chinese Influence.

Of this recipe,	More appropriate,
Kapha, enjoy one at most	any change would alter the recipe
Pitta, enjoy some	use fewer nuts and aniseed; use maple syrup and a small amount of lemon juice as glaze
Vata, enjoy more	

AROMATIC WALNUT MIX EMBEDDED IN RICE DOUGH AND BOILED.

TOOR DAL

During eating the mind and life force energy open to the environment. What is that environment?

1 1/2 cups oiled or dry toor dal
1 tbsp split white lentils (urad dal) or split mung
1 tsp fenugreek seed

<u>The Seasonings</u>
1 tbsp ghee
1 1/2 tsp cumin seed
1 tsp nigella seed
1 1/2 tsp fennel seed
a sprinkle of asafoetida
1/2 tsp turmeric
1 tsp earth or sea salt

1 tsp amchoor or lemon juice
coriander leaves

1. Inspect the dal and remove inedibles and inferior specimens. Wash the oil off and soak for 2 hours.
2. Rinse the urad dal, pat dry and air dry.
3. Rinse and bring toor dal to boil in fresh water. Rinse foam away and replace with more fresh boiling water. Or skim off all the foam and continue cooking in the same liquid. Cover and cook 1 hour, until quite soft, smooth and the consistency of pancake batter.
4. Meanwhile, warm a small skillet over medium heat. Add the white dal and roast until just starting to darken. Add fenugreek seeds for another half a minute, lowering heat. Transfer both to a mortar.
5. Warm ghee in the same skillet and add cumin, nigella, fennel and asafoetida. Sauté for 2 minutes. Meanwhile, crush the mortar mix coarsely and add to the skillet with the turmeric. Remove from heat and add salt and amchoor. Let cool.
6. When dal is soft, add skillet seasonings. Cook another 5 minutes.
7. Garnish with coriander leaves and a squeeze of lemon juice if using.

Serves 4. Indian Influence, Bengal.

Of this recipe,	To fine tune,
Kapha, enjoy more	decrease ghee, salt and amchoor/lemon
Pitta, enjoy less	replace toor with mung dal, decrease nigella, salt and amchoor/lemon
Vata, enjoy some	just now and then

A SMALL YELLOW PULSE COOKED WITH A DEFINITIVE SPICE BLEND.

TWICE-COOKED RICE

A visit to the market or the generosity of a friend may decide what's for dinner.

2 cups basmati or long grain rice
3 3/4 cups water
1 tsp licorice powder
2 1/2 cm = 1 inch fresh ginger

More Seasonings
1 tbsp coriander seed
1 tsp fenugreek seed
2 tbsp ghee
a scant tsp cumin seed
1 tsp earth or sea salt

coriander leaves
citrus juice

1. Inspect rice and remove inedibles. Rinse and combine with water, licorice powder or a shave of licorice root and grated ginger in a medium saucepan. Bring to boil, stir once, cover and cook on low heat 15 minutes. Remove from heat and cool 10 minutes, undisturbed.
2. Tease cooked rice out with a fork as individual grains onto a flat surface to cool and firm, about 30 minutes. Remove licorice root.
3. Warm a wok or large skillet over medium low heat. Dry roast coriander seeds for 1 minute and add the fenugreek for another minute. Transfer to mortar and grind seeds to powder. Fenugreek needs some persuasion.
4. Warm ghee in the wok over medium low heat.
5. Add rice and sauté without mashing the grains. Heat for several minutes, then add the crushed spices, cumin seed and salt. Toss gently for several minutes.
6. Garnish with coriander and complement the tastes with sour, in this case, citrus.

Serves 4. Indian Influence

Of this recipe,   To fine-tune,
Kapha, enjoy some .... basmati rice is O.K. on occasion; decrease the ghee, licorice and use minimal citrus
Pitta, enjoy more .... decrease ginger and citrus
Vata, enjoy more

SOME OF THE SPICES IN THIS UNCTUOUS RICE DISH ARE TRADITIONAL SKIN CLEANSERS.

VAL DAL

The simplicity of sattwic cooking and eating will help achieve simplicity in mind-life.

1/2 cup split val or mung beans

The Seasonings
1 tbsp ghee
1/2 tsp cumin seed
1 1/2 tsp cumin powder
1 tsp cinnamon powder
3/4 tsp turmeric
a sprinkle of asafoetida
a sprinkle of ajowan (wild celery) seed
1/2 tsp earth or sea salt

1 tsp dried oregano or 2 tsp fresh
1 tbsp pumpkin seeds
lemon juice
1 tbsp fresh savory

1. Inspect dal and remove non-edibles, inferior specimens, etc. and soak 8 hours.
2. Rinse and bring to boil in fresh water and change this water with fresh boiling water when foam arises. Or skim off all the foam and continue cooking in the same liquid. Cover pot and cook 1 hour. Stir occasionally to help disintegrate.
3. Warm the ghee in a small skillet over medium heat. Add the cumin seed and lower heat. Sauté for 1 minute. Swirl in the cumin, cinnamon, turmeric and ajowan seeds if using, heating for 2 minutes. Remove from heat and add salt.
4. Dry roast or toast the pumpkin seeds.
5. When dal is like a thick soup add dried oregano and skillet mix.
6. Let cool and add lemon juice. Garnish with the pumpkin seeds and by snipping fresh herbs over the top. Savory is the herb that helps digest beans, has a mild ajowan taste and can be used in its place.
7. If this dish cools long enough it will become a bean dip.

Serves 3-4. Indian/Mexican Influence.

Of this recipe,	It would be better to,
Kapha, enjoy more	use less lemon
Pitta, enjoy more	decrease spices, herbs and use less lemon
Vata, enjoy less	use mostly mung beans and add more ghee

LAB-LAB, AN AGREEABLE-TASTING BEAN, COOKED WITH DIGESTIVE SPICES.

VEGETABLE BESAN

In Ayurvedic practices, excess superficial oil is removed with besan sprinkled on the skin and then scraped off.

The Seasonings
2 tbsp ghee
1 tsp allspice
1 tsp cinnamon
1/2 tsp nutmeg
2 tsp coriander
1 tsp ginger
a sprinkle of asafoetida
1 tsp amchoor or lemon juice

1 tsp earth or sea salt
1 3/4 cups chickpea flour (besan)
3 tbsp pumpkin seeds
1 tbsp coconut

The Vegetables
1 medium sweet potato, option of 2
   more
1 zucchini
1/2 medium cauliflower

1. Warm ghee in a small skillet over medium-low heat and introduce all seasonings except lemon juice. Swirl for 1 minute, remove from heat and set aside.
2. Preheat oven to 350°F (180°C, Gas 4).
3. Grate the vegetables into a large mixing bowl, collecting juice as well.
4. Add the salt, skillet savories and 2 tablespoons of the pumpkin seeds. Add the besan, mixing until it moistens and holds the vegetables together.
5. Oil a 22 x 33 cm = 9 x 13 inch dish and add the paté. Separate into 8 pieces which will make serving easier later. Bake for 45 minutes. As an option, bake 2 more sweet potatoes during this time.
6. Meanwhile, toast in the oven the last tablespoon of pumpkin seeds and separately toast the coconut until lightly colored.
7. To assemble, slice, dice or mash the 2 sweet potatoes, if using, and divide onto the scored besan rectangles. Sprinkle with lemon juice if using, a few drops per serving, and the seeds and coconut.

Serves 8 as a side dish, 4 as a main meal. Caribbean Influence.

Of this recipe,   If only serving your dosha,
Kapha, enjoy some .... decrease the sweet potato
Pitta, enjoy some .... decrease the amount of allspice and ginger powders
Vata, enjoy some .... use a teaspoon more ghee to offset the drying quality of besan; choose more sweet potato and zucchini and less of everything else

GRATED VEGETABLES BAKED INTO A PATÉ, GARNISHED
WITH SEEDS AND COCONUT.

WHEAT BERRY PORRIDGE

The porridge from the grain, the grain from the sun, the sun from abundance Divine. May that light also shine in this heart of mine
— German Prayer

1 cup wheat, spelt or triticale berries
1/2 cup almonds
4 cups water
1/2 tsp earth or sea salt
1 tsp grated orange rind
juice of that orange
1 tbsp ghee
1-2 tbsp palm, unrefined cane sugar or maple syrup

1. If you have a slow cooker: inspect the "korns" to remove anything inedible. Place in cooker, add water and turn to low overnight, about 8 hours. Soak almonds in water overnight.
2. Heat almonds in a small amount of warm water until skins swell. When cooler, remove skins.
3. Chop almonds coarsely.
4. Remove excess liquid from the porridge and add almonds to the cooker.
5. Add the rest of the ingredients, stir to blend and serve.
6. For stovetop cooking, clean and soak the korns overnight. Soak the almonds in a separate vessel.
7. To cook, place the berries in just 3 cups of water, bring to boil and simmer 45 minutes to one hour, covered, until soft, chewy, swelled and opened. Add more water if necessary.
8. Proceed from step 2 above.

Serves 4-5. Russian Influence.

Of this recipe,   Better yet,
Kapha, enjoy less .... use barley instead of wheat; decrease the juice and ghee; use sunflower or pumpkin seeds instead of nuts and use honey to sweeten when the porridge has cooled
Pitta, enjoy more .... decrease the nuts and juice, sweeten with sugar or maple syrup
Vata, enjoy more .... alternate sweeteners, including honey when cooled

CHEWY WHEAT, CRUNCHY NUTS AND SWEET ORANGE.

WHEAT NOODLES

It is appropriate to shop for food more than once a week.

500 gm = 1 lb wheat noodles, handmade is best

<u>**Vata Churna**</u>
1 generous tsp cumin seed
1 tsp fenugreek seed
3 tbsp ghee
1 tsp ginger
1 tsp turmeric
**1/4 tsp pure asafoetida or 1 tsp compounded with turmeric
    and rice flour**

1/2 tsp rock salt

fresh coriander

1. Prepare noodles according to directions.
2. Meanwhile, dry roast both varieties of seeds in a large skillet or wok over medium low heat for 2 minutes. Transfer to mortar and grind fenugreek as fine as possible.
3. Warm ghee in the same skillet over medium low heat. Add all spices. Warm for 2 minutes, remove from heat and mix salt in well.
4. Mince coriander.
5. Place cooked noodles in the skillet, using two forks to lift them rather than stir them, coating them with the ghee and spices.
6. Garnish with coriander.

Serves 4-5.

This is a vata-specific dish. The spice blend is tailored to supply the warming and grounding effect and proper tastes on the palate. You can buy it as Vata Churna, which will have cane sugar in it as well. We use the sweetness of wheat instead. Vata, use this spice blend often.

THE DEFINITIVE VATA-FRIENDLY SPICE AND GRAIN BLEND.

WHITE BEANS and HERBS

It takes some time to turn an ocean liner around and real boats rock.

1 cup Great Northern or other
   white beans
1 bay leaf

The Vegetables
1 carrot
1/2 celeriac or 1 cup celery
1 parsnip
1 kohlrabi
1 leek

3 tbsp olive oil
1/3 tsp caraway seed
a sprinkle of asafoetida
1 tsp earth or sea salt

The Herbs
1 tbsp fresh or 1 tsp dried:
marjoram, lovage, savory, basil
3 tbsp fresh parsley

2 tbsp lemon juice
a grating of nutmeg

1. Remove debris and inferior specimens and soak beans for 8 hours. Rinse and bring to boil with fresh water in a large saucepan. When water foams, rinse and replace with fresh boiling water. Or skim off all the foam and continue cooking in the same liquid. Add bay leaf and cook 1 hour, covered.
2. Peel and cut the first four vegetables into pieces. Add to beans to cook for 20 minutes, covered.
3. Slice leek thinly. Warm olive oil in a small skillet and sauté for 5 minutes. Add caraway and asafoetida and sauté 2 minutes. Add to beans.
4. Mix in salt and remove from heat. Allow the cooling to begin.
5. Chop all the fragrant green fresh herbs together except parsley. Chop that separately. Add fresh or dried herbs to beans.
6. Add lemon juice.
7. Garnish with nutmeg and parsley.

Serves 4-6. European Influence, Poland.

Of this recipe,   To further accommodate your dosha,
Kapha, enjoy more .... use sunflower, mustard oil or ghee and less of it;
use less lemon juice
Pitta, enjoy more .... decrease herbs, caraway and lemon juice
Vata, enjoy less .... decrease beans and caraway; increase cooked
vegetables

VEGETABLES AND BEANS WITH FRESH HERBS THROUGHOUT.

WILD RICE and PECANS

The personal touch of the cook is of utmost importance.

    1 cup wild rice
    1/4 cup pecans, about 8 nuts
    3 large crisp apples, Granny Smiths if possible
    lemon juice
    3/4 tsp earth or sea salt
    2 tsp ghee
    1 tbsp minced fresh parsley
    1 tsp fresh marjoram or 1/4 tsp dried
    black peppercorns

1. Inspect grains to remove debris, wash and boil uncovered in a medium-sized pot in ample water. If water level gets too low add some more boiling water. After 45 minutes check that the grain is soft; if not, continue cooking.
2. Chop coarsely and dry roast or toast pecans. Set aside.
3. Peel and cut the apples into small-medium pieces and sprinkle with lemon juice.
4. When the grain is soft, drain most of the cooking liquid (as stock if desired) and mix in salt and ghee. Place apples on top of the rice and cook uncovered over low heat for 5 minutes.
5. Chop the parsley and marjoram.
6. To serve, set the rice and apples out, garnish with herbs and pecans.
7. Pass the pepper grinder at the table.

Serves 4. North Amerindian Influence, Canada and the United States.

Of this recipe,	Better for your dosha,
Kapha, enjoy some	decrease pecans substantially
Pitta, enjoy some	decrease pecans and marjoram, minimize black pepper
Vata, enjoy some	decrease wild rice by half and add white rice to cook 20 minutes; cook apple well and enjoy more pecans

WELL-COOKED RUSH SEEDS ARE MELLOWED WITH APPLE AND NUTS.

YELLOW DAL

Sunrise and sunset are auspicious times of the day.

The Seasonings
1 tsp black peppercorns
1 tsp caraway seed
1 tbsp ghee
1 tsp cumin seed
a sprinkle of asafoetida
1 tsp turmeric
1/4 tsp ground cardamom
1/2 tsp earth or sea salt

lemon wedges

1 1/2 cups split yellow peas, toor or mung

1 tbsp milk or water
1 pinch saffron stigmas

1. Inspect the dal and remove inedibles and inferior specimens. Wash the oil off if using oily toor. Soak for 2 hours.
2. Rinse and bring to boil in fresh water in a small saucepan. Rinse foam away and replace with more fresh boiling water to cover. Or skim off all the foam and continue cooking in the same liquid. Cover the pot and cook 1 hour, until quite soft. Mash more towards the end of cooking. Split mung will require less cooking time.
3. Meanwhile, warm the milk just below boiling, remove from heat and float the saffron on top, vibrance developing slow motion.
4. Grind the peppercorns and caraway together.
5. Warm the ghee in a small skillet over medium heat. Add the cumin seed and asafoetida and lower heat. Add the turmeric, pepper and caraway. Remove from heat and add cardamom and salt.
6. When the dal is cooked, continue mashing it in the pot and add the skillet masala. Add the saffron. Let the flavors blend for several minutes.
7. Serve with lemon wedges available.

Serves 4. Middle Eastern Influence, Yemen.

Of this recipe	For your dosha,
Kapha, enjoy more	choose split peas or toor dal, use less lemon
Pitta, enjoy some	choose toor and mung dal and decrease pepper, caraway and lemon
Vata, enjoy some	choose mung and toor dal and decrease caraway and pepper

A MAJORITY OF BLACK PEPPER AND CARAWAY, AN
UNDERCURRENT OF SAFFRON.

YELLOW SPLIT PEA SPREAD

The word 'simple' is vastly superior to the word 'fast' when it comes to cooking.

The Dressing
1 tsp earth or sea salt
1/2 tsp black pepper
1 tbsp dried oregano
1/2 cup olive oil
1/2 cup lemon juice

2 cups yellow split peas
2 bay leaves

The Garnish
Choose from fresh coriander, rocket, cress, watercress, lamb's lettuce, lettuce, dandelion, salad burnet, parsley, fennel fronds, sorrel, chia or other herbs and leaves as garnish and/or choose from nasturtium, borage, rose, hibiscus, chamomile, mint, fennel, rosemary, thyme or other edible flowers/petals and/or various sprouts.

1. Inspect peas and remove anything foreign or inferior, soak them for 3 hours and then rinse and cook, using fresh water. When water foams, rinse and replace with fresh boiling water. Or skim off all the foam and continue cooking in the same liquid. Cook covered for 1 hour with the bay leaves.
2. Chop the various garnishes if necessary and amass separately.
3. After the one hour, notice if the peas are soft and able to disintegrate. When they are, drain and save cooking liquid to change the consistency of the spread if desired. Remove bay leaves.
4. Meanwhile, whisk salt, pepper, oregano, oil and lemon juice into a dressing. Let rest 10 minutes.
5. Put the cooked peas into a large bowl, whisk and add most of the dressing. Stir vigorously. Taste for sour and pungent, neither overpowering.
6. Sculpt onto a serving platter and pour over remaining dressing if needed.
7. Garnish with design of different herbs, leaves, petals and/or sprouts.

Serves 4. Mediterranean Influence.

Of this recipe,   To accommodate your dosha,
Kapha, enjoy some .... decrease the oil and lemon juice substantially; use bitter and pungent greens
Pitta, enjoy some .... decrease the oil, lemon juice, oregano and pepper; use bitter rather than pungent or sour greens
Vata, enjoy some .... the large amount of oil offsets the drying quality of the peas; use less garnish and enjoy now and then

SALAD DRESSING WHIPPED INTO SPLIT PEAS WITH LEAF, PETAL AND SPROUT GARNISH.

VEGETABLES

APPLESAUCE VEGETABLES

We have power in choice.

The Vegetables
1 cauliflower
2 medium carrots
2 small beetroots
200 gm = 7 oz snow peas
2 bunches spinach (or other
    greens)

The Sauce
1 tbsp juniper berries *
1 tbsp sunflower oil
8 medium apples
2 tsp lemon juice
1 tsp palm or unrefined cane sugar
1/2 tsp earth or sea salt
1/4 tsp black pepper

1. Trim cauliflower leaves and cut stem short and flat. Steam whole for 20 minutes, covered, turning over after 10 minutes. Add snow peas for another 6 minutes, turning cauliflower over again. Test that cauliflower is soft to the center before removing from steamer.
2. Meanwhile low boil whole beetroot, covered, for 15 minutes and add whole carrots, cooking both for another 15.
3. Chop the greens into short ribbons, wash well and steam for 3 minutes when you have removed the cauliflower and snow peas.
4. For the applesauce, warm a medium skillet or saucepan over low heat. Dry roast juniper berries 2 minutes. Remove and mash or mince, returning to skillet with sunflower oil.
5. Finely grate apples into skillet and mix in lemon juice.
6. Cook several minutes, until soft. Add sugar, salt and pepper.
7. The Scandinavian serving suggestion is to spread the applesauce into an open ring on the serving platter. Place the whole cauliflower in the center. Remove peel and cut the carrots and beetroot into pieces. Arrange with the snow peas and greens in a mandala or landscape. Drizzle on a glaze of oil or ghee.

A simpler method is to steam the cauliflower as flowerets with chunky carrots for 10 minutes. Add snow peas for 5, add greens for 3. The beetroot, if being used, still needs to cook on its own unless magenta is your preferred color for everything. Place all vegetables in a serving dish and provide the applesauce in a serving bowl.

* Juniper is not recommended during pregnancy or with kidney disease.

Serves 6. Scandinavian Influence, Norway.

Of this recipe,   To favor your dosha further,
Kapha, enjoy more .... minimize oil
Pitta, enjoy more .... minimize oil; choose less beetroot and spinach
Vata, enjoy some .... choose mostly carrot and snow peas

WHOLE CAULIFLOWER IS THE CENTERPIECE OF VEGETABLES. JUNIPER FLAVORS THE APPLES.

ARTICHOKE and BROAD BEANS

Ayurveda describes how to rid the mind-body of that which causes disruption.

500 gm = 1 lb whole artichokes
500 gm = 1 lb broad beans in shell

The Seasonings
2 tbsp olive oil
2 tsp coriander powder
1 tsp ginger powder
1/2 tsp earth or sea salt

fresh parsley
fresh coriander leaves
a few drops of lemon juice

1. Steam artichokes with a small amount of stem for 15 minutes.
2. Shell beans and add to artichokes for another 15 minutes.
3. Warm the olive oil in a small skillet over medium low heat. Add coriander and ginger. Sauté 1 minute. Add salt and remove from heat.
4. Mince parsley and coriander to the amount of 2 tablespoons each.
5. To collect the artichoke hearts, kitchen botany suggests that we peel away the leaves from the stem upwards until we come to the hairy, sometimes prickly fibers in the centre. The base of most leaves have a small amount of edible vegetable that can be pulled off through your teeth, the base first dipped in ghee maître d'hotel in the continental way. To remove the hairy center, cull it with a spoon. The fibers will lift out of the base, leaving tiny indentations where each fiber was inserted. It is this base of each thistle that we eat. Cut this into bean-sized pieces.
6. Remove loosened skins from broad beans and press the beans out. Discard skins.
7. Combine all ingredients.

Serves 4 as side dish. North African Mediterranean Influence.

Of this recipe,	To further respect your dosha,
Kapha, enjoy more	use sunflower oil and less of it
Pitta, enjoy more	decrease ginger
Vata, enjoy less	neither artichoke nor broad beans are on your 'best' list

STEAMED, THEN TOSSED WITH HERBS, LEMON AND SPICES.

ASPARAGUS East and West

Recipes are references. Make adjustments from there.

EAST
1 bunch asparagus, about 16, or fiddlehead fern shoots
3/4 cup coconut milk
1 tbsp dried tamarind
less than 1/2 tsp earth or sea salt
1/2 tsp peppercorns

1. Snap off the tough ends of the asparagus. Cut stalks into short lengths separating tops from lower stalks.
2. Soak the tamarind in 2 tablespoons hot water.
3. Heat the coconut milk in a medium pot over medium low heat.
4. Add the lower ends of the spears. Simmer 5 minutes, uncovered.
5. Add the tops, cook another 5 minutes.
6. Collect 1 tablespoon of sieved tamarind puree and add to pot.
7. Add the salt and 1/4 teaspoon fresh ground pepper and mix through.

WEST
1 bunch asparagus, about 16, or fiddlehead fern shoots
1/2 tsp mustard seed
1 tbsp olive oil
1 tsp dried tarragon or 2 tsp fresh leaves
less than 1/2 tsp earth or sea salt
1 tbsp orange juice
1 tsp orange rind

1. Snap off the tough ends of the asparagus. Leave lengths uncut.
2. Warm a skillet over medium heat that will accommodate the stalks' length. Dry roast the mustard for 2 minutes. Transfer to a mortar.
3. Warm the oil in the skillet and add the young shoots.
4. Cook for about 7 minutes, turning and repositioning occasionally.
5. Rehydrate dried tarragon in the smallest amount of warm water.
6. Grind mustard seeds into powder. Combine with tarragon and salt.
7. Sprinkle seasonings into the skillet, cook another minute, remove from heat.
8. Place asparagus on serving platter and distribute orange rind and juice on top, then the savory skillet oil, finally freshly snipped tarragon if using.

Each variation serves 4.

Of these recipes,
Kapha, choose the west version with less orange juice and oil
Pitta, choose both with somewhat less tamarind or orange juice
Vata, choose a smaller portion of either

ASPARAGUS PRESENTS ITSELF THROUGHOUT ALL
SEASONINGS.

BAKED GRATED VEGETABLES

Greet each ingredient.

2 yellow summer squash
sea salt

The Seasonings
1 tbsp ghee
1/2 tsp nigella seed
1/2 cup sunflower seeds

1 medium carrot
2 small parsnips
1/2 tsp earth or sea salt
1/2 tsp black pepper
1/2 cup wheat flour, any variety

extra liquid ghee

1. Preheat oven to 375°F (190°C, Gas 5) and oil/ghee a 20 x 20 cm = 8 x 8 inch baking dish or equivalent.
2. Grate summer squash and dust with sea salt. Let stand in colander to sweat out some of the liquid while you continue.
3. In a small skillet over medium low heat warm the ghee and sauté the nigella and sunflower seeds for 5 minutes, until the sun seeds start to become golden. Remove from heat.
4. Grate the carrot and parsnip.
5. Rinse the grated squash briefly, squeeze and dry.
6. Combine vegetables, half the skillet seeds, salt, pepper and flour. Place in the baking dish and divide into servings before baking.
7. Bake uncovered for 30 minutes, drizzling with the extra ghee halfway through.
8. When the vegetables are cooked, garnish with the remaining seeds.

Serves 4 or 2 as a good part of a main meal. European/American Influence.

Of this recipe,   To customize,
Kapha, enjoy less .... use carrot, potato, celery or celeriac; no need to use the flour or extra ghee; decrease sun seeds
Pitta, enjoy more .... decrease the nigella, and black pepper; use less sun seeds
Vata, enjoy more

A SOFT VEGETABLE SLICE, TEXTURED BY SUN SEEDS.

BAMBOO SHOOT

Despite equal employment opportunity and political correctness, there are still people more naturally suited to certain jobs.

1 bamboo shoot
salt water made with 1 tsp sea salt in 2 cups water

It takes 5 days of soaking to prepare the bamboo shoot for cooking and is different in taste, color and texture from processed bamboo shoots.

1. Remove tough outer portion of shoot piece by piece until you get to a pliable inner core. Cut into short narrow lengths and place in salt water to cover. Replace salt water every day for 5 days.
2. To cook, steam for 20-30 minutes.
3. Add to vegetables, staples or soups.

Serves 4. Chinese Influence.

Of this ingredient,
Kapha, enjoy more
Pitta, enjoy some
Vata, enjoy less

AFTER FIVE DAYS OF SOAKING, THE YOUNG SHOOT IS COOKED AND ADDED TO OTHER DISHES.

BEETROOT PUDDING

To assist digestion, sit like royalty for five minutes after eating and then walk 108 paces. Allow the next hour to be relaxing.

> 1 medium beetroot
> 4 cm = less than 2 inches fresh ginger
> 1 lemon
> 4 tbsp palm or unrefined cane sugar
> 1 cup water
> 1/2 tsp sea salt
> 7 tbsp kudzu powder
>
> 1 tsp sesame seeds

1. Have ready 4 custard cups that will sit in a baking dish in an ice water bath.
2. Peel and grate beetroot. Place in medium saucepan.
3. Grate ginger and squeeze out 1 1/2 teaspoons of juice. Add to pot.
4. Grate some of the lemon rind and add 1 teaspoon to pot.
5. Add sugar and water and bring everything to boil.
6. Cook 5-8 minutes, covered, until beetroot is soft. Add salt. Add 2 teaspoons lemon juice.
7. Add kudzu powder, and mix vigorously. You cannot overmix. Continue to cook over medium heat until thick, elastic and an incredible sheen develops, about 3-5 minutes.
8. Fill baking dish with ice water.
9. Rinse the custard cups in the cold water, empty and leave wet. Divide the pudding between them. Shake and bounce each cup to eliminate air bubbles and place in the bath. When all custard cups are in, the water should reach the height of the pudding. Let cool 1 hour.
10. Warm a small skillet over medium heat and add sesame seeds. Toast until lightly colored.
11. Run a butterknife around the edge of each pudding and invert onto a platter. Garnish with sesame seeds. Complement with color.

Serves 4. Japanese Influence.

Of this recipe,   To customize,
Kapha, enjoy less .... enjoy the beets steamed with ginger, less lemon juice, less sugar, less salt, not as a pudding
Pitta, enjoy some .... beets can be unbalancing if eaten in excess, enjoy occasionally; use less ginger juice
Vata, enjoy more

BEETROOT COLOR GROWS TRANSLUCENT WITH KUDZU AND MOLDS WELL.

BOILED SALAD

The Vegetables
1 carrot
3 stalks celery
1 broccoli
1 handful green beans

The Sauce
2 tbsp ghee
4 tbsp wheat flour
1 1/2 cups stock or water
1 tsp dried parsley or 2 tbsp minced fresh parsley
2 tsp dried tarragon or 3 tbsp minced fresh tarragon
1/2 tsp earth or sea salt

peppercorns
lemon wedges

1. Prepare the vegetables by cutting the carrot, celery and broccoli stems into bite-size pieces. Separate the broccoli flowerets. Trim the beans. Set aside.
2. Set a large pot of water to boil for the vegetables. Alternatively, prepare a vegetable steamer.
3. To prepare the sauce warm the ghee over medium heat in a medium sauce-pan.
4. Add the flour and sauté for 2 minutes.
5. Add the 1 1/2 cups stock and bring to boil, whisking constantly.
6. Lower heat and add the dried parsley, tarragon and salt and cook another 2 minutes. Remove from heat and cover. If using fresh herbs add just before covering.
7. When the large pot of water is boiling add the vegetables. The ideal is that the quantity of that water is large enough that adding the vegetables does not lose the boil. Boil gently uncovered for 5 minutes, then drain. Or steam for five.
8. Pour sauce over vegetables.
9. Serve with a lemon wedge and pass the pepper grinder.

Serves 6. English Influence.

Of this recipe,   To enjoy more,
Kapha, enjoy less .... delete the sauce itself and use its herbs and pepper on the vegetables; baking the vegetables is more appealing to kapha
Pitta, enjoy more .... decrease tarragon; use minimal pepper and lemon
Vata, enjoy some .... broccoli and celery in this amount is O.K.

COOKED VEGETABLES WITH A TARRAGON SAUCE.

BROCCOLI

From temperate to tropical, all lands have been provided with healing herbs and spices.

2 medium heads of broccoli, with stalks if possible
1 tbsp linseed, pumpkin or sunflower seeds
1 tbsp ghee
1 small knob fresh ginger
a sprinkle of asafoetida
a small amount of earth or sea salt
1 lemon wedge

1. Preheat oven to 350°F (180°C, Gas 4).
2. Peel off tougher outer layers of broccoli stalks carefully with a knife. Slice broccoli in half longitudinally through the stem and flowerets. Also slice down the flowerets on two opposite sides, making the outsides flat as well. From each head you will have 2 flat longitudinal sections. Save what you have trimmed for another meal.
3. Place the 4 sections in one or two baking dishes and add water to just cover the bottom. Bake covered for 35 minutes, until tender. Alternatively, steam in a bamboo steamer for 15 minutes, turning once in that time.
4. Warm a small skillet over medium low heat. Dry roast the seed(s) of choice, shaking the pan until slightly darker or a few have popped. Linseed toasts quickly.
5. Add the ghee to the skillet and grate on the ginger. Sauté over medium low heat for several minutes, adding the asafoetida. Remove from heat and add the salt.
6. Place broccoli on a serving dish and distribute the skillet mix along the surface. Sprinkle on the seeds.
7. A very few drops of lemon juice completes the six tastes.

Serves 4 as a vegetable side dish. Asian Influence.

Of this recipe,	To further modify,
Kapha, enjoy more	use less linseed
Pitta, enjoy more	decrease the ginger substantially, use less linseed
Vata, enjoy some	occasionally

LONGITUDINAL SECTIONS OF BROCCOLI, BAKED OR STEAMED, WITH GINGER AND SEEDS.

BURDOCK and CARROT

We can cultivate refinement in our diet and eating habits.

Cooking Liquid
less than 1 cup water
1 mandarin or orange
1/2 tsp aniseed

1 cup sliced carrot
1 cup sliced burdock root
1 tbsp sesame oil
1/4 tsp earth or sea salt

1 small knob fresh ginger
1 tsp ghee
1 tbsp sesame seeds

fresh coriander leaf

1. Create the cooking liquid by bringing the water to boil. Add peel from a quarter of the organic mandarin and aniseed, remove from heat, cover and steep. Set mandarin aside to be juiced later.
2. Slice carrots into thin rounds or half rounds.
3. Prepare burdock: wash roots. Place them in water. Remove one at a time and reveal the inner white by peeling. Place in fresh water to cover. Continue until all the burdock is peeled. Next, slice burdock into thin rounds, one root at a time and place in a bowl in fresh water. Continue until all the root is sliced very thin. Water prevents browning prior to cooking. This water can have a small amount of lemon juice added.
4. Warm the oil in a medium skillet over medium heat. Pat the burdock dry and add, along with the carrot. Lower heat and sauté 10 minutes, stirring often.
5. Strain mandarin tea and add ½ cup to skillet. Cover and cook over low heat 15 minutes. Check that the roots are poaching in a small amount of liquid and add more if needed.
6. Meanwhile peel and grate ginger.
7. Warm ghee in small skillet over medium heat. Add ginger, add sesame seeds and sauté until golden. Add to vegetables.
8. Sprinkle salt onto the cooked roots and mix through. When cooler squeeze some mandarin juice on top.
9. Chop coriander to the amount of 1 tablespoon as garnish.

Serves 4. Japanese Influence. I couldn't find burdock in the shops so I grew my own.

Of this recipe,   to improve for your dosha,
Kapha, enjoy some .... minimize sesame seeds
Pitta, enjoy more .... minimize ginger, aniseed and sesame
Vata, enjoy more

ROOT VEGETABLES BRAISED IN MANDARIN TEA TOPPED WITH
GINGER AND SESAME.

BZAR POTATOES

It is amazing how words on a page transform into a delectable dish.

4 large potatoes
3 tbsp olive oil
1 cup water

The Skillet Masala
4 spring onions
2 tbsp olive oil
1 tsp turmeric
1 tsp coriander
1/2 tsp cumin
1/4 tsp cloves
1/4 tsp cinnamon
1/4 tsp ginger
1/2 tsp earth or sea salt
a sprinkle of black pepper

lemon wedges

1. Peel and cube the potatoes. Warm the 3 tablespoons of oil in a large sauce-pan or skillet over medium heat. Sauté potatoes, uncovered, until golden.
2. Add water and bring to boil. Simmer 10 minutes, covered.
3. Meanwhile, slice the spring onions reserving a few greens as garnish.
4. In a small skillet heat the remaining oil over medium low heat and sauté the onions 5 minutes, then add the ground spices. Sauté for 1 minute. Add salt.
5. When the potatoes are cooked and the water has evaporated, coat with the skillet masala. Cook another 3-5 minutes. The more you mix, the creamier this will become. Add black pepper.
6. Garnish with spring onion greens and lemon wedges.

Serves 4-6. Afghani Influence.

Of this recipe,   Better yet,
Kapha, enjoy more .... use less oil and make it mustard oil
Pitta, enjoy more .... use less onions, cloves, ginger, pepper
Vata, enjoy less .... potatoes are considered drying; there is enough oil in this already so choose this dish occasionally

CUBES OF POTATO AND ROUNDS OF SPRING ONION
COATED WITH SPICES.

CABBAGE and SEEDS

The tamasic mind looks no further than its own needs; the rajasic mind cannot help but act; the sattwic mind embraces the big picture and organizes according to a multi-dimensional understanding.

1 small head cabbage
2 medium apples
1 tbsp ghee
barely a sprinkle of ajowan seed
a sprinkle of asafoetida
1/2 tsp earth or sea salt

1. Slice cabbage into ribbons, composting harder core or use for stock. Peel, core and cube apples.
2. In a skillet large enough for the cabbage, warm the ghee over medium heat.
3. Introduce the ajowan and asafoetida, then the cabbage and apple.
4. Sauté until the cabbage has relaxed, stirring occasionally, about 20 minutes.
5. Add the salt and mix through.

The seeds in this recipe would be poppy seeds. They are somewhat tamasic, leading to drowsiness and heaviness. Sprinkle on a teaspoon of them as you wish.

Serves 4 as side dish. Russian Influence.

Of this recipe,   To further refine,
Kapha, enjoy more .... omit the poppy seeds
Pitta, enjoy some .... use more ghee
Vata, enjoy less .... use more ghee and cook the cabbage and apple
until completely softened. Be aware if indigestion occurs in the form of
excess flatulence and then try it at another time of day. If no better, pass
on this recipe.

ALSO APPLE IN STOVE TOP COOKING.

CABBAGE SAUTÉ

If we are genetic material wrapped in food, what is your wrapper made of?

The Vegetables
1/2 medium red cabbage
6 spring onions
1 bunch dark leafy greens

The Seasonings
2 tbsp sesame oil
1/2 tsp ginger powder
a sprinkle of ajowan seed
1 tsp Chinese 5-spice powder
1/2 tsp earth or sea salt

2 sheets of nori sea vegetable

1. Slice cabbage leaves, removing harder core. Slice spring onions, separating bulb portion from tops in separate piles. Chop the dark leafy greens once the cabbage is cooking.
2. Warm the oil in a medium skillet over medium low heat and sprinkle on the ginger powder and ajowan seeds. Sauté 1 minute.
3. Add the 5-spice powder and incorporate its essence and aroma. Add the spring onion bottoms and cabbage and cook over slightly higher heat, turning the vegetables occasionally for about 15 minutes.
4. Chop the greens.
5. Add the spring onions tops and greens to cook 3 minutes.
6. Mix the salt through and begin cooling.
7. Toast nori very briefly and tear into ribbons as garnish.

Serves 4 over rice. Chinese Influence.

Of this recipe,   To modify,
Kapha, enjoy more .... use less oil and nori
Pitta, enjoy some .... use less ginger, ajowan and nori; use bitter rather than pungent greens, for instance dandelion rather than mustard greens
Vata, enjoy less............... enjoy cabbage only occasionally and do use the ajowan seeds

PURPLE AND GREEN VEGETABLES.

CELERIAC with SPINACH SAUCE

If we eat a variety of foods with the seasons of harvest, neither deficiencies nor excesses are apt to arise.

2 cups chopped celeriac or celery	**The Sauce**
1 tbsp sunflower oil	2 tbsp ghee
2 bay leaves	1 tsp black mustard seed
8 peppercorns	a sprinkle of asafoetida
1 1/2 cups water	4 tbsp wheat flour
1 bunch spinach/other greens,	1 cup celeriac cooking liquid
about 350 gm = 12 oz	less than 1 tsp earth or sea salt

1 tsp grated orange rind and 1 tbsp orange juice

1. Remove outer layer of celeriac with a knife. Cut celeriac or celery into pieces.
2. Warm oil in a medium saucepan over medium heat, adding bay, pepper and vegetable. Sauté for several minutes while you heat the water to boiling.
3. Add the water to the saucepan, stir, and simmer, covered, for 20 minutes until soft.
4. Cut the spinach into short strips by cutting leaves lengthwise and crosswise. Wash, drain and place in a saucepan. Heat the spinach uncovered, with just the water clinging to the leaves. Rotate occasionally to cook all leaves evenly until wilted. Drain any excess liquid and set aside.
5. When the celeriac/celery is cooked, collect the liquid to make the sauce, bringing quantity up to 1 cup with water if necessary.
6. To make the sauce warm the ghee in a small saucepan over medium heat. Add the mustard seeds and asafoetida to cook for 1 minute, then the flour, turning the heat down to sauté the flour for 2 minutes.
7. Add the cooking liquid and raise the heat to bring the sauce to boil, whisking continuously. Add the salt and spinach and combine with another minute of heat.
8. Layer celeriac, spinach sauce, orange juice and zest.

Spinach sauce can be a vegetable dish on its own.

Serves 6. European Influence, France.

Of this recipe,	Better yet,
Kapha, enjoy more	prepare the "sauce" without the ghee, flour or cooking liquid
Pitta, enjoy some	decrease pepper, spinach and mustard seed
Vata, enjoy some	with less spinach

A GREEN SAUCE SERVED ON THE ROOT RELATIVE OF CELERY.

CHINESE CABBAGE and CHESTNUTS

The color of the raw chestnut husks, what do you make of it?

12 fresh chestnuts

2 tbsp sesame oil
1/2 cup water
a sprinkle of asafoetida
3 cm = 1 inch fresh ginger
1 tsp earth or sea salt

1 Chinese cabbage
lime wedges

1. Carefully peel chestnuts with a sharp knife.
2. Immerse the chestnuts in boiling water to cover and blanch for 1 minute.
3. Remove the membranes, exposing the yellow nuts. This is easier when hot so shield your hands. Slice each nut into about 4 sections lengthwise or crumble/mash totally.
4. In a small skillet warm 2 tablespoons sesame oil over medium heat. Add the nuts, asafoetida and grate the fresh ginger in. Sauté one minute. Add about 1/2 cup hot water poaching chestnuts uncovered over low heat until water reduces and creates a thin sauce. Incorporate salt and remove from heat.
5. Meanwhile, slice the cabbage leaves into ribbons and the mid-ribs into small dice. Place in steamer over boiling water, uncovered, for 5 minutes, then cover until cooked, several minutes more.
6. Arrange the cabbage on a platter and garnish with the chestnut mix.
7. Add the lime wedges.

Serves 4. Asian Influence.

Of this recipe,	To customize,
Kapha, enjoy more	use less nuts and less oil; use a few drops of lime
Pitta, enjoy more	use less ginger and lime
Vata, enjoy less	use some ajowan seed in the sauté

STEAMED CABBAGE WITH CHESTNUT TOPPING.

CHOKO SALSA

Enter vegetable-dicing contemplation.

1 chayote (choko)
1 red pepper (capsicum)
1 stalk celery
1 tsp grated fresh ginger

The Fresh Herbs
2 sprigs mint
2 stalks flat leaf parsley
2 sprigs thyme
1 coriander plant

1 tbsp lime or lemon juice
a drizzle of almond or other mild-flavored oil
1/2 tsp earth or sea salt

1. Peel the choko, then cut apart on the seams and finish peeling.
2. Prepare the pepper in the same way.
3. Remove the strings from the celery.
4. Cut all of the above into small dice and combine.
5. Grate the ginger very fine; remove the herb leaves from the stems and mince leaves. You could use stalks for soup stock flavoring.
6. Combine all ingredients except salt and toss occasionally for 10 minutes. Mix in salt just before serving and toss again.

Serves 6-8. South American Influence, Brazil.

Of this recipe,   To enjoy more,
Kapha, enjoy some .... increase celery relative to choko; increase fresh herbs and ginger, decrease citrus
Pitta, enjoy more .... delete the ginger, decrease the citrus; use a small pepper
Vata, enjoy some .... sauté the diced vegetables and ginger in 1 tablespoon ghee for 5 minutes and cool before adding the remaining ingredients, thus omitting the drizzle of oil

FINE DICING ALLOWS ALL JUICES TO EXUDE AND BLEND.

CHOKO, LIME and THYME

Trying to burn protein for energy is like trying to burn the bricks of a fireplace for heat.

1 christophene (choko)
1 tsp sunflower oil
a sprinkle of earth or sea salt
1/2 lime
fresh thyme
coriander leaves, optional

1. Peel christophene, then slice along seams and finish peeling.
2. Cut into thick matchstick lengths of 5 cm = 2 inches. The young seed can be included.
3. In a medium skillet, warm oil over medium heat.
4. Add christophene and sauté over lower heat for several minutes.
5. Add a small amount of water and cover, cooking until more tender, 10-15 minutes. If using dried thyme add 3/4 teaspoon now.
6. Grate zest from the lime half and then juice it.
7. Collect thyme leaves from stems to the amount of 1 1/2 teaspoons.
8. Towards the end of cooking, check that the water is evaporated. Add the salt to the choko.
9. To serve, toss with lime juice, fresh thyme and lime zest and garnish if desired with a sprig of coriander.

Serves 2-3. Caribbean Influence.

Of this recipe,   To adjust,
Kapha, enjoy some .... use less lime juice
Pitta, enjoy some .... use less lime juice and thyme
Vata, enjoy more

CHOKO, A MILD VINE VEGETABLE, IS SEASONED IN
CARIBBEAN FASHION.

CILANTRO-MINT DRESSING

Gather ingredients and self into this recipe.

1 orange
2 tbsp cilantro (coriander) leaves, generously measured
1 tbsp mint leaves, generously measured
almond or other oil
1 1/2 tsp unfired honey
a few grains of sea salt
1/4 tsp ginger powder

1. Collect 1/2 teaspoon of grated zest from the orange and then collect the juice.
2. Finely mince the cilantro and mint leaves.
3. Combine the juice, 1/2 - 2 tablespoons oil, herbs and remaining ingredients together with gently shaking or whisking. Let rest at least 15 minutes, then mix again.

This can dress 4 salads or 2 servings of cooked, cooled rice. Asian Influence.

Of this recipe,   To enjoy more,
Kapha, enjoy some .... use a minimum of mustard or sunflower oil and use less juice
Pitta, enjoy some .... use less juice and substitute cane sugar for the honey; use a drizzle of almond oil
Vata, enjoy more............ use palm sugar sometimes instead of honey; for non-cooked dressings also try the freshest macadamia, walnut or hazelnut oil

FRESH GREEN INFILTRATING ORANGE AND GINGER.

COOKED GREENS

It is easier for the body to claim these nutrients if the cellulose plant wall is opened by heat.

1 tbsp shelled pistachios

1 kg = about 2 lbs assorted greens choosing from collard greens, spinach, dandelion, Swisschard, beet greens, Chinese greens, mustard greens, rocket, corn salad, Egyptian spinach, mountain spinach, Ceylon spinach, Japanese greens, turnip greens or local greens

1/2 cup coriander leaves
1/4 cup fresh basil
1/4 cup Thai basil or 1/8 tsp aniseed
1/2 tsp earth or sea salt
a wedge of lemon
mustard, ghee, olive or sesame oil

1. Toast the pistachios.
2. Tear or chop the assorted greens into small pieces and wash well.
3. Wash and mince into a separate area the coriander and basils.
4. Into a large skillet over medium heat, place the assorted greens with the water clinging to the leaves. Cook, rotating the leaves until they are all wilted. With a variety of greens you will need to cook the more fibrous ones longer. Remove from heat. Drain any remaining liquid.
5. Add salt and the herbs and mix through so they wilt as well.
6. Garnish with pistachios and squeeze on a few drops of lemon juice.

Serves 4. Asian Influence.

Of this recipe,   Still better,
Kapha, enjoy some .... decrease the nuts and use less lemon; drizzle on a small amount of mustard oil
Pitta, enjoy some .... use bitter and astringent greens, decrease nuts and use less lemon; dissolve a small amount of ghee on your cooling greens
Vata, enjoy less.............. add a drizzle of ghee, olive or sesame oil to your serve and still enjoy less

HERBS MINGLE WITH OTHER STEAMED GREENS.

CUCUMBER and APPLE SALAD

Appreciation of nature and cooking are on the same coin.

1 cup diced cucumber
1 tbsp dried or 2 tbsp fresh chives
1 1/2 cups diced red apples
a sprinkle of sea salt
a drizzle of mild-flavored oil

1. Peel and seed cucumbers if necessary and dice.
2. Add chopped chives and toss occasionally for 15 minutes.
3. Just before serving, peel and dice apple.
4. Add apple with the salt and oil, mixing thoroughly.

Serves 4. Irish Influence.

Of this recipe,   Even better,
Kapha, enjoy some .... decrease cucumber
Pitta, enjoy more
Vata, enjoy some .... enjoy something denser as well

AN EARLY AUTUMN RECIPE, THE LAST OF THE CUCUMBERS, THE
FIRST OF THE APPLES.

CUCUMBER SALAD

There are many different ways to do things better.

2 average sized cucumbers

Dry Roast
1/2 tsp mustard seed
1/2 tsp dill seed
1/2 tsp coriander seed
a scant 1/4 tsp peppercorns

4 tsp fresh or 2 tsp dried dill
1 tbsp almond or other mild oil
a scant 1/4 tsp earth or sea salt

1. Peel cucumbers if necessary and cut into spears or dice.
2. Warm a small skillet over medium heat. Add mustard seeds and dry roast until the first few pop. Lower heat and add the other seeds for half a minute. Transfer all to a mortar and grind.
3. Toss cucumber with spices, dill and oil. Toss occasionally for 10 minutes.
4. Add salt before serving and mix in.

Serves 4-6. Eastern European Influence, Czechoslovakia.

Of this recipe,   To fine-tune,
Kapha, enjoy less .... omit cucumbers and substitute celery and sprouts; use a lesser amount of oil
Pitta, enjoy more .... decrease mustard and pepper; use a lesser amount of almond oil
Vata, enjoy some .... experiment with varieties of oil on the uncooked salad or sauté the spices in the oil, substituting 1/2 teaspoon coriander powder for the coriander seeds and a few turns of the pepper grinder for the whole peppercorns. The cucumber can be sautéed briefly. Then remove from heat and add the dill and salt.

WITH DILL FRONDS, SEEDS AND SPICES.

CURRIED GREENS

Any spice blend can become a broth or tea, any broth seasoning can become a staple or vegetable flavoring, any garnish can top a different dish and so on.

Whole Spices
3/4 tsp coriander seed
1/4 tsp cumin seed
1 cardamom pod, lightly crushed
1/8 tsp fenugreek seed
1/8 tsp mustard seed
1 clove

1/2 tsp turmeric

1 kg = about 2 lbs leafy greens
1 tbsp ghee
1/4 tsp earth or sea salt
citrus quarter rounds

1. Warm a small skillet over medium heat. Dry roast the whole spices.
2. Transfer cardamon to a mortar and grind first, discarding pod. Grind the rest of the seeds. Add turmeric.
3. Cut, wash and drain greens. These will vary with your locale.
4. In a large skillet or medium soup pot warm the ghee. Add the spice mix and sauté 1 minute.
5. Add the greens and keep them moving, cooking them evenly until wilted and the liquid has evaporated. Add salt and mix through.
6. Serve with citrus garnish.

Serves 4. African Influence, Malawi.

Of this recipe,   A few changes,
Kapha, enjoy more .... decrease salt, ghee and citrus
Pitta, enjoy more .... use bitter greens, decreasing salt and citrus
Vata, enjoy less

PAN-STEAMED GREENS AND A CURRY BLEND.

CURRIED PLANTAINS

What ambiance do you create around yourself while cooking?

2 plantains

The Seasonings
1 tbsp ghee
1 tsp cumin powder
1 tsp coriander powder
1/2 tsp ginger powder
1/4 tsp turmeric powder
a sprinkle of asafoetida

1 tbsp coconut
1/4 tsp earth or sea salt
a grating of nutmeg
a wedge of lime or lemon

1. To handle plantains rub hands with a little ghee. Peel and cut or cut and peel plantains into rounds.
2. Warm remaining ghee in medium skillet over medium low heat.
3. Sprinkle in spice powders and make a homogenous slurry.
4. Place plantain rounds in a single layer over the spice base and cook for 5 minutes.
5. Turn the rounds over, sprinkling skillet with coconut to cook another 5 minutes.
6. Sprinkle with salt and toss in the skillet.
7. To serve, grate nutmeg over the top and squeeze on a few drops of lime juice.

Serves 4. Caribbean Influence.

Of this recipe	To modify
Kapha, enjoy less	plantain is heavy, use a lighter vegetable such as cauliflower; decrease the coconut and lime
Pitta, enjoy some	decrease nutmeg and citrus juice
Vata, enjoy some	make sure the plantains are well cooked

PLANTAINS PAN-SAUTÉED OVER SPICES.

EGGPLANT and BASIL

The Japanese temple cook brings the 3 virtues to the meal: lightness and softness, cleanliness and freshness, precision and care.

3 small eggplants
sea salt

1 tbsp sesame seeds

2 tbsp sesame oil
2 tbsp ghee
a sprinkle of asafoetida
1/4 tsp earth or sea salt

1/2 cup chopped fresh basil

1. Peel and slice the eggplant into sticks.
2. Toss with salt and leave in colander over sink for 1 hour, tossing now and then. Cooks find that salting a vegetable removes some of the bitterness and firms the texture. We use salt here for the latter outcome.
3. Rinse and dry eggplant sticks.
4. Warm a medium skillet over medium low heat. Dry roast sesame seeds to golden brown and transfer to bowl.
5. Warm oil and ghee in wok or the same skillet over medium heat.
6. Add eggplant, stirring to absorb oils. Cook for a few minutes, flipping the sticks. Add asafoetida. Add a small amount of water, lower heat, cover and steam until eggplant is soft, about 5-8 minutes. Add salt.
7. Let cool 5-10 minutes. Chop the basil and toss through.
8. Garnish with sesame seeds.

Serves 2 as a vegetable, 4 if over rice. South East Asian Influence, Thailand.

Of this recipe,   To modify,
Kapha, enjoy some .... decrease oils, sesame and salt
Pitta, enjoy less .... eggplant is O.K. rarely; fresh basil is O.K. on occasion; decrease salt and sesame
Vata, enjoy less.............. eat eggplant rarely; add lemon juice

EGGPLANT STICKS GARNISHED WITH BASIL AND SESAME.

EXOTICALLY SPICED VEGETABLES

Blessings on the cook and the meal.

The Vegetables
1 cauliflower
1 zucchini

The Spices
4 tsp ghee
1 tsp cumin seed
1 tsp fennel seed
a sprinkle of asafoetida
1/4 tsp fenugreek powder
3/4 tsp turmeric
1 tsp coriander

3/4 tsp earth or sea salt
1/2 tsp fresh ground black pepper
1 tsp garam masala
lemon

1. Cut the cauliflower into flowerets. Cut the zucchini into 2 cm = 1 inch shapes.
2. Steam the cauliflower uncovered for 5 minutes, covered, for 5 minutes. Add the zucchini, cover and steam everything 5 minutes more.
3. Warm the ghee in a small skillet over medium heat.
4. Sprinkle the 2 seed varieties and asafoetida into the ghee and swirl. When the seeds begin to crackle, remove from heat.
5. Swirl in the fenugreek, turmeric and coriander. Let cool.
6. Blend the spices through the vegetables with the salt, pepper and garam masala. Serve with lemon wedges.

Garam Masala is a variable blend of pungent, delicate spices. One such blend suggests we use scant quarter teaspoons of the following: cinnamon powder, cardamom seeds, whole black pepper and whole cloves, all dry roasted on low heat for a minute and ground together with 1/4 tsp mace or nutmeg.

Serves 4. Pakistani Influence.

Of this recipe,   To refine,
Kapha, enjoy more .... decrease the zucchini
Pitta, enjoy more
Vata, enjoy less.............. decrease cauliflower

STEAMED CAULIFLOWER AND ZUCCHINI TOSSED WITH INFUSED SPICES.

FENNEL, CUCUMBER and CARROT

If in preparing a recipe you find an ingredient missing, maintain your sense of humor and keep cooking.

1 medium cucumber
1 large carrot
1/2 fennel bulb

The Seasoned Oil
1 tbsp sunflower oil
2 tbsp tamarind purée
1/4 tsp earth or sea salt
1/4 tsp black pepper

1. Peel cucumber and carrot.
2. Dice the three vegetables.
3. Combine the remaining ingredients into a seasoned oil and pass it at the table. Because we don't combine lemon with cucumber, tamarind provides a tang. Use 1 tablespoon dried fruit, soaked in 2 tablespoons hot water. When cooler, work tamarind off its seeds and press through a sieve.

Serves 4. Mediterranean Influence.

Of this recipe,   Even better,
Kapha, enjoy some .... replace cucumber with celery; use less dressing except pepper
Pitta, enjoy some .... use a small carrot and less dressing
Vata, enjoy some .... enjoy as a small summer salad with more dressing, otherwise cook the vegetables using zucchini instead of cucumber

LIGHT AND CRUNCHY DICED VEGETABLES WITH
SEASONED OIL.

GINGER SYRUP

A traditional medicine guideline is that activity overcomes stagnation but over-activity hastens deterioration.

1 tbsp peeled, grated fresh ginger
1 cup water
1/4 cup unrefined cane or palm sugar

1. Peel and grate ginger and combine with the water in a small saucepan over medium heat.
2. Bring to boil and simmer, covered, 30 minutes.
3. Strain and squeeze out the ginger and combine liquid and sugar in the same pot.
4. Bring to boil and simmer uncovered until condensed, anywhere from 1/2 to 1 hour. Be aware that the transition between thick syrup and taffy happens quickly.
5. Use 1/4 - 1 teaspoon in synthesis with bakery, beverage, fruit, soup, staples or vegetables.

Fully condensed makes 1/8 cup. Indian and Asian Influence.

Of this recipe,   Even better,
Kapha, enjoy less .... ginger powder is your better condiment
Pitta, enjoy less .... ginger is heating, sugar is cooling; the heating is more dominant
Vata, enjoy some .... heating is also drying; use a small amount as a topping to pancakes, porridge, flatbread, etc.

FRESH GINGER ESSENCE IS CONDENSED IN SUGAR SYRUP.

GREEN BEANS and WALNUTS

Take three slow, relaxed breaths, starting…now.

250 gm = 1/2 lb green beans
1/4 cup walnut pieces
3 spring onions
1 tbsp olive oil
1 tsp mustard seed
1/2 tsp earth or sea salt
1 lemon

1. Trim the beans and steam for 10 minutes.
2. Chop the walnuts.
3. Slice the spring onions finely. Reserve some of the tops as garnish.
4. Warm the oil in a small skillet over medium heat and sauté the mustard seeds until they just begin to pop.
5. Add the spring onions and sauté until soft over lower heat, about 5 minutes. Add the salt, mixing in well.
6. Toss the green beans with the skillet sauté and a squeeze of lemon juice.
7. Garnish with the spring onion greens and walnuts.
8. This can be blended into a dip or spread. Did your mind allow you those three breaths or was it too impatient?

Serves 4. Eastern European Influence, Hungary.

Of this recipe,	To enjoy more,
Kapha, enjoy some ………	use less oil and far fewer nuts
Pitta, enjoy some ……….	use ghee + olive oil, fewer spring onions and nuts
Vata, enjoy some ……….	cook the beans well and enjoy occasionally

STEAMED BEANS HIGHLIGHTED WITH SPRING ONIONS
AND LEMON.

GRILLED VEGETABLES

Enjoy yourself cooking.

The Spices
8 tsp paprika
4 tsp celery seed
2 tsp mustard seed or powder
2 tsp thyme, dried
2 tsp marjoram, dried
2 tsp earth or sea salt
4 tsp unrefined cane sugar
4 tsp ground black pepper

The Vegetables
1 bunch asparagus or fiddlehead ferns
small carrots, peeled, trimmed and halved
small parsnips, peeled, trimmed and halved
zucchini/summer squash, cut in 4 lengths
eggplant, 1 cm = 1/4 inch lengths or rounds
sweet pepper (capsicum), quartered, seeds and membranes
    removed
sweet potato, 1 cm = 1/4 inch rounds
potato, 1 cm = 1/4 inch rounds

oil or ghee

1. Prepare barbecue, grill, charcoal burner, camp fire grilling racks or use a skillet for stove top cooking.
2. Mix all the spices together. What is not used can be stored in a jar.
3. Choose amongst the vegetables listed or choose your own. Coat them lightly with oil or ghee, sprinkle on the spice mix and grill. If appropriate brush the uncooked side with oil or ghee and sprinkle with spices before flipping.
4. The heat, size of vegetables and grill used will factor into cooking time. Please don't eat anything burnt and favor a lower cooking temperture.

Serves 8-10 using all the vegetables listed. American Influence.

Of this recipe,
Kapha, choose less parsnip, zucchini and sweet potato and less sugar in the spice mix; use minimal oil
Pitta, choose less pepper (capsicum) and use less oil and spice mix altogether
Vata, choose less eggplant and potato

THE FUEL COOKING THESE VEGETABLES ALSO CONTRIBUTES TO THE FLAVOR.

JICAMA SALAD

It takes time to find lesser amounts of salt, sugar, sourness or hot spices perfect.

1 jicama (yam bean) or 2 choko
200 gm = 7 oz snow peas
1 red or yellow pepper (capsicum)

The Dressing
1 sweet orange
1 tbsp almond or other mild oil
1/4 tsp earth or sea salt
1/2 tsp cinnamon
a grating of nutmeg

1. Cut jicama along seams and peel, then dice.
2. Cut snow peas into similar size in its own pile.
3. Peel pepper, cut along seams and finish peeling. Dice and add to snow peas.
4. Prepare steamer and bring its water to boil. Steam jicama for 5 minutes, covered, add snow peas and capsicum on top for 3 minutes more, also covered. Cool.
5. Grate orange rind and collect 2 teaspoons. Combine juice of half the orange with oil, rind and salt and mix through vegetables.
6. Sprinkle vegetables with spices and mix again.

Serves 4-6. Central American-Asian Influence.

Of this recipe,   To enjoy more,
Kapha, enjoy some .... use cooked potato instead of jicama; mustard is your best oil in small amounts
Pitta, enjoy more .... sweet pepper in this amount is already "less"
Vata, enjoy more

STEAMED VEGETABLES WITH SIMPLE DRESSING.

JUNIPER and VEGETABLES

Our taste buds do not register levels of carbohydrate and protein.

12 asparagus spears or fiddlehead ferns
3 parsnip

The Seasonings
6 juniper berries *
5 cm = 2 inches fresh rosemary
2 tsp fresh or 1 tsp dried marjoram
2 tsp ghee
1/2 tsp earth or sea salt

1. Snap off woody ends of asparagus.
2. Trim, peel and cut parsnip into quarters lengthwise.
3. Steam parsnip, covered, for 5 minutes and add asparagus or fern shoots for another 5. If using dried herbs sprinkle them onto the steaming vegetables in the last two minutes.
4. Crush and mince juniper, chop fresh rosemary and marjoram, removing stems.
5. Warm ghee in medium skillet over low heat and add juniper. Heat for 2 minutes and add salt.
6. Add steamed vegetables to seasoned ghee, add rosemary and marjoram and mix through. Blend with another minute of heat.

Serves 4. Eastern European Influence, Romania.
* Juniper is not recommended during pregnancy or with kidney disease.

Of this recipe,	Better yet,
Kapha, enjoy more	decrease parsnip
Pitta, enjoy some	use less herbs and berries
Vata, enjoy some	use less herbs and berries

VEGETABLE SPEARS WITH ASSERTIVE HERBS.

KOHLRABI STEW

Let us not eat leftovers. Let us not overeat to avoid creating leftovers.

> 2 cups water or stock
> 1 kg = 2 lbs kohlrabi, mild turnip or rutabaga
> 1/2 kg = 1 lb potatoes
> 1/2 tsp earth or sea salt
> 1 tbsp ghee
> 1 tbsp minced parsley
> black peppercorns
> lemon wedges

1. Begin to bring water or stock to boil in a large covered pot.
2. Remove kohlrabi leaves and set aside. Slice off root prop.
3. Peel and dice kohlrabi.
4. Add kohlrabi to simmering stock and cook, covered, 15 minutes.
5. Peel and dice potatoes.
6. Add potatoes and cook, covered, another eight.
7. Slice kohlrabi leaves or a few cabbage leaves and add, cooking uncovered until they are tender. Mix in salt and ghee. Mash some of the kohlrabi and potato into any remaining stock and mix through the stew.
8. Garnish with parsley, a grind of pepper and a few drops of lemon.

Serves 6. European Influence, Germany.

Of this recipe,	Better for your dosha,
Kapha, enjoy more	more pepper, less salt and lemon
Pitta, enjoy more	less salt, pepper and lemon
Vata, enjoy less..............	kohlrabi and potato can be unbalancing too often

VEGETABLES FEATURING AS THEMSELVES, SIMPLE AND TASTY.

LEEKS and RICE

Your kitchen is an asset when you can work in it easily.

1 kg = 2 lbs leeks
2 carrots
3/4 cup water
1/2 cup olive oil
3 tbsp rice
1 tsp palm or unrefined cane sugar
3/4 tsp earth or sea salt

black peppercorns
several thin strips of lemon rind
4 thin lemon wedges

1. Cut the whites of the leeks into 5 cm = 2 1/2 inch sections.
2. Peel and cut the carrots into thin slices.
3. Heat the water to boiling and keep hot, covered, on low heat.
4. Warm the oil in a saucepan and sauté the leeks and carrots for 10 minutes.
5. Add the rice and sauté for a few minutes.
6. Add the hot water, sugar and salt, stirring to mix. Cook over low heat, covered, 25 minutes.
7. Remove from heat and let stand for 5 minutes.
8. Decorate with a few turns of black pepper, lemon rind, lemon wedges and other colors.

Serves 4. Mediterranean Influence, Turkey.

Of this recipe,   Better yet,
Kapha, enjoy less .... use black pepper with your portion and decrease oil substantially
Pitta, enjoy more .... use more rice, some leek, some carrot and less oil
Vata, enjoy more .... add something pungent

LEEKS AND CARROTS STEWED IN OLIVE OIL.

263

LEEKS with GINGER

In the plane of duality it is possible to compare and choose the better option.

4 cups sliced leek
2.5 cm = 1 inch fresh ginger
2 tbsp ghee
1 lime
1/2 tsp earth or sea salt

1 tbsp raw nuts of choice

1. Slice the leeks into 2 cm = 1 inch rounds.
2. Peel the ginger and dice in small pieces.
3. In a skillet to accommodate the leeks, warm ghee over medium heat. Sauté ginger.
4. Add the leeks to the skillet and slow cook, about 15-20 minutes.
5. Grate the lime zest and then juice the lime.
6. Take skillet off heat. Add salt, all of the lime juice, 1 teaspoon zest and mix in well.
7. Roast or toast nuts and sprinkle on as garnish.

Serves 4. Asian Influence.

Of this recipe,   To refine,
Kapha, enjoy some .... use less ghee, citrus juice and use pumpkin or sunflower seeds instead of nuts
Pitta, enjoy some .... use less ginger and citrus juice and make sure the leeks are well cooked
Vata, enjoy more .... cook the leeks well

SIMPLE SAUTÉING, PIQUANT LIME AND CRUNCHY NUTS.

LOTUS ROOT SALAD

Savor the sensation of an occupation completed.

300 gm = about 10 oz fresh lotus root
2 tbsp raisins
1 cup snow pea or other sprouts

<u>The Dressing</u>
1 tbsp lemon juice
1 tbsp sesame oil
1/4 tsp earth or sea salt
1 tsp palm or unrefined cane sugar

2 tsp sesame seeds

1. Prepare steamer and have water in it at a simmer.
2. Peel and slice young roots into thin rounds, circles within circles. Without delay, place directly into the steamer.
3. Steam for 1 hour. It's not that amazing that they hold their shape, seeing as they live in water. Add raisins for the last 5 minutes and sprouts 3 minutes before cooking is complete. Let cool, covered. Transfer to serving dish.
4. Shake together lemon juice, oil, salt and sugar and toss through.
5. In a small skillet toast sesame over medium heat until golden. Sprinkle over the salad.

If all the salad is not finished at lunch, heat a small amount of ghee and sauté the marinated lotus root in it for a snack later in the day.

Serves 4. Asian Influence, China and Japan.

Of this recipe,   To support your dosha,
Kapha, enjoy less .... have just the sprouts, translating as "enjoy less"
Pitta, enjoy some
Vata, enjoy some

LOTUS ROOT HAS A UNIQUE CROSS-SECTION AND
STAYS FIRM WITH COOKING.

OKRA and PUMPKIN

It is easier to stay well than to get well.

The Stew
500 gm = 16 oz pumpkin or winter squash
300 gm = 12 oz okra
1 cup fresh coconut milk, optional
1/2 - 1 cup water
100 gm = small bunch spinach, dasheen or amaranth leaf
3 tbsp fresh parsley
leaves of 5 celery stalks
1 tsp fresh thyme

Final Additions
2 tbsp pumpkin seeds
1/2 tsp earth or sea salt
1 lime
black peppercorns

1. Cut pumpkin into large chunks and steam for 15 minutes to loosen peel. Let cool until you can scoop the pumpkin out of the peel and into a large saucepan or skillet.
2. Trim okra and cut into 1 cm = 1/2 inch rounds and add.
3. Add the coconut milk and water. See Coconut Soup recipe for description of making coconut milk. Alternatively use 1 1/2 cups water and 1 tablespoon ghee.
4. Bring vegetables to boil, lower heat, cover and simmer 20 minutes. Stir occasionally.
5. Cut greens into small segments and add with chopped parsley, celery leaves and thyme leaflets or 1/2 teaspoon dried thyme.
6. Cook another few minutes. Some of the pumpkin will be disintegrated and form a sauce.
7. Dry roast the pumpkin seeds over medium low heat until a few pop. Let cool.
8. Mix salt into the callaloo. Garnish with lime wedges and pumpkin seeds. Pass the pepper grinder at the table.

Serves 4. Caribbean Influence.

Of this recipe,   To modify,
Kapha, enjoy less .... decrease the pumpkin and okra and use all water instead of coconut milk; so leave the recipe as is and enjoy less
Pitta, enjoy more .... decrease thyme
Vata, enjoy some .... decrease the pumpkin unless your digestion is strong

EACH CARIBBEAN COUNTRY HAS ITS OWN VERSION OF THIS ONE-POT VEGETABLE STEW, CREAMY ORANGE AND GREEN.

OVEN-BAKED VEGETABLES

Check on the state of energy in the kitchen where your meals are being prepared. You are consuming that too.

The Vegetables
2 large potatoes
1 beetroot
1 carrot
2 stalks celery
1 parsnip
1 turnip

The Seeds
4 tbsp olive oil
1 tsp mustard seed
1 tsp fennel seed
1 tsp coriander seed
1/2 tsp nigella seed
1/2 tsp crushed or powdered fenugreek seed
1 tsp earth or sea salt

1. Cut the vegetables into pieces. Beet, carrot, celery, parsnip and turnip require small pieces to cook in the time suggested. Potato pieces can be slightly larger. All chopped vegetables can be collected together except beetroot. Collect that separately.
2. Preheat the oven to 400°F (200°C, Gas 6).
3. Place your baking casserole in the oven with olive oil, seeds and salt for several minutes, then remove and add the vegetables, except for the beetroot, coating them with the seasoned olive oil. Toss beetroot with a little unseasoned oil and place on top of the rest of the vegetables using their color to design the dish.
4. Place the casserole in the oven, uncovered, and bake until the potatoes are done. Test the potato and parsnip at 30 minutes to decide.

Serves 4 as side dish. North American/European Influence with Indian spices.

Of this recipe,   Even better,
Kapha, enjoy more .... use sunflower oil and less of it
Pitta, enjoy more .... choose less carrot, beetroot and turnip; use half ghee, half oil; decrease nigella and mustard seeds
Vata, enjoy more .... choose less potato; half ghee, half oil is an option. If the vegetables seem too dry, use more ghee/oil or cover while baking.

ASSORTED COLORED VEGETABLES BAKED WITH VARIOUS SEEDS.

PAN-SAUTEED EGGPLANT

The act of nourishing ourselves with food is an act of respect
to that which gives us life.

The Coating
3 tbsp flour, any type
2 tsp cumin powder
2 tsp coriander powder
1 1/2 tsp ginger powder
1 tsp turmeric
2 tsp paprika
1 1/2 tsp black pepper
1 1/4 tsp earth or sea salt
1 1/2 tsp dried organic sugar

6 Japanese eggplants (long, thin) or equivalent
olive oil
a few thyme leaflets

1. Combine flour with the spices, salt and sugar, making sure all are finely ground.
2. Peel and trim eggplant and cut lengthwise into 1 cm = just under 1/2 inch thick slices.
3. Sprinkle some of the coating mix onto a flat surface and press each eggplant section onto it, both sides. There may be some mix left which can be stored a few days.
4. In a large skillet, warm a thin film of olive oil over medium heat.
5. Pan cook the eggplant until the under sides are golden, then flip. Add another small amount of oil under the second sides. Adjust heat to prevent smoking of the oil. Re-flip as needed until the eggplant is soft.
6. Garnish with thyme.

Serves 4. Caribbean Influence.

Of this recipe,   To refine,
Kapha, enjoy some .... use minimal ghee instead of olive oil; use rye or barley flour and less salt and sugar in the mix
Pitta, enjoy some .... use more ghee and less olive oil and enjoy only occasionally; use wheat flour, decrease ginger, paprika and black pepper
Vata, enjoy less.............. eggplant must be drying, observe how much oil it soaks up if it has the chance; use wheat flour and enjoy now and then

EGGPLANT IS COATED WITH A SEASONED FLOUR.

PEAS, LETTUCE, POTATOES

If you are not joyful about cooking, offer the opportunity to someone else.

4 small potatoes
1 1/2 cups peas
1 small cos lettuce
1 tbsp fresh mint or 1 tsp dried
1/4 cup fresh parsley
2 tsp sunflower oil
1/2 tsp earth or sea salt

lemon rounds
nasturtium or other flowers

1. Add potatoes to just boiling water and cook covered until soft, about 20 minutes.
2. Pop pods and remove peas.
3. Chop lettuce, mint and parsley together.
4. In a medium saucepan warm the sunflower oil over medium low heat.
5. Add peas and sauté, uncovered, for 15 minutes, until peas are softer, adding water if needed to prevent sticking.
6. Add lettuce and herbs and sauté 1 minute.
7. Peel and cut potatoes into pieces and mix in.
8. Mix in salt and combine with heat for another minute.
9. Garnish with lemon twists and nasturtiums.

Serves 4. North American - European Influence.

Of this recipe,   To enjoy more,
Kapha, enjoy more .... use less lemon juice
Pitta, enjoy more .... use a nasturtium petal rather than whole flower and a small amount of lemon
Vata, enjoy some .... reduce potatoes and lettuce and make sure the peas are well cooked; use more oil

A COOKED SALAD, VARIED SHAPES, FLAVORS AND TEXTURES.

PINE NUTS and VEGETABLES

Gesture to nourish at least one other being before eating, for instance, water a plant.

The Vegetables
1 medium sweet potato or yam
1 large carrot
3 cm = 1 inch fresh ginger
6 spring onions
250g = 8 oz snow peas

1 tbsp sesame oil
1/4 tsp earth or sea salt
1/4 tsp black pepper
1 tsp sesame oil
1/4 - 1/2 cup pine nuts

1. Peel and grate sweet potato and carrot together.
2. Grate ginger and finely slice spring onions from root to tip.
3. Trim the snow peas and leave entire. These will be steamed later.
4. Warm oil in pot or skillet and sauté ginger and spring onions, infusing their attributes into the sesame oil and softening their pungency.
5. Add grated orange vegetables and cook until done, stirring occasionally, about 15 minutes.
6. Meanwhile in a small skillet heat the last teaspoon of oil and roast the pine nuts until light brown, 1-2 minutes. Also set up your steamer and bring its water to boil.
7. Steam the snow peas for 3 minutes. Arrange on a serving platter.
8. Mold the cooked vegetables into mounds or other shapes and landscape them amongst the snow peas.
9. Garnish with pine nuts.

Serves 3-4 as a meal in itself, 6-8 if accompanied with rice. Asian Influence, China.

Of this recipe,   Even better,
Kapha, enjoy less .... use potato instead of sweet potato, minimum oil and next to no nuts; then it is a good vegetable meal
Pitta, enjoy some .... use ghee instead of sesame oil and decrease nuts
Vata, enjoy more

ORANGE VEGETABLES SITTING AMONGST GREEN SNOW PEAS.

POTATO and PARSNIP

We are already standing on sacred ground.

4 medium or large potatoes
2 parsnip
1/4 cup almonds

For the potato
2 tbsp generously packed fresh chives (or parsley)
2 tbsp ghee
1/4 tsp earth or sea salt

For the parsnip
1 tbsp ghee
1/2 tsp nigella seed
2 tsp sumac powder
a sprinkle of earth or sea salt
1/4 tsp black pepper

1. Bake the potatoes in a 400°F (200°C, Gas 6) oven or in a stove-top potato baker, or add to boiling water until done, between 60-90 minutes.
2. Peel and dice the parsnip and poach in a small amount of water in a covered saucepan until soft, about 10 minutes.
3. Heat almonds in a small amount of warm water until skins swell. When cooler, remove skins. Chop the nuts into medium pieces and toast.
4. To season the parsnip, warm the ghee in a small skillet over medium heat and add the black seeds. Lower the heat and add the sumac, rocking gently. Add the salt, pepper and parsnip, mixing all with the ghee seasoning. Keep warm.
5. Mash the cooked potato with the fresh herbs, ghee and salt.
6. To serve, layer potato, then parsnip and garnish with toasted almonds.

Serves 4-8.   North American, European and Middle Eastern Influence.

Of this recipe,   To enjoy more,
Kapha, enjoy some ……… decrease the parsnip, nuts and ghee
Pitta, enjoy some ………. decrease the nuts
Vata, enjoy some ………… increase the parsnip relative to the potato

MASHED HERBED POTATO, PARSNIP CUBES AND TOASTED ALMONDS.

PUMPKIN and FENNEL

Potential precedes manifestation.

1 kg = 2 lb pumpkin or winter squash
1/2 tsp earth or sea salt
1 fennel bulb
1 tbsp olive oil
1/2 tsp fennel seed
less than 1/2 tsp earth or sea salt
1/4 tsp black pepper
1 tbsp lemon juice
1/2 tbsp fresh marjoram or 3/4 tsp dried

1. Cut the pumpkin into pieces and steam, covered, until soft, about 15-20 minutes.
2. Remove the skin and mash when it is cool enough to handle. Add the salt and dried marjoram (if using) and place in an ovenproof serving dish. Keep warm in a low oven, uncovered if too moist, covered if just right.
3. Cut the fennel bulb into small pieces, about 3 cups.
4. Warm the olive oil in a large skillet over medium heat, sauté the fennel seed and add the fennel pieces. Cook for 5 minutes, stirring so that it cooks evenly. Add salt.
5. Layer the fennel on top of the pumpkin when ready to serve.
6. Top with the black pepper, lemon juice and marjoram leaves.

Serves 4-6. Mediterranean Influence.

Of this recipe,   To further refine,
Kapha, enjoy less .... bake the pumpkin and use more black pepper and marjoram, less salt and lemon juice. Make sure your digestion feels strong enough to digest pumpkin; midday is the best time and still have less
Pitta, enjoy some .... use less lemon juice and marjoram
Vata, enjoy some .... decrease pumpkin, increase fennel

DICED FENNEL SITS ON A BED OF MASHED PUMPKIN.

PUMPKIN SAUCE

Sage and nutmeg have such an affinity for each other they probably were together in a past life.

500 gm = 1 lb pumpkin or winter squash
2 tbsp olive oil
2 tsp dried sage or 4 tsp fresh, lightly packed
1 tsp nutmeg
3/4 tsp earth or sea salt
2 tsp orange juice
1 tbsp pine nuts

1. Preheat oven to 350°F (180°C, Gas 4).
2. Cut the pumpkin into 8 cm = 3 inch pieces. You can leave the skin on.
3. Place the pumpkin into a covered casserole dish, add the olive oil, cover and bake for about 40 minutes, until soft. Turn the pieces about twice during this time.
4. Remove the pumpkin skins, mash the pumpkin into the casserole juices, chop the sage and add. Add nutmeg, salt and juice.
5. Toast or dry roast the pine nuts for the garnish.
6. Serve as a vegetable, a sauce for pasta or add water to make soup.

Serves 3-4. Mediterranean Influence.

Of this recipe,   To fine-tune,
Kapha, enjoy less .... bake the pumpkin uncovered with very little oil to make it drier. Use fewer pine nuts and still have less.
Pitta, enjoy some .... use less spicing and nuts
Vata, enjoy some .... have a small portion

PUMPKIN IS BAKED AND MASHED WITH SAGE AND NUTMEG.

ROASTED RED PEPPER DIP

Our organism works in the modes of thinking, feeling and willing.

3 sweet red peppers (capsicum)
1 cup walnut kernels
1 pomegranate
2 tsp palm or raw cane sugar
1 tsp cumin
1/4 tsp sea salt
olive oil

1. Slice peppers in half lengthwise and remove stem, seeds and inner membranes. Roast peppers to char the skin in a hot oven, under the grill or over an open flame. Cover with a towel and cool.
2. Rub or wash off charred peel. Chop the peppers into small dice reserving 2 strips as garnish.
3. Crush walnuts with a mortar and pestle, reserving 2 if using as garnish.
4. Squeeze pomegranate halves over a sieve, collecting the juice into a bowl.
5. Add juice, walnuts, sugar, cumin and salt to peppers. Taste for sweet and sour with an undertone of bitter.
6. To serve, drizzle on some olive oil and adorn with the pepper strips and/or chopped walnuts.

Serves 6-8. Middle Eastern Influence, Lebanon.

Of this recipe,   To improve,
Kapha, enjoy less .... minimize nuts substantially and also the olive oil
Pitta, enjoy less .... maximize pomegranate and minimize nuts and peppers
Vata, enjoy more

DICED SWEET PEPPER AND CRUSHED WALNUTS MOISTENED
WITH POMEGRANATE JUICE.

SESAME SEED SALAD

Teflon-coated cookware will go out the same window as aluminum cookware.

The Seasonings
1/2 cup sesame seeds
1/4 tsp cumin seed
3/4 cup packed parsley leaves
1/2 cup hot water
1/4 cup lemon juice
1/2 tsp earth or sea salt
a sprinkle of asafoetida
1 tbsp olive oil

2 large potatoes
1 small head cauliflower

1. Peel and cut the potatoes into cubes. Separate the cauliflower into flowerets and cube the upper stem.
2. Steam the potatoes, covered, about 10 minutes and add the cauliflower for another 10, uncovered for the first few minutes.
3. Toast or dry roast 1 teaspoon of the sesame seeds with the cumin seeds over medium heat until the cumin aromatizes the air. Transfer to holding dish and set aside.
4. Toast or dry roast the remainder of the sesame seeds until golden, lowering heat if necessary.
5. Mince the parsley leaves, saving stems to flavor other dishes.
6. With a mortar and pestle, crush 1 tablespoon of the sesame seeds with 1 tablespoon hot water. When mostly crushed add 2 tablespoons of parsley and continue crushing until a paste is formed. Empty mortar and continue until all seeds and parsley are used. It is possible to use an electric appliance for this step.
7. Combine that seed paste, lemon juice, salt, asafoetida and olive oil to a creamy, pourable consistency, adding more water if necessary. If using fresh tahini, add the minced parsley directly and then the lemon, etc. Be prepared to add water later to adjust consistency.
8. Arrange the steamed vegetables and sprinkle with the toasted seeds. Provide the sauce in a pitcher à la table.

Serves 4. Middle Eastern Influence.

Of this recipe,   Ideally,
Kapha, enjoy some .... enjoy more vegetables, less dressing
Pitta, enjoy some .... use less dressing
Vata, enjoy some .... enjoy less of these particular vegetables, more dressing

STEAMED VEGETABLES WITH PARSLEY SESAME SAUCE.

SPINACH CROWNS

Combinations change the initial effect of any one ingredient.

16 spinach crowns
a sprinkle of earth or sea salt
1 tbsp sesame seeds
1 tsp ghee
a turn of the black pepper grinder
a sprinkle of sumac or lemon juice

1. Crowns are the part of the spinach plant which contains the bottoms of the stalks and the tops of the root, where the stalk joins the root. Wash these carefully to remove soil.
2. Sauté the salt and sesame seeds in the ghee until the seeds are golden brown.
3. Steam the crowns 4 minutes uncovered watching them turn bright green.
4. Sprinkle with the pepper and sumac and garnish with the seed-salt mix.
5. Serve as a side dish or on top of steamed, chopped spinach.

Serves 2. Japanese Influence.

Of this recipe,   To customize,
Kapha, enjoy some .... decrease the salt and seeds, increase the pepper
Pitta, enjoy some .... decrease the salt and seeds
Vata, enjoy some .... add a teaspoon of sesame oil in step 4

THIS WINS A PRIZE FOR UNUSUAL VISUAL.

STEAMED SPROUTED LENTILS

The fire of the sun grew this food; the fire of the hearth cooked it. We offer this to our digestive fire.

The Vegetables
2 cups brown lentil sprouts, 3-4 days growing
1 medium zucchini
1 bunch rocket greens

1/4 cup basil leaves

The Dressing
2 tbsp olive oil
1 tbsp lemon juice
1/4 tsp earth or sea salt
1/4 tsp freshly ground black pepper

1. Pick over lentils before sprouting and remove debris and broken ones or inferior ones. Soak in water for 8 hours, then drain and place in sprouter or mesh-covered jar on its side. Rinse twice a day. Remove any that are not up to sprouting.
2. To prepare, cube and steam the zucchini for 5 minutes uncovered, then add the sprouts and rocket, torn into pieces and washed. Distribute evenly and steam uncovered 2 minutes more.
3. Let cool.
4. Cut basil into short ribbons and arrange over the top.
5. Combine oil, lemon juice, salt and pepper together and pass the dressing at the table.

Serves 4. Mediterranean Influence.

Of this recipe,   To fine-tune,
Kapha, enjoy more .... use less zucchini and dressing; you could have this as a raw salad in summer
Pitta, enjoy some .... use less rocket, more bitter greens, less dressing, and also enjoy as a raw salad in summer
Vata, enjoy some .... use more dressing and enjoy occasionally in summer

GREEN LEAVES AND ZUCCHINI CUBES AMIDST ROBUST SPROUTS.

STUFFED POTATO PATTIES

Alert without mental tension, calm without mental dullness

1 kg = about 2 lbs potatoes

The Stuffing	The Dough
2 tbsp ghee	2 tbsp flour
4 spring onions	1/2 tsp earth or sea salt
1/2 tsp turmeric	1/4 tsp fresh ground pepper
1/4 tsp cinnamon	
a sprinkle of asafoetida	ghee
4 tbsp minced parsley	fresh lemon juice
2 tbsp chopped nuts or seeds of choice	
1/2 tsp earth or sea salt	
1/4 tsp fresh ground pepper	

1. Add potatoes whole and unpeeled to boiling water. Cook until done.
2. Meanwhile, prepare the stuffing or call it filling: warm ghee in a small skillet over medium low heat. Slice spring onion and sauté until soft. Add turmeric, cinnamon and asafoetida, cook for 1 minute and remove from heat.
3. Reserve one generous teaspoon of the minced parsley and add the rest with the nuts to the skillet mix along with the salt and pepper. Set stuffing aside.
4. Peel and mash the potatoes, adding the flour, salt and pepper. A less elaborate option: don't add the flour; combine the stuffing directly with the mashed potatoes and serve as in step seven.
5. Divide the potato mix into 20 parts. Roll each part into a sphere and remember those pinch pots made of clay? Indent your thumb almost to the bottom and widen the space, making it more wide than deep. Fill this with 1 teaspoon of stuffing and work the potato closed around it or close with the potato dough from the twentieth sphere.
6. When all spheres have been filled, cook as follows: Kapha, place in oven on a lightly greased baking sheet at 300°F (160°C, Gas 2) for 20 minutes. Pitta and vata, heat a small amount of ghee in a skillet and heat both sides at 5 minutes each.
7. Sprinkle with a few drops of lemon juice and garnish with the remaining parsley.

Serves 4. Middle Eastern Influence, Iraq.

Of this recipe,   Better yet,

Kapha, enjoy more .... decrease the oil and salt and use seeds instead of nuts; use rye or barley flour

Pitta, enjoy more .... decrease the spring onion and parsley, use seeds and wheat flour

Vata, enjoy some .... potatoes are drying, use oily nuts; use wheat flour

MASHED POTATO DOUGH ENCLOSES A SPICED AND TEXTURED FILLING.

SUNCHOKES and BRUSSELS SPROUTS

Once heat is added, a change begins to take place in food.
The life force begins to decrease and disorder begins to
increase. A refrigerator or freezer cannot forestall this.

The Sauce:
1 small carrot
1 small stick celery
500 ml = 2 cups water

1 bay leaf
a few parsley stalks, using leaves below

1 sprig fresh thyme or 1/2 tsp dried
1 clove, crushed, or sprinkle powder
6 peppercorns, crushed

1 blade mace or 1/4 tsp nutmeg
1/2 tsp earth or sea salt

3 tbsp ghee
1/2 tsp cumin seed
a few ajowan seeds
5 tbsp wheat flour

1. Thinly slice carrot and celery, adding to the water in a saucepan.
2. Heat, adding the other ingredients up to and including the pepper. Cover
   and simmer for 15 minutes. Remove from heat, add nutmeg and infuse 30
   minutes, rocking occasionally. Add salt.
3. Strain to obtain 2 cups of stock. The carrot and celery can be served with
   the other vegetables.
4. Warm the ghee in a medium saucepan on medium low heat. Add the cumin
   and ajowan seeds. After 1 minute add the flour. Sauté for 2 minutes. Add
   the stock slowly and bring to boil, whisking constantly.
5. When it has boiled and thickened, remove from heat and whisk for another
   half a minute. Set aside.

The Vegetables:
700 gm = 1 1/2 lb Jerusalem artichokes
450 gm = 1 lb Brussels sprouts

fresh lemon juice
fresh parsley or thyme

1. Simmer the sunchokes unpeeled, covered, 20 minutes, until soft.
2. Quarter the Brussels sprouts removing some of the tougher core and steam
   for 15 minutes in a separate pot, uncovered for the first 10, then covered
   for 5 minutes.
3. To combine: Split and scoop out the sunchokes onto a serving dish or just
   split and leave the scooping to the diner. Place the Brussels sprouts around
   the sunchokes and sprinkle both with a few drops of lemon juice. Garnish
   with some snipped parsley and/or fresh thyme. Provide the sauce at the
   table.

Serves 6-8. European Influence, France.

Of this recipe,   To enjoy more,
Kapha, enjoy less .... use no sauce and so infuse the spices from the
sauce into a small amount of heated sunflower, mustard oil or ghee; add
more minced parsley and thyme
Pitta, enjoy more... .... always consider decreasing the pungent taste,
in this case the thyme, clove, pepper and mace
Vata, enjoy some .... chose more of the sunchokes and less of the
Brussels sprouts, they are noted for wind production; the ajowan and
cumin may counter this tendency for you

BASED ON THE ORIGINAL MARQUIS LOUIS de BÉCHAMEL SAUCE.

SWEET BEETS

All that we can apprehend and all that we cannot even imagine is part of the one system, there is nothing on the 'outside'.

Per person:
1 small beetroot
2 tsp palm or unrefined cane sugar
1/2 tsp grated ginger root
1 tsp ghee
1 thin round of lemon or other citrus
a small amount of earth or sea salt
unprocessed honey
fresh mint

1. Peel and grate beets and combine with sugar and ginger in an appropriately sized saucepan.
2. Bring to steaming over medium low heat, adding a small of water if necessary to start the release of beet juice. Tease beet ribbons apart. Add ghee.
3. Slice lemon round into quarters and remove seeds.
4. Add lemon, turn heat to low, cover and stir occasionally until the beets are soft and pulpy.
5. Add salt and when cool add honey to taste.
6. Garnish with chopped and whole mint leaves.

Eastern European Influence.

Of this recipe,	To balance your dosha,
Kapha, enjoy some	omit sugar and when cool add more honey
Pitta, enjoy less	beets, ginger and honey are heating, enjoy rarely
Vata, enjoy more	use half sugar and when cool, half honey

GRATED AND COOKED WITH TONES OF PUNGENT, BITTER AND SOUR.

TARO ROUNDS

Diet affects the mind, affects the way we perceive things.

1 taro, 500 gm = 1 lb

The Seasonings
1/4 tsp black peppercorns
1/2 tsp aniseed
1/4 tsp ginger
1 tbsp ghee
a sprinkle of earth or sea salt

fresh coriander
lemon wedges

1. Create a bed of coals for traditional preparation. Otherwise preheat oven to 375°F (190°C Gas 5).
2. Surround taro by coals and bake for 1 hour, or until knife is easy to insert. If using an oven, bake for 75 minutes and then test with a knife.
3. Meanwhile, warm a small skillet over medium low heat and add whole peppercorns. Dry roast for 1 minute and transfer to mortar. Add aniseed to skillet while you grind the pepper. After 1 minute add the aniseed to mortar and grind, now adding the ginger powder.
4. Warm the ghee in the same skillet over medium low heat and add the mortar mix. Sauté for 2 minutes, then remove from heat and add the salt.
5. Chop the fresh coriander.
6. When the taro is thoroughly cooked, slice into rounds and remove peel with a knife.
7. Place on a platter and garnish with the skillet mix and fresh coriander. Pass the lemon at the table.

Serves 2 as a side dish. Choose a larger taro for more people and increase baking time and seasonings accordingly. Polynesian-Hawaiian-Caribbean Influence.

Of this recipe,   To enjoy more,
Kapha, enjoy less .... use potato instead of taro, less ghee and a few drops of lemon; the spices are good with any food or as a digestive tea using 1/4 teaspoon of the mix
Pitta, enjoy some .... use less skillet spices in the same amount of ghee; use a few drops of lemon
Vata, enjoy more............ a small amount of the spices are also good as a digestive tea

TARO IS BAKED AND COATED WITH A TRADITIONAL DIGESTIVE TRIO OF SPICES.

TURNIP

The karate teacher used to say, "Think about what you're doing."

Per person
1 turnip
1 tbsp dandelion, endive or other bitter greens
2 tsp ghee
1/4 tsp cardamom
less than 1/4 tsp earth or sea salt
lemon wedge

1. Cut turnip into cubes and steam, uncovered, for 5 minutes, covered for 10, until cooked.
2. Cut fine the green/s of your choice.
3. In the last minute of steaming the turnip add the greens and cook until wilted.
4. Meanwhile, warm ghee in small skillet over medium low heat. Introduce cardamom, Add cooked vegetables and toss. Add salt.
5. Provide the lemon wedge for a few drops of juice.

European Influence, England.

Of this recipe,   Even better,
Kapha, enjoy more .... choose a robust-flavored turnip
Pitta, enjoy less .... find a variety of turnip that is more mild than pungent
Vata, enjoy some .... choose a small turnip and less greens. All greens should be cooked.

MILD TURNIP IS STEAMED WITH GREENS.

VEGETABLE PARCELS

Sleeping after eating weakens digestion. Resting is not the
same as sleeping.

The Seasonings
7 cm = 3 inches lower lemon grass stalk
1 bi-lobed Kaffir lime leaf
4 cm = 1 1/2 inches galangal or ginger root
1 tbsp ghee
1 tbsp sesame oil
2 tsp black or white sesame seeds
1/2 tsp earth or sea salt

The Vegetables
2 small sweet potatoes
1/2 small celeriac or 2 stalks celery
half a broccoli

4 sprigs coriander

4 rectangles of baking paper 30 x 40 cm = 12 x 15 inches

1. Peel off outer lemon grass leaves and remove root. Slice from the base of
   the stalk up in very thin rings. When the purple inner ring disappears, slice
   no further. Use the remaining stem to make stock or tea. Mince lime leaf
   and grate the galangal.
2. In a large skillet warm the ghee and oil over medium low heat. Add the
   above seasonings and sesame seeds and sauté 3 minutes.
3. Remove from heat and add salt.
4. Preheat oven to 375°F (190°C, Gas 5). Have 2 baking trays handy.
5. Peel and cut the sweet potato into small-medium cube-type shapes.
6. Remove celeriac peel by slicing it off with a knife. Cube as above.
7. Cut broccoli stem into similar size, leaving small flowerets whole, halving
   larger ones.
8. Toss the vegetables into the spice ghee mix and coat well.
9. Lay out the rectangles of baking paper vertically and place one quarter of
   the vegetables just above the center. Fold paper in half. Fold the three sides
   in, in small turns, pressing the folds down as you go. Fold until the paper is
   almost up to the vegetables. Consider using an origami book to learn how to
   make decorative parcels, or vary the shapes.
10. Place parcels on the baking sheet, folds down if they are unrolling.
11. Bake for 30 minutes.
12. Remove from oven and snip paper open in a pattern of your choice.
13. When the steam has dissipated garnish with a sprig of coriander.

Serves 4 as side dish. Southeast Asian Influence.

If you don't want to use paper for ecological reasons, bake in a covered casserole dish or use banana leaves and a steamer for additional flavor. This can also be sautéed, covered, for 15 minutes.

Of this recipe,	In your parcel,
Kapha, enjoy some	decrease sweet potato, oil and seeds and bake uncovered for a drier dish
Pitta, enjoy more	use less galangal or ginger
Vata, enjoy more	

VEGETABLES STEAM WHEN WRAPPED IN BAKING PAPER.

VEGETABLE SAUTÉ

Don your alchemical apron.

The Vegetables
1 large carrot
1/2 head broccoli
2 tbsp ghee
1 star anise
2 stalks celery
1 medium zucchini

The Seasonings, Dried or Fresh
1 tsp dried oregano or 1 tbsp fresh
1/2 tsp dried thyme or 1/2 tbsp fresh
1 tsp dried basil or a generous tablespoon fresh

More Seasonings
1 tsp ghee
6 cloves
1/4 tsp nutmeg
1/4 tsp aniseed or 1 tbsp fresh Thai
    basil
1/2 tsp earth or sea salt
1 cup fresh coriander leaves, lightly
    packed
1/2 cup fresh parsley leaves, lightly
    packed

lemon or lime wedges

1. Cut the carrot and broccoli into small even size.
2. In a large skillet warm the 2 tablespoons ghee over medium heat. Add the carrots, broccoli and star anise and cook for 5 minutes, uncovered, stirring occasionally. Adjust heat as necessary.
3. Chop the celery into small pieces and add. Cook for another 5 minutes.
4. Chop the zucchini into small pieces and add. Cook another five, this time with the cover on.
5. Sprinkle on the dried herbs and mix through. If the vegetables are still not soft to the center add a little water to the skillet and leave the cover on. Simmer until softer.
6. Make a space in the skillet and dissolve the 1 teaspoon of ghee.
7. Crush the cloves and add to the pool of ghee with the nutmeg and aniseed. Turn off heat and begin to cool. Add the salt after 5 minutes and then stir seasonings through the vegetables.
8. Gather the fresh herbs. Chop and mix them through the vegetables.
9. Pass the citrus wedges at the table.

Serves 4 as a side dish. Can be served over rice. Asian Influence, Malaysia.

Of this recipe,   To further align,
Kapha, enjoy more .... use less ghee and decrease zucchini
Pitta, enjoy some .... decrease the oregano, thyme, cloves, nutmeg
and anises; fresh basil is O.K. in moderation
Vata, enjoy some .... decrease broccoli and celery

FRESH HERBS MIXED THROUGH ASSORTED VEGETABLES.

VEGETABLES ZA'ATAR

Do your kitchen utensils make your craft easy?

The Vegetables
3 small potatoes
1 red, yellow or orange pepper (capsicum)
125 gm = 4 oz green or long beans
125 gm = 4 oz okra

1 tbsp sesame seeds

The Seasonings
2 tbsp olive oil
1/2 tbsp dried thyme
1 tsp dried oregano
1/2 tbsp sumac powder
1/2 tsp earth or sea salt

1. Begin by cooking the whole potatoes, covered, in just boiling water.
2. Peel if desired and slice the pepper.
3. Trim the beans and cut into short lengths.
4. Warm the olive oil in a medium skillet or saucepan over medium heat and sauté the intact okra, the beans and capsicum for 10 minutes stirring occasionally.
5. Warm a small skillet over medium low heat and dry roast the sesame seeds until light brown. Let cool.
6. When the potato is cooked, peel, cut into cubes and mix into the other vegetables.
7. Sprinkle the herbs, sumac and salt onto the vegetables. Toss through evenly and gently. Sumac has a wonderful tangy taste but squeeze on some lemon if you can't locate sumac. Use 1 tablespoon fresh thyme leaflets and 2 teaspoons fresh chopped oregano leaves if possible.
8. Cook on low heat for 5 minutes, tossing occasionally.
9. Mix in the sesame seeds, the final taste of the za'atar blend.

Serves 4. North African-Mediterranean Influence.

Of this recipe,   Better yet,
Kapha, enjoy some .... instead of olive oil, use mustard seed or sunflower oil and less of it and decrease the seeds and sumac
Pitta, enjoy some .... some of these spices are heating or sour, use less of the za'atar mix
Vata, enjoy some .... use less potatoes

SESAME AND HERBS COAT ASSORTED VEGETABLES.

READING and REFERENCE

Food Charts are found in the following books:

Ayurveda: A Life of Balance   Maya Tiwari
Healing Arts Press, 1995

The Ayurveda Cookbook   Amadea Morningstar
Lotus Press, 1990

Ayurveda for Women   Dr Robert Svoboda
Simon and Schuster, 1999

Ayurveda and Panchakarma   Dr Sunil Joshi
Lotus Press, 1997

Ayurveda: the Science of Self-Healing   Dr Vasant Lad
Lotus Press, 1984

Ayurvedic Healing: A Comprehensive Guide Dr David Frawley
Lotus Press

Body, Mind and Sport   John Douillard
Harmony Books, 1994

The Chopra Center Cookbook Nourishing Body and Soul Dr Deepak Chopra,
Rider, 2000   David Simon,
and Leanne Backer

Heaven's Banquet   Miriam Kasin Hospodar
Plume Books, 2001

Further Reading

Agriculture   Rudolf Steiner
Bio-dynamic Agricultural Association, London, 1974

Ancient Secrets of Modern Health   Dr Rajen Cooppan
Logo Australia 1999

Ayurvedic Balancing   Joyce Bueker
Llewellyn Publications, 2002

Ayurveda Healing for Women   Atreya
Samuel Weiser, Inc. 1999

Ayurveda: Life, Health and Longevity   Dr Robert Swoboda
Arkana 1992

Ayurveda Revolutionized   Edward Tarabilda
Lotus Press, 1999

Ayurveda the Right Way to Live   Gopi Warrier
Carlton 2002

The Heart of Yoga, Developing a Personal Practice   T.K.V. Desikachar
Inner Traditions International, 1995

Organic and Wholefoods Naturally delicious cuisine   André Dominé, editor
Culinaria Könemann 1997

Perfect Digestion   Dr Deepak Chopra
Harmony Books, 1995

Religiousness in Yoga, Lectures on Theory and Practice   T.K.V. Desikachar
Edited by Mary Louise Skelton and John Ross Carter
University Press of America, 1980

Textbook of Ayurveda, Fundamental Principles   Dr. Vasant Lad
The Ayurvedic Press, 2002

The Vegetable Bible   Christian Teubner
Penguin Books, 1998

What Are We Seeking?   T.K.V. Desikachar
Krishnamacharya Yoga Mandiram, 2001

Yoga and Ayurveda   Dr David Frawley
Lotus Press, 1999

Yoga and the Healing of Consciousness   Dr David Frawley
Lotus Press, 1997

Yoga and the Living Tradition of Krishnamacharya
                           T.K.V. Desikachar with R.H. Cravens
Aperture, 1998

Yoga for your Type   Dr. David Frawley and Sandra S. Kozak
Lotus Press, 2001

The Yoga of Herbs: An Ayurvedic Guide to Herbal MedicineDr Vasant Lad &
Lotus Press, 1998   Dr David Frawley

Yogayajnavalkya Samhita   translated by T.K.V. Desikachar
Krishnamacharya Yoga Mandiram, 2000

Open any of these books and discover a wealth of additional books for reading and reference.

APPENDICES

RECIPES by COUNTRY and REGION

-Afghanistan: Bzar Potatoes
-Africa: (and see individual countries): Artichokes and Broad Beans, Green
  Split Peas and Aubergine, Lime-Aide, Nuts in Mung Flour, Papaya and Cape
  Gooseberries, Red Lentil Soup, Rye Flatbread, Vegetables Za'atar
-Algeria: Math Beans, Beets and Kumquats
-The Americas (and see individual countries): Barley Tonic, Cornbread, Multi-
  Colored Soups
-Central: Broiled Pineapple, Jicama Salad, Papaya and Cape Gooseberries
-North: Baked Grated Vegetables, Buckwheat-Grain Pancakes, Grilled Vegeta-
  bles, Marmalade Syrup, Mulberry Tarts, Oven-Baked Vegetables, Pear Cake,
  Peas, Lettuce, Potato, Potato and Parsnip, Red Lentils, Savory Cake with
  Herbs, Savory Milk Casserole, Seeds, Figs and Apples, Stonefruit Spread
-South: Quinoa
-Argentina: Feijoas
-Armenia: Sculpted Aduki Beans
-Asia (and see individual countries): Baked Broccoli, Barley Tea, Barley Tonic,
  Chinese Cabbage and Chestnuts, Cilantro-Mint Dressing, Cooked Greens,
  Ginger Syrup, Honey Shapes, Jicama Salad, Leeks and Ginger, Multi-Colored
  Soups, Nut Porridge, Pineapple and Coconut, Steamed Buns, Vegetable Par-
  cels
-Austria: Loquat Tart, Pumpkin Soup
-Australia: Lily-Pillie and Mulberries, Macadamia Pesto, Multi-Colored Soups,
  Oat Biscuits, Seed Crackers
-Bali: Black-Eyed Pea Salad-East, Dark Yellow Rice
-Belgium: Mixed Vegetable Soup
-Bosnia: Donuts in Rose Syrup
-Brazil: Choko Salsa, Taro and Sorrel Hotpot
-Bulgaria: Sunchoke Soup
-Burma: Pancake-Wrapped Vegetables
-Canada: Wild Rice and Pecans (and see North America)
-Caribbean: Black Beans, Choko, Lime and Thyme, Coconut Cookies, Curried
  Plantains, Custard Apple, Jerk Broth, Lime-Aide, Mung and Okra, Nut Slice,
  Okra and Pumpkin, Pan-Sautéed Eggplant, Pineapple and Coconut, Soybean
  Salad, Taro Rounds, Vegetable Besan
-China: Cabbage Sauté, Flavorpot, Fruit in Agar-Agar, Lotus Root Salad, Pan-
  cake-Wrapped Vegetables, Pine Nuts and Vegetables, Sweet Mung Soup, Sweet
  Rice Dumplings, Tamarind Chutney
-Croatia: Plum Dumplings
-Cuba: Papaya
-Czechoslovakia: Cucumber Salad
-Denmark: Chestnut Sauce
-Egypt: Chickpeas Dukkah, Nut and Seed Garnish, Quince Spread
-England: Blueberry Lemon Mini Cakes, Boiled Salad, Leek and Oat Soup, Tur-
  nip

-Ethiopia: Millet Berbere
-Europe (and see individual countries): Applesauce Vegetables, Baked Grated Vegetables, Barley and Dill Soup, Barley Tonic, Buckwheat Flatbread and Pasta, Buckwheat-Grain Pancakes, Choko, Celeriac and Broccoli Broth, Ghee Mâitre d'Hotel, Green Beans and Walnuts, Green Topping, Honey Shapes, Marmalade Syrup, Mulberry Tarts, Multi-Colored Soups, Oven-Baked Vegetables, Pear Cake, Pears and Anise, Peas, Lettuce, Potato, Plum Sauce, Potato and Parsnip, Savory Milk Casserole, Stonefruit Spread
-Finland: Thick Vegetable Soup
-France: Celeriac with Spinach Sauce, Puy Lentils, Sunchokes and Brussels Sprouts
-Germany: Kohlrabi Stew, Steamed Apples
-Greece: Bean and Vegetable Casserole, Filled Flatbread, Lemon Mint Rice, Quinoa, Saffron Crackers
-Guatemala: Peach and Cherry Compote
-Hong Kong: Nut Porridge
-Hungary: Berry Stew, Red Broth
-India: Barley Dumpling Soup, Basic Gourmet Milk, Buckwheat-Besan Crepes, Carrot and Milk Pudding, Chef's Kichuri, Chyawanprash and Milk, Condensed Milk, Date-Mint Chutney, Festive Rice, Ginger Syrup, Lemon Rind Chutney, Lime-Aide, Multi-Colored Soups, Mung and Okra, Mung Dal, Nuts in Mung Flour, Oven-Baked Vegetables, Pan-Cooked Chickpea Snack, Pear Cake, Plum Sauce, Prune Chutney, Pumpkin Seeds, Rice, Rice and Urad Dal Patties, Sautéed Celery Pancakes, Soft Cheese with Spices, Toasted Sunflower Seeds, Toor Dal, Twice-Cooked Rice, Val Dal
-Indonesia: Dark Rice and Sweet Potato
-Iran: Bean Hotpot, Millet and Rice
-Iraq: Stuffed Potato Patties
-Ireland: Cucumber and Apple Salad, Hazelnut Biscuits
-Israel: Grape-Fruit Juice, Nut Chutney
-Italy: Cornbread, Pesto Pasta, Pine and Thyme, Savory Cake with Herbs, Semolina Dumplings
-Japan: Barley Tea, Beetroot Pudding, Fruit in Agar-Agar, Lotus Root Salad, Rice and Sweet Aduki Beans, Spinach Crowns, Steamed Rice in Mugs, Sticky Rice Balls
-Jordan: Lentils and Noodles
-Kenya: Mung Dal Too
-Korea: Buckwheat Flatbread or Pasta, Pine Nut and Rice Porridge
-Lebanon: Pistachio Dressing, Sesame, Almonds and Dates
-Malawi: Curried Greens
-Malaysia: Vegetable Sauté
-Mediterranean-North Africa (and see individual countries): Artichoke and Broad Beans, Baked Rice and Vine Leaves, Fennel, Cucumber and Carrot Salad, Filled Orange Crescents, Marmalade Syrup, Pumpkin and Fennel, Pumpkin Sauce, Steamed Sprouted Lentils, Vegetables Za'atar, Yellow Split Pea Spread

-Mexico: Avocado, Mango, Pumpkin Seed Sauce, Sweet Walnuts, Val Dal

-Middle East (and see individual countries): Carrot and Milk Pudding, Cream of Rice, Date Slice, Festive Rice, Green Split Peas and Aubergine, Pomegranate Lentil Soup, Potato and Parsnip, Roasted Red Pepper Dip, Sesame Seed Salad

-Morocco: Filled Orange Crescents

-Netherlands: Oat Biscuits

-New Zealand: Multi-Colored Soups, Oat Biscuits, Potato Soup

-Norway: Applesauce Vegetables

-Pakistan: Chickpea Flour Sauce, Exotically Spiced Vegetables, Mulberry Tarts

-Peru: Avocado Soup

-Philippines: Coconut Soup, Pineapple and Coconut, Steamed Yam Cake, Sweet Mung Soup

-Polynesia: Taro Rounds

-Portugal: Kale Soup

-Poland: White Beans and Herbs

-Republic of South Africa: Melon

-Romania: Juniper and Vegetables

-Russia: Beet and Cabbage Soup, Buckwheat-Besan Crepes, Buckwheat Flatbread or Pasta, Cabbage and Seeds, Cucumber Salad, Kasha Flatbread, Spiced Honey Drink, Steamed Buns, Toasted Sunflower Seeds, Wheat Berry Porridge

-Scandinavia: Applesauce Vegetables, Chestnut Sauce, Rye Rounds, Thick Vegetable Soup

-Scotland: Oatcakes, Potato Cakes

-Singapore: Noodle Soup

-Spain: Broad Bean Soup, Brown Lentil Hotpot, Orange Muffin Cakes

-Sweden: Rye Rounds

-Switzerland: Stove-Top Cooked Grain

-Syria: Chickpeas Kebsa

-Tibet: Barley Dumpling Soup

-Thailand: Eggplant and Basil, Flavored Almonds, Kaffir Noodles, Sweet Mung Soup

-Tunisia: Bean and Rye Patties

-Turkey: A Customable Platter, Leeks and Rice

-United States: Black-eyed Pea Salad-West, Broccoli Pastries, Peach Cake

-Vietnam: Sweet Mung Soup

-Yemen: Yellow Dal

RECIPES by FOOD TYPES

Adolescent-Approved: Broccoli Pastries, Filled Flatbread, Potato Cakes, Savory Cake with Herbs, Seed Crackers, all Sweet Bakery recipes, Savory Milk Casserole, Plum Dumplings, Stonefruit Spread, (generally fruit is preferred on its own without spices), Flavored Almonds, Pumpkin Seeds, Noodle Soup, Potato Soup, Thick Vegetable Soup, Adaptable Flatbread, Buckwheat-Grain

Pancakes, Sweet Griddlecakes, Handmade Pasta, Lentils and Noodles, Pancake-Wrapped Vegetables, Pesto Pasta, Spice and Nut Flatbread, Steamed Buns, Baked Grated Vegetables, Broccoli, Bzar Potatoes, Oven-Baked Vegetables, Sesame Seed Salad, Stuffed Potato Patties, Vegetables Za'atar and Chef's Kichuri now and then.

Barbecue: Bean and Rye Patties, Broiled Pineapple, Flatbreads, Grilled Vegetables, Millet and Rice, Rice and Urad Patties.

Children's Parties: Sweet Bakery items, Potato Cakes, Fruit in Agar-Agar, Honey Shapes, Sweet Walnuts, Flatbreads, Rice and Sweet Aduki Beans, Steamed Buns with less buckwheat and more fruit in the filling, Sticky Rice Balls, Sweet Rice Dumplings, Beetroot Pudding, Grilled Vegetables and Stuffed Potato Patties all made with the size of small mouths in mind.

Chutneys: Date-Mint Chutney, Lemon Rind Chutney, Macadamia Pesto, Nut Chutney, Pineapple and Coconut, Plum Sauce, Prune Chutney, Rhubarb and Strawberries, Tamarind Chutney.

Dips/Dressings/Sauces: Chestnut Sauce, Chickpea Flour Sauce, Cilantro-Mint Dressing, Ghee Maître D'Hotel, Green Topping, Macadamia Pesto, Nut and Seed Garnish, Pistachio Dressing, Pumpkin Seed Sauce, Roasted Red Pepper Dip, Sesame Seed Salad.

Finger Food: not that long ago all food was finger food; over one third of these recipes are already that. Cut savory and sweet bakery items into small pieces; fruit can be cut to size appropriate for a mouthful; nuts and seeds can be sprinkled into you; prepare bean recipes to dip consistency; staples and vegetables can be put on a platter and all flatbreads and crackers can accompany them.

Kapha-Friendly, random selection: Beverage: Aloe Aperitif, Digestive Teas, Flower Waters, Hot Water, Spiced Honey Drink. Fruit: Dried Fruit in Green Tea, fresh apple or pear. Breakfast: Barley-Millet Porridge, Buckwheat-Grain Pancakes, Oatcakes. Lunch or Dinner: Borlotti Beans, Chef's Kichuri, Lemon Rind Chutney, Millet Berbere, Prune Chutney, Rye Flatbread, Rye Rounds, Brown Lentil Hotpot, Broccoli, Oven-Baked Vegetables, Steamed Sprouted Lentils. Snack: Pumpkin Seeds, Toasted Sun Seeds.

One-Pot or Skillet Meals: All flatbreads, Barley-Millet Porridge, Bean and Vegetable Casserole, Black Beans, Borlotti Beans, Chickpeas Dukkah, Chickpeas Kebsa, Dark Rice and Sweet Potato, Festive Rice, Green Split Peas and Aubergine, Griddlecakes, Sweet and Savory, Kaffir Noodles, Lemon Mint Rice, Lentils and Noodles, Math Beans, Beets and Kumquats, Millet Berbere, Millet and Rice (as a moister version), Mung Dal, Mung Dal Too, Okra and Pumpkin, Pan-Cooked Chickpea Snack, Pesto Pasta, Pigeon Peas, Pine Nuts and Rice Porridge, Puy Lentils, Quinoa, Red Lentils, Rice, Rice Ras el Hanout, Rice Pudding, Sautéed Celery Pancakes, Sculpted Aduki Beans, Semolina Dumplings, Soybean Salad, Sticky Rice Balls, Stove-Top Cooked Grain, Sweet Rice Dumplings, Toor Dal, Val Dal, Wheat Berry Porridge, Wheat Noodles, Wild Rice and Pecans, White Beans and Herbs, Yellow Dal, Yellow Rice and Yellow Split Pea Spread are adaptable to being cooked in one vessel. Refer to the camp meal instructions in Chef's Kichuri for general directions. So you only have one pot, but do you have a few bowls? One can be for toasted seeds and one for the sauce that you cooked first. One-Pot Meals also imply minimal steps in preparation and cooking. Set the longest cooking ingredients to cook first, adding ingredients based on the time required to cook them. To grace the dish with the ghee and spice component, an option is to dissolve the ghee on top of the ingredients in the pot in the last several minutes, infuse the spices in the pool of molten ghee and then mix it in.

Pitta-Friendly, random selection: Beverage: Barley Tonic, Digestive Teas, Flower Waters. Fruit: Custard Apple, Dried Fruit in Green Tea, Melon. Breakfast: Basic Gourmet Milk, Cream of Rice, Stove-Top Cooked Grain. Lunch or Dinner: Adaptable Flatbread, Broccoli Pastries, Chef's Kichuri, Date-Mint Chutney, Filled Flatbread, Kaffir Noodles, Mung Dal Too, Rice, Sweet Mung Soup, Choko Salsa, Curried Greens, Okra and Pumpkin in Coconut Milk. Snack: Date Slice, Pear Cake, Pumpkin Seeds, Toasted Sun Seeds.

Premier Recipe: Chef's Kichuri. When you need a tridoshic meal that is prepared in 30 minutes, this is it.

Salad Possibilities using grains, legumes and/or vegetables: Black-Eyed Pea Salad-East, Black-Eyed Pea Salad-West, Boiled Salad, Borlotti Beans, Chickpeas Dukkah, Chickpeas Kebsa, Choko, Lime and Thyme, Choko Salsa, Cucumber and Apple Salad, Cucumber Salad, Fennel, Cucumber and Carrot, Green Beans and Walnuts, Jicama Salad, Math Beans, Beet and Kumquat, Millet Berbere, Peas, Lettuce and Potato, Pigeon Peas, Puy Lentils, Quinoa, Red Lentils, Sesame Seed Salad, Soybean Salad, Steamed Sprouted Lentils, White Beans and Herbs, Yellow Rice.

Simple and Introductory: Savory Cake with Herbs, Pear Cake, Dried Fruit in Green Tea, Melon, Pumpkin Seeds, Toasted Sun Seeds, Thick Vegetable Soup, Buckwheat Grain Pancakes, Chef's Kichuri, Cream of Rice, Griddlecakes, Sweet and Savory, Lemon Mint Rice, Mung Dal, Yellow Split Pea Spread, Asparagus-West, Curried Greens, Oven-Baked Vegetables, Vegetables Za'atar.

Steamer Cooking: Broccoli, Exotically Spiced Vegetables, Jicama Salad, Juniper and Vegetables, Nuts in Mung Flour, Sesame Seed Salad, Steamed Apples, Steamed Buns, Steamed Rice in Mugs, Steamed Sprouted Lentils, Steamed Yam Cake, Turnip.
Tridosha-Friendly, random selection: Beverage: Digestive Teas, Flower Waters.

Fruit: Pears and Anise, Seeds, Figs and Apples or make a seasonal fruit platter and enjoy it well before the meal. Breakfast: Griddlecakes, Sweet and Savory. Lunch or Dinner: Chef's Kichuri, Millet and Rice, Mixed Vegetable Soup, Thick Vegetable Soup, Applesauce Vegetables, Fennel, Cucumber and Carrot, Green Beans and Walnuts. Snack: Pumpkin Seeds, Toasted Sun Seeds.

Vata-Friendly, random selection: Beverage: Digestive Teas, Flower Waters, Hot Water, Lime-Aid. Fruit: Avocado, Berry Stew, Rhubarb and Strawberries. Breakfast: Cream of Rice, Nut Porridge, Pine Nut and Rice Porridge. Lunch or Dinner: Chef's Kichuri, Green Topping, Pesto Pasta, Soft Cheese, Spice and Nut Flatbread, Wheat Noodles, Leek and Oat Soup, Baked Grated Vegetables, Pine Nuts and Vegetables, Roasted Red Pepper Dip. Snack: Filled Orange Crescents, Flavored Almonds, Hazelnut Biscuits, Honey Shapes.

RECIPES by INGREDIENTS

This listing allows one to choose any ingredient and find all the recipes that use it. Refer to Recipe Index for page numbers.

Asafoetida (Ferula assa-foetida), ghee, lemon (Citrus limon), peppercorns (Piper nigrum) and earth and sea salt are ubiquitous and not listed specifically here. Earth Salt is harvested from earth deposits, also called mineral salt, pink salt, black salt or Himalayan salt. It can be used with savory dishes.

All recipes were prepared at sea level. One teaspoon is five milliliters, one tablespoon is 15 milliliters and one cup is 8 ounces/250 milliliters.

-Agar-Agar (Gelidium amansii) Fruit in Agar-Agar

-Ajowan Seeds (Trachyspermem ammi, Carum ajowan): Brown Lentil Hotpot, Cabbage and Seeds, Cabbage Sauté, Millet Berbere, Pigeon Peas, Puy Lentils, Sunchokes and Brussels Sprouts, Val Dal

-Allspice (Pimenta dioica): Jerk Broth, Nut Slice, Pepper Fruit Syrup, Saffron Crackers, Vegetable Besan

-Almonds (Prunus dulcis): Basic Gourmet Milk, Broad Bean Soup, Donuts in Rose Syrup, Filled Orange Crescents, Flavored Almonds, Loquat Tart, Mulberry Tarts, Nut Chutney, Nut Porridge, Oat Biscuits, Potato and Parsnip, Quince Spread, Seeds, Figs and Apples, Steamed Apples, Sesame, Almonds and Dates, Steamed Rice in Mugs, Wheat Berry Porridge
-Oil: Choko Salsa, Cilantro-Mint Dressing, Cucumber Salad, Jicama Salad, Loquat Tart, Nut Slice, Wheat Berry Porridge

-Aloe: (Aloe barbadensis): Aloe Aperitif, Papaya and Cape Gooseberries

-Amaranth (Amaranthus gangeticus) Greens: Cooked Greens, Curried Greens,

Multi-Colored Soups, Okra and Pumpkin
-Seeds (Amaranthus tricolor/Achyranthes bidentata): Seed Crackers

-Amchoor (Green Mango) Powder: Dark Rice and Sweet Potato, Multi-Colored
Soups, Noodle Soup, Toor Dal, Val Vegetable Soup, Vegetable Besan

-Aniseed (Pimpinella anisum): Brown Lentil Hotpot, Burdock and Carrot,
Cooked Greens, Cream of Rice, Flavorpot, Mung Dal, Noodle Soup, Pears
and Anise, Pigeon Peas, Rice and Sweet Aduki Beans, Spice and Nut Flatbread, Sweet Rice Dumplings, Taro Rounds, Vegetable Sauté

-Apples (Malus sp.): Dried: Dried Fruit in Green Tea
-Fresh: Applesauce Vegetables, Barley Tonic, Cabbage and Seeds, Cucum-
ber and Apple Salad, Nut Chutney, Potato Cakes, Seeds, Figs and Apples,
Steamed Apples, Wild Rice and Pecans

-Apricots (Prunus armeniaca) Dried: Dried Fruit in Green Tea, Festive Rice, Orange Muffin Cakes, Pomegranate Lentil Soup
-Fresh: Loquat Tart, Orange Muffin Cakes, Steamed Buns

-Arrowroot (Maranta arundinacea): Nut Porridge, Pumpkin Seed Sauce

-Artichokes (Cynara cardunculus): Artichoke and Broad Beans

-Asparagus (Asparagus officinalis): Asparagus, East and West, Grilled Vegetables, Juniper and Vegetables, Noodle Soup

-Aubergine: see Eggplant

-Avocado (Persea americana): Avocado, Avocado Soup

-Bamboo (Phyllostachys pubescens): Bamboo Shoot

-Barley (Hordeum vulgare): Barley and Dill Soup, Barley Dumpling Soup, Barley-Millet Porridge, Barley Tea, Barley Tonic
-Flour: Buckwheat-Grain Pancakes, Filled Flatbread, Griddlecakes, Sweet
and Savory

-Basil (Ocimum basilicum): Baked Rice and Vine Leaves, Cooked Greens, Egg-
plant and Basil, Filled Flatbread, Green Topping, Kaffir Noodles, Melon,
Multi-Colored Soups, Pesto Pasta, Potato Cakes, Quinoa, Red Broth,
Steamed Sprouted Lentil Salad, Vegetable Sauté, White Beans and Herbs

-Basil, Sacred (Ocimum tenuiflorum): Flower Waters and Infusions, Pigeon Peas

-Basil, Thai (O. basilicum var. anise): Broiled Pineapple, Cooked Greens, Sweet

Mung Soup, Vegetable Saute

-Bay Leaves (Laurus nobilis): Beet and Cabbage Soup, Celeriac with Spinach
Sauce, Digestive Teas. Kale Soup, Leek and Oat Soup, Math Beans, Beets
and Kumquats, Mixed Vegetable Soup, Multi-Colored Soups, Potato Soup,
Red Broth, Sunchokes and Brussels Sprouts, Yellow Split Pea Spread, White
Beans and Herbs

-Beans:
    Aduki (Vigna angularis): Rice and Sweet Aduki Beans, Sculpted Aduki Beans
    Black: Black Beans
    Black-eyed peas: Black-Eyed Pea Salad-East, Black-Eyed Pea Salad-West
    Borlotti: Borlotti Beans
    Broad (Vicia faba): Artichoke and Broad Beans, Broad Bean Soup
    Chickpeas (Cicer arietinum): A Customable Platter, Chickpeas Dukkah,
    Chickpeas Kebsa
    Chickpea Flour: Buckwheat-Besan crepes, Chickpea Flour Sauce, Sautéed
    Celery Pancakes, Pan-Cooked Chickpea Snack, Vegetable Besan
    Green (Phaseolus vulgaris): Boiled Salad, Coconut Soup, Green Beans and
    Walnuts, Noodle Soup, Pancake-Wrapped Vegetables, Pigeon Peas, Soybean
    Salad, Taro and Sorrel Hotpot, Vegetables Za'atar
    Kidney (Phaseolus vulgaris): Bean and Vegetable Casserole, Kale Soup
    Lima (Phaseolus lunatus): Bean and Rye Patties
    Math (Dew) (Vigna aconitifolius): Math Beans, Beets and Kumquats
    Mung (Vigna mungo/radiata): Chef's Kichuri, Mung Dal, Mung Dal Too, Sweet
    Mung Soup, Val Dal, Val Vegetable Soup, Yellow Dal
    Mung Flour: Mung and Okra, Nuts in Mung Flour
    Pigeon Peas (Cajanus canus): Pigeon Peas
    Pinto: Bean Hotpot
    Soy (Glycine max): Soybean Salad
    White: White Beans and Herbs
    Yard Long (Vigna unguiculate): Coconut Soup, Noodle Soup, Soybean Salad,
    Vegetables Za'atar

-Beet (Beta vulgaris) Greens: Cooked Greens
    -Root: Applesauce Vegetables, Beet and Cabbage Soup, Beetroot Pudding,
    Math Beans, Beets and Kumquats, Multi-Colored Soups, Oven-Baked Veg-
    etables, Sweet Beets

-Berries: Berry Stew, Blueberry Lemon Mini-Cakes, Lily-Pillies and Mulberries,
    Mulberry Tarts

-Besan: see Beans, Chickpea Flour

-Blueberries (Vaccinium corybosum): Blueberry Lemon Mini Cakes

-Bitter Melon (Momordica charantia): Barley Dumpling Soup

-Bok Choi (Brassica chinensis): Cooked Greens, Curried Greens, Multi-Colored Soups

-Boniato: See Sweet Potato

-Borage (Borago officinalis) Flowers: Yellow Split Pea Spread

-Brazil Nuts (Bertholletia excelsa): Custard Apple, Nut Porridge

-Broccoli (Brassica oleracea convar. botyris var italica): Boiled Salad, Broccoli, Broccoli Pastries, Choko, Celeriac and Broccoli Broth, Kaffir Noodles, Vegetable Parcels, Vegetable Sauté

-Brussels Sprouts (Brassica oleracea convar. fruticose var. gemmifera): Sunchokes and Brussels Sprouts

-Buckwheat (Fagopyrum esculentum): Kasha Flatbread, Steamed Buns
-Flour: Buckwheat-Besan Crepes, Buckwheat Flatbread and Pasta, Buckwheat-Grain Pancakes, Pine and Thyme

-Butter, sweet: Broccoli Pastries, Ghee, Mulberry Tarts

-Cabbage, Chinese (Brassica pekinensis): Chinese Cabbage and Chestnuts, Cooked Greens, Curried Greens, Multi-Colored Soups

-Cabbage, White (Brassica oleracea convar. capitata var. capitata f. alba): Beet and Cabbage Soup, Cabbage and Seeds

-Cabbage, Red (Brassica oleracea convar. capitata var. capitata f. rubra): Cabbage Sauté

-Cape Gooseberry: (Physalis peruviana): Papaya and Gooseberries

-Capsicum (Capsicum annum): (sweet pepper) Black-Eyed Pea Salad-West, Choko Salsa, Coconut Soup, Grilled Vegetables, Jicama Salad, Mung and Okra, Noodle Soup, Red Lentils, Roasted Red Pepper Dip, Vegetables Za'atar

-Carambola: see Star Fruit

-Caraway (Carium carvi): Barley and Dill Soup, Bean and Rye Patties, Cream of Rice, Plum Dumplings, Pumpkin Soup, Red Broth, Rye Flatbread, Sautéed Celery Pancakes, White Beans and Herbs, Yellow Dal

-Cardamom, Black (Amomum subulatum): Pigeon Peas

-Green (Elletaria cardmomum): Basic Gourmet Milk, Carrot and Milk Pudding, Chickpeas Kebsa, Curried Greens, Dark Yellow Rice, Digestive and Doshic Teas, Flavorpot, Griddlecakes, Sweet and Savory, Millet Berbere, Nut Chutney, Nut Porridge, Oat Biscuits, Pigeon Peas, Pine Nut and Rice Porridge, Plum Sauce, Rice, Sesame, Almonds and Dates, Spiced Honey Drink, Stonefruit Spread, Turnip, Yellow Dal

-Carob (Ceratonia siliqua): Carob Ginger, Hazelnut Biscuits, Honey Shapes

-Carrots (Daucus carota): A Customable Platter, Applesauce Vegetables, Baked Grated Vegetables, Bean and Vegetable Casserole, Beet and Cabbage Soup, Boiled Salad, Burdock and Carrot, Carrot and Milk Pudding, Chef's Kichuri, Fennel, Cucumber and Carrot, Grilled Vegetables, Kale Soup, Leeks and Rice, Multi-Colored Soups, Oven-Baked Vegetables, Pancake-Wrapped Vegetables, Pine Nuts and Vegetables, Pomegranate Lentil Soup, Red Lentil Soup, Steamed Rice in Mugs, Sunchokes and Brussels Sprouts, Thick Vegetable Soup, Val Vegetable Soup, Vegetable Sauté, White Beans and Herbs

-Cashews (Annacardium occidentale): Carrot and Milk Pudding, Festive Rice, Nuts in Mung Flour, Nut Porridge

-Cauliflower (Brassica oleracea convar.botyris var.botyris): Applesauce Vegetables, Bean and Vegetable Casserole, Exotically Spiced Vegetables, Sesame Seed Salad, Vegetable Besan

-Celeriac (Apium graveolens): Celeriac with Spinach Sauce, Choko, Celeriac and Broccoli Broth, Vegetable Parcels, White Beans and Herbs

-Celery (Apium graveolens): Avocado Soup, Boiled Salad, Celeriac with Spinach Sauce, Chef's Kichuri, Chestnut Sauce, Choko Salsa, Coconut Soup, Mixed Vegetable Soup, Okra and Pumpkin, Oven-Baked Vegetables, Pancake-Wrapped Vegetables, Potato Soup, Sautéed Celery Pancakes, Savory Milk Casserole, Sunchoke Soup, Sunchokes and Brussels Sprouts, Thick Vegetable Soup, Val Vegetable Soup, Vegetable Parcels, Vegetable Sauté, White Beans
  - Seed: Chestnut Sauce, Grilled Vegetables, Sautéed Celery Pancakes

-Chamomile (Matricaria recutata): (German): Flower Waters, Yellow Split Pea Spread

-Chard (Beta vulgaris var vulgaris/flavescens): Cooked Greens, Curried Greens, Multi-Colored Soups

-Cherries (Prunus avium): Dried: Dried Fruit in Green Tea
  - Fresh, Sweet: Fruit in Agar-Agar, Peach and Cherry Compote
  - Fresh, Sour: Berry Stew

-Chervil (Anthriscus cerfolium): Ghee with Herbs

-Chestnuts (Castanea sativa): Chestnut Sauce, Chinese Cabbage and Chestnuts

-Chia (Salvia rhyacophilia): Yellow Split Pea Spread

-Chickpeas and Chickpea Flour: see Beans

-Chicory (Witlof, radicchio) (Cichorium intybus): Cooked Greens, Curried Greens, Multi-Colored Soups, Yellow Split Pea Spread

-Chives (Allium tuberosum/schoenprasum): Cornbread, Cucumber and Apple Salad, Millet and Rice, Multi-Colored Soups, Potato and Parsnip, Savory Cake with Fresh Herbs, Soybean Salad

-Choko (Sechium edule): Choko, Celeriac and Broccoli Broth, Choko, Lime and Thyme, Choko Salsa, Soybean Salad

-Chrysanthemum (Chrysanthemum coronarium) Greens: Cooked Greens, Curried Greens, Multi-Colored Soups

-Chyawanprash: Chyawanprash and Milk

-Cinnamon (Cinnamonum verum): A Customable Platter, Bean and Rye Patties, Bean and Vegetable Casserole, Berry Stew, Black Beans, Borlotti Beans, Broad Bean Soup, Bzar Potatoes, Chickpea Flour Sauce, Chickpeas Dukkah, Chickpeas Kebsa, Coconut Cookies, Cream of Rice, Dark Yellow Rice, Digestive Teas, Festive Rice, Filled Orange Crescents, Flavorpot, Grape-Fruit Juice, Griddlecakes, Sweet and Savory, Jerk Broth, Jicama Salad, Leek and Oat Soup, Loquat Tart, Math Beans, Beets and Kumquats, Nut Chutney, Nut Porridge, Oat Biscuits, Pancake-Wrapped Vegetables, Papaya, Peach and Cherry Compote, Pepper Fruit Syrup, Pigeon Peas, Potato Cakes, Quince Spread, Red Lentil Soup, Rice, Rice and Sweet Aduki Beans, Seeds, Figs and Apples, Spiced Honey Drink, Stonefruit Spread, Stove-Top Cooked Grain, Stuffed Potato Patties, Sweet Rice Dumplings, Sweet Walnuts, Val Dal, Vegetable Besan

-Cloves (Syzgium aromaticum): Black Beans, Bzar Potatoes, Chickpeas Kebsa, Coconut Cookies, Dark Yellow Rice, Flavorpot, Grape-Fruit Juice, Millet Berbere, Nut Chutney, Oat Biscuits, Peach and Cherry Compote, Pigeon Peas, Potato Soup, Rhubarb and Strawberries, Rice and Sweet Aduki Beans, Spiced Honey Drink, Sunchokes and Brussels Sprouts, Vegetable Sauté

-Coconut (Cocus nucifera): Black-Eyed Pea Salad-East, Coconut Cookies, Coconut Soup, Curried Plantains, Dark Rice and Sweet Potato, Honey Shapes, Kaffir Noodles, Mung Dal Too, Mung and Okra, Noodle Soup, Nut Slice, Oat

Biscuits, Pineapple and Coconut, Stove-Top Cooked Grain, Vegetable Besan

-Cream or Milk: Asparagus, East and West, Coconut Soup, Okra and Pumpkin, Steamed Yam Cake
-Oil: Coconut Cookies, Okra and Pumpkin, Steamed Yam Cake

-Collard Greens (Brassica oleracea var. accphala): Cooked Greens, Curried Greens, Kale Soup, Multi-Colored Soups

-Coriander (Coriandrum sativum): Leaves: Artichoke and Broad Beans, Avocado Soup, Bean and Rye Patties, Burdock and Carrot, Chef's Kichuri, Chickpeas Kebsa, Choko, Lime and Thyme, Choko Salsa, Cilantro-Mint Dressing, Cooked Greens, Dark Yellow Rice, Festive Rice, Green Split Peas and Aubergine, Jerk Broth, Lentils and Noodles, Macadamia Pesto, Mango, Math Beans, Beets and Kumquats, Millet Berbere, Millet and Rice, Multi-coloured Soups, Mung Dal, Mung Dal Too, Pancake-Wrapped Vegetables (roots), Pigeon Peas, Pineapple and Coconut, Pomegranate Lentil Soup, Rice, Rice and Urad Dal Patties, Savory Cake with Herbs, Taro Rounds, Taro and Sorrel Hotpot, Toor Dal, Twice-Cooked Rice, Val Vegetable Soup, Vegetable Parcels, Vegetable Sauté, Wheat Noodles, Yellow Split Pea Spread
-Seeds or ground: Artichoke and Broad Beans, Avocado, Avocado Soup, Barley Dumpling Soup, Barley Tonic, Bean and Rye Patties, Bean Hotpot, Borlotti Beans, Broiled Pineapple, Buckwheat-Besan Crepes, Bzar Potatoes, Chef's Kichuri, Chickpea Flour Sauce, Chickpeas Dukkah, Chickpeas Kebsa, Cucumber Salad, Curried Greens, Curried Plantains, Dark Yellow Rice, Digestive Teas, Exotically Spiced Vegetables, Festive Rice, Lemon Rind Chutney, Lily-Pillies and Mulberries, Mango, Millet Berbere, Multi-Colored Soups, Mung Dal, Noodle Soup, Nut and Seed Garnish, Oatcakes, Oven-Baked Vegetables, Pancake-Wrapped Vegetables, Pan-Sautéed Eggplant, Peach Cake, Pear Cake, Pigeon Peas, Plum Sauce, Pumpkin Seeds, Rice, Red Broth, Rye Flatbread, Sculpted Aduki Beans, Steamed Buns, Twice-Cooked Rice, Val Vegetable Soup, Vegetable Besan, Wheat Noodles

-Cornmeal (Zea mays): (polenta, ground maize) Cornbread

-Cranberries (Vaccinium macrocarpon): Dried: Dried Fruit in Green Tea

-Cress (Lepidium sativum): Multi-Colored Soup, Yellow Split Pea Spread

-Cucumber (Cucumis sativa): Black-Eyed Pea Salad-East, Cucumber and Apple Salad, Cucumber Salad, Fennel, Cucumber and Carrot

-Cumin (Cuminum cyminum): Seeds or ground: A Customable Platter, Adaptable Flatbread, Bean and Rye Patties, Bean and Vegetable Casserole, Beet and Cabbage Soup, Black-Eyed Pea Salad-West, Broccoli Pastries, Buckwheat-Besan Crepes, Bzar Potatoes, Chef's Kichuri, Chickpea Flour Sauce,

Chickpeas Dukkah, Chickpeas Kebsa, Curried Greens, Curried Plantains, Dark Yellow Rice, Date-Mint Chutney, Digestive Teas, Exotically Spiced Vegetables, Festive Rice, Green Split Peas and Aubergine, Griddlecakes, Sweet and Savory, Macadamia Pesto, Millet Berbere, Multi-Colored Soups, Mung Dal, Mung Dal Too, Noodle Soup, Nut and Seed Garnish, Nuts in Mung Flour, Pancake-Wrapped Vegetables, Pan-Cooked Chickpea Snack, Pan-Sautéed Eggplant, Pigeon Peas, Plum Dumplings, Pomegranate Lentil Soup, Pumpkin Seeds, Puy Lentils, Rice, Rice and Urad Dal Patties, Roasted Red Pepper Dip, Sautéed Celery Pancakes, Sesame Seed Salad, Soft Cheese with Spices, Spice and Nut Flatbread, Sunchokes and Brussels Sprouts, Toor Dal, Twice Cooked Rice, Val Dal, Val Vegetable Soup, Wheat Noodles, Yellow Dal

-Currants (Ribes nigrum): Dried Fruit in Green Tea, Festive Rice

-Curry Leaves (Murraya koenigii): Festive Rice, Noodle Soup, Pan-Cooked Chickpea Snack

-Custard Apple (Asimina triloba): Custard Apple

-Daikon (Raphanus sativus var. sativus): Barley Dumpling Soup, Pancake-Wrapped Vegetables
-Dal: see Lentils

-Dandelion Greens (Taraxacum officinale): Cooked Greens, Curried Greens, Digestive and Doshic Teas, Multi-Colored Soups, Turnip, Yellow Split Pea Spread

-Dates (Phoenix dactylefera): Date-Mint Chutney, Date Slice, Dried Fruit in Green Tea, Sesame, Almonds and Dates

-Dates, Chinese (Ziziphus jujube): Dark Rice and Sweet Potato, Dried Fruit in Green Tea, Pine Nut and Rice Porridge

-Dill (Anethum graveolens): Fresh: Barley and Dill Soup, Bean Hotpot, Cucumber Salad, Multi-Colored Soups, Pumpkin Soup
-Seeds: Cucumber Salad

-Dragon Fruit (Hylocereus undatus): Fruit in Agar-Agar

-Drumsticks (Moringa oleifera): Pigeon Peas

-Eggplant: Aubergine or Japanese (Solanum melongena): A Customable Platter, Eggplant and Basil, Green Split Peas and Aubergine, Grilled Vegetables, Pan-Sautéed Eggplant

-Endive (Cichorium endive): Cooked Greens, Curried Greens, Multi-Colored Soups, Turnip, Yellow Split Pea Spread

-Feijoa (Acca sellowana): Feijoas

-Fennel (Foeniculum vulgare): Bulb: Brown Lentil Hotpot, Fennel, Cucumber and Carrot, Mixed Vegetable Soup, Pumpkin and Fennel
 -Flowers: Yellow Split Pea Spread
 -Fronds: Yellow Split Pea Spread
 -Seeds: Beet and Cabbage Soup, Choko, Celeriac and Broccoli Broth, Digestive Teas, Exotically Spiced Vegetables, Filled Flatbread, Flavorpot, Oven-Baked Vegetables, Pear Cake, Plum Dumplings, Pumpkin and Fennel, Quinoa, Rice, Rye Rounds, Steamed Buns, Sweet Mung Soup, Toor Dal

-Fenugreek (Trigonella foenum-graecum): Leaves: Millet and Rice
 -Seeds: Barley and Dill Soup, Buckwheat-Besan Crepes, Curried Greens, Exotically Spiced Vegetables, Millet Berbere, Multi-Colored Soups, Mung Dal, Oven-Baked Vegetables, Pigeon Peas, Toasted Sun Seeds, Toor Dal, Twice-Cooked Rice, Wheat Noodles

-Fiddlehead Fern (Pteridium aquilinum): Asparagus East and West, Grilled Vegetables, Juniper and Vegetables, Noodle Soup

-Figs (Ficus carica): Dried Fruit in Green Tea, Nut Slice, Seeds, Figs and Apples

-Five Spice Powder: Cabbage Sauté

-Flours: see individual grains, lentils and beans

-Galangal (Alpinia galangal): Dark Yellow Rice, Fruit in Agar-Agar, Noodle Soup, Pancake-Wrapped Vegetables, Vegetable Parcels

-Garam Masala: Exotically Spiced Vegetables

-Ginger (Zingiber officinale): Fresh: Aloe Aperitif, Beetroot Pudding, Black Beans, Broccoli, Buckwheat Besan Crepes, Burdock and Carrot, Chef's Kichuri, Chinese Cabbage and Chestnuts, Choko, Celeriac and Broccoli Broth, Dark Yellow Rice, Digestive Teas, Dried Fruit in Green Tea, Feijoas, Flavorpot, Ginger Syrup, Ginger Tea, Leek and Oat Soup, Leeks with Ginger, Lemon Rind Chutney, Math Beans, Beets and Kumquats, Multi-Colored Soups, Noodle Soup, Pancake-Wrapped Vegetables, Pan-Cooked Chickpea Snack, Papaya, Pigeon Peas, Pineapple and Coconut, Pine Nuts and Vegetables, Plum Sauce, Spiced Honey Drink, Sweet Beets, Twice-Cooked Rice, Vegetable Parcels
 -Ground: Adaptable Flatbread, Artichoke and Broad Beans, Avocado, Blueberry Lemon Mini Cakes, Borlotti Beans, Broiled Pineapple, Buckwheat Flat-

bread and Pasta, Buckwheat-Grain Pancakes, Bzar Potatoes, Cabbage Sauté, Carob Ginger, Cilantro-Mint Dressing, Coconut Cookies, Coconut Soup, Cream of Rice, Curried Plantains, Dark Rice and Sweet Potato, Date Slice, Digestive Teas, Donuts in Rose Syrup, Flavored Almonds, Fruit in Agar-Agar, Green Split Peas and Aubergine, Honey Shapes, Millet Berbere, Multi-Colored Soups, Noodle Soup, Nut Porridge, Oatcakes, Oat Biscuits, Pan-Sautéed Eggplant, Pear Cake, Pine Nut and Rice Porridge, Prune Chutney, Red Lentil Soup, Rice and Sweet Aduki Beans, Spice and Nut Flatbread, Steamed Buns, Steamed Yam Cake, Taro Rounds, Val Vegetable Soup, Vegetable Besan, Wheat Noodles

-Grapefruit (Citrus grandis): Flower Waters, Grape-Fruit Juice, Marmalade Syrup, Pears and Anise

-Grapes (Vitis vinifera): Grape-Fruit Juice

-Grape Vine Leaves: Baked Rice and Vine Leaves

-Green Beans: see Beans

-Greens: Applesauce Vegetables, Cabbage Sauté, Celeriac with Spinach Sauce, Coconut Soup, Cooked Greens, Curried Greens, Leek and Oat Soup, Multi-Colored Soups, Turnip, Val Vegetable Soup, Yellow Split Pea Spread

-Guava (Psidium guajava): Fruit in Agar-Agar

-Hazelnuts (Corybus avellana/maximus): Broad Bean Soup, Hazelnut Biscuits, Nut and Seed Garnish, Nut Slice

-Hibiscus (Hibiscus rosa-sinensis): Flower Waters and Infusions

-Honey, unprocessed, unfired: Aloe Aperitif, Basic Gourmet Milk, Borlotti Beans, Buckwheat-Grain Pancakes, Carob Ginger, Cilantro-Mint Dressing, Cream of Rice, Digestive Teas, Feijoas, Ginger Tea, Griddlecakes, Sweet and Savory, Honey Shapes, Lemon Rind Chutney, Lime-Aide, Math Beans, Beets and Kumquats, Nut Porridge, Pepper Fruit Syrup, Quince Spread, Spiced Honey Drink, Sweet Beets, Sweet Rice Dumplings

-Honeysuckle (Lonicera japonica): Flower Waters and Infusions

-Jasmine (Jasminium grandiflorum or officinale): Flower Waters and Infusions

-Jerusalem Artichokes: see Sunchokes

-Jicama (Pachyrhizus erosus): (yam bean) Jicama Salad

-Jujubes: see Dates, Chinese

-Juniper Berries (Juniperus communis): Applesauce Vegetables, Juniper and
  Vegetables
-Kaffir Lime Leaves (Citrus hystrix): Flavored Almonds, Kaffir Noodles, Noodle
  Soup, Pancake-Wrapped Vegetables, Vegetable Parcels

-Kale (Brassica oleracea convar. acephala var. sabellica): Kale Soup

-Kiwi Fruit (Actinidia deliciosa): Steamed Buns

-Kohlrabi (Brassica oleracea convar. acephala var. gongylodes): Kohlrabi Stew,
  White Beans and Herbs

-Kudzu (Pueraria lobata): Beetroot Pudding

-Kumquats (Eremocitrus glauca): Math Beans, Beets and Kumquats

-Lamb's Lettuce, Corn Salad or Mache (Valerianella locusta): Cooked Greens,
  Curried Greens, Multi-Colored Soups, Yellow Split Pea Spread

-Lavender (Lavandula angustifolia): Flower Waters, Mixed Vegetable Soup

-Leeks (Allium porrum): Brown Lentil Hotpot, Leek and Oat Soup, Leeks and
  Rice, Leeks with Ginger Root, Thick Vegetable Soup, White Beans and Herbs

-Legumes: see Lentils

-Lemon Grass (Cymbopogon citriatus): Dark Yellow Rice, Flavored Almonds,
  Noodle Soup, Pancake-Wrapped Vegetables, Vegetable Parcels

-Lettuce (Lactuca sativa): Barley and Dill Soup, Coconut Soup, Peas, Lettuce,
  Potatoes, Yellow Split Pea Spread

-Lentils (Lens culinaris):
  Brown: Brown Lentil Hotpot, Lentils and Noodles, Pomegranate Lentil Soup,
  Steamed Sprouted Lentils
  Green Split Peas (Pisum sativum): Green Split Peas and Aubergine, Multi-
  Colored Soups
  Puy: Puy Lentils
  Red: Red Lentils, Red Lentil Soup
  Toor: Toor Dal, Yellow Dal
  Urad (Vigna mungo): Toor Dal
  Urad Flour: Rice and Urad Dal Patties
  Val: (Lab Lab): Bean and Rye Patties, Val Dal, Val Vegetable Soup
  Yellow Split Peas (Pisum sativum): Multi-Colored Soups, Yellow Dal, Yellow

Split Pea Spread

-Licorice Root (Glycyrrhiza glaubra): Barley Tonic, Flavorpot, Twice-Cooked Rice

-Lily-Pillies (Syzgium australe): Lily-Pillies and Mulberries

-Lime (Citrus aurantifolia): Avocado Soup, Chinese Cabbage and Chestnuts, Choko, Lime and Thyme, Choko Salsa, Curried Plantains, Dark Yellow Rice, Flower Waters, Ghee Maitre D'Hotel, Jerk Broth, Kaffir Noodles, Leeks with Ginger, Lime-Aid, Mango, Marmalade Syrup, Mung and Okra, Noodle Soup, Okra and Pumpkin, Pumpkin Seed Sauce, Soybean Salad, Vegetable Sauté

-Linseed (Linum usitatissimum): (Flax) Broccoli, Mung and Okra, Oat Biscuits, Pears and Anise, Prune Chutney, Savory Cake with Herbs, Seed Crackers, Seeds, Figs and Apples, Stove-Top Cooked Grain

-Lovage (Levisticum officinale): White Beans and Herbs

-Loquats (Eriobotrya japonica): Loquat Tart

-Lotus (Nelumbo nucifera) Root: Lotus Root Salad
    -Seeds: Tamarind Chutney

-Lychees (Litchi chinensis.): Fruit in Agar-Agar

-Macadamia Nuts (Macadamia integrifolia/tetraphylla): Dark Yellow Rice, Macadamia Pesto, Peach Cake

-Mace (Myrstica fragrans): Sunchokes and Brussels Sprouts

-Malanga (Xanthosoma sp.): use in Taro recipes

-Mandarin (Citrus deliciosa): Burdock and Carrot, Flower Waters, Marmalade Syrup, Orange Muffin Cakes, Tamarind Chutney

-Mango (Mangifera indica) Dried: Dried Fruit in Green Tea
    -Fresh: Fruit in Agar-Agar, Mango

-Mango, Green: see Amchoor

-Maple Syrup (Acer saccharum): Barley-Millet Porridge, Basic Gourmet Milk, Berry Stew, Buckwheat-Grain Pancakes, Carrot and Milk Pudding, Cream of Rice, Custard Apple, Griddlecakes, Sweet and Savory, Nut Porridge, Papaya and Cape Gooseberries, Pineapple and Coconut, Plum Sauce, Sweet Rice Dumplings, Tamarind Chutney, Wheat Berry Porridge

-Marjoram (Origanum spp.): Grilled Vegetables, Juniper and Vegetables, Mixed Vegetable Soup, Multi-Colored Soups, Potato Soup, Pumpkin and Fennel, Red Broth, White Beans and Herbs, Wild Rice and Pecans

-Melon (Cucumis melo): Melon

-Milk, raw or non-homogenized: Basic Gourmet Milk, Berry Stew, Carob Ginger, Carrot and Milk Pudding, Chyawanprash and Milk, Condensed Milk, Mung Dal Too, Savory Milk Casserole, Soft Cheese, Soft Cheese with Spices, Spiced Honey Drink, Yellow Dal

-Millet (Panicum miliaceum and African var.): Barley-Millet Porridge, Buckwheat-Grain Pancakes, Griddlecakes, Sweet and Savory, Millet Berbere, Millet and Rice, Potato Soup, Stove-Top Cooked Grain
  -Flour: Cornbread, Savory Cake with Herbs

-Mint (Mentha sp): Flowers: Yellow Split Pea Spread
  -Leaves: Bean Hotpot, Black-Eyed Pea Salad-East, Broiled Pineapple, Buckwheat-Besan Crepes, Choko Salsa, Cilantro-Mint Dressing, Date-Mint Chutney, Dried Fruit in Green Tea, Filled Flatbread, Flower Waters, Fruit in Agar-Agar, Grape-Fruit Juice, Lemon Mint Rice, Melon, Millet and Rice, Rice, Peas, Lettuce, Potatoes, Quinoa, Spiced Honey Drink, Sweet Beets, Sweet Mung Soup, Yellow Split Pea Spread
-Mitsuba (Cryptotaenia japonica): Cooked Greens, Curried Greens, Multi-Colored Soups

-Mizuna (Brassica juncea var. japonica): Cabbage Sauté, Cooked Greens, Curried Greens, Multi-Colored Soups

-Mulberries (Morus alba/nigra): Lily-Pillies and Mulberries, Mulberry Tarts

-Mustard (Brassica juncea var.): Greens: Cooked Greens, Curried Greens, Multi-Colored Soups
  -Oil: a good oil for Kapha in small amounts
  -Seeds: Asparagus, East and West, Beet and Cabbage Soup, Black Beans, Black-Eyed Pea Salad-West, Celeriac with Spinach Sauce, Chef's Kichuri, Chickpea Flour Sauce, Cucumber Salad, Festive Rice, Green Beans and Walnuts, Grilled Vegetables, Lemon Rind Chutney, Multi-Colored Soups, Mung Dal, Oven-Baked Vegetables, Pumpkin Seeds, Pumpkin Seed Sauce, Rice and Urad Dal Patties, Steamed Rice in Mugs

-Nasturtium (Tropaeolum majus): Barley and Dill Soup, Barley Dumpling Soup, Flower Waters, Peas, Lettuce, Potatoes, Yellow Split Pea Spread

-Nectarines (Prunus persica var): Stonefruit Spread

-Nigella Seeds (Nigella sativa) (Kalonji): Baked Grated Vegetables, Baked Potato Cakes, Barley and Dill Soup, Chickpea Flour Sauce, Mung Dal, Oven-Baked Vegetables, Potato and Parsnip, Toor Dal, Val Vegetable Soup

-Noodles: Lentils and Noodles, Noodle Soup, Wheat Noodles

-Nori: see Sea Vegetables

-Nuts: see individual varieties, also: Barley-Millet Porridge, Leeks with Ginger, Stuffed Potato Patties

-Nutmeg (Myrstica fragrans): Basic Gourmet Milk, Broccoli Pastries, Broiled Pineapple, Buckwheat-Grain Pancakes, Chickpeas Kebsa, Coconut Cookies, Curried Plantains, Custard Apple, Dark Yellow Rice, Digestive Teas, Hazelnut Biscuits, Jerk Broth, Jicama Salad, Millet Berbere, Nut Chutney, Nut Slice, Oat Biscuits, Peach Cake, Pigeon Peas, Pumpkin Sauce, Quince Spread, Saffron Crackers, Spiced Honey Drink, Steamed Apples, Sunchokes and Brussels Sprouts, Taro and Sorrel Hotpot, Vegetable Besan, Vegetable Sauté, White Beans and Herbs

-Oats (Avena sativa) Rolled: Date Slice, Leek and Oat Soup, Multi-Colored Soups, Oat Biscuits, Oatcakes
  -Whole: Stove-top Cooked Grain

-Okra (Abelmoschus esculentus): A Customable Platter, Mung and Okra, Okra and Pumpkin, Vegetables Za'atar

-Olive Oil (Olea europaea): A Customable Platter, Artichoke and Broad Beans, Asparagus, East and West, Avocado Soup, Baked Rice and Vine Leaves, Bean and Vegetable Casserole, Black-Eyed Pea Salad-West, Broad Bean Soup, Brown Lentil Hotpot, Bzar Potatoes, Chickpeas Dukkah, Filled Flatbread, Green Beans and Walnuts, Green Split Peas and Aubergine, Green Topping, Kale Soup, Lemon Mint Rice, Leeks and Rice, Lentils and Noodles, Macadamia Pesto, Oven-Baked Vegetables, Pan-Sautéed Eggplant, Pesto Pasta, Pine and Thyme, Pistachio Dressing, Pomegranate Lentil Soup, Pumpkin and Fennel, Pumpkin Sauce, Puy Lentils, Roasted Red Pepper Dip, Savory Cake with Herbs, Sculpted Aduki Beans, Sesame Seed Salad, Soybean Salad, Steamed Sprouted Lentils, Vegetables Za'atar, White Beans and Herbs, Yellow Split Pea Spread

-Oranges (Citrus aurantifolia var. sinensis): Asparagus, East and West, Avocado, Bean Hotpot, Buckwheat-Grain Pancakes, Burdock and Carrot, Carrot and Milk Pudding, Celeriac with Spinach Sauce, Cilantro-Mint Dressing, Date Slice, Filled Flatbread, Filled Orange Crescents, Flower Waters, Jicama Salad, Marmalade Syrup, Mulberry Tarts, Orange Muffin Cakes, Papaya, Plum Dumplings, Prune Chutney, Pumpkin Sauce, Quinoa, Rhubarb and Straw-

berries, Tamarind Chutney, Wheat Berry Porridge
-Blossoms: Filled Orange Crescents, Flower Waters

-Oregano (Origanum vulgare spp.): Filled Flatbread, Multi-Colored Soup, Puy
Lentils, Quinoa, Sautéed Celery Pancakes, Val Vegetable Soup, Val Dal, Vegetable Sauté, Vegetables Za'atar, Yellow Split Pea Spread
-Cuban O. (Coleus amboinicus): a small amount of fresh leaf can be substituted for oregano in any of the above recipes

-Papaya (Carica papaya): Dried: Dried Fruit in Green Tea
-Fresh: Papaya, Papaya and Cape Gooseberries

-Paprika (Capsicum tetragonum): A Customable Platter, Baked Rice and Vine
Leaves, Barley Dumpling Soup, Bean and Rye Patties, Broccoli Pastries,
Green Split Peas and Aubergine, Grilled Vegetables, Macadamia Pesto, Pan-
Sautéed Eggplant, Pine and Thyme, Red Broth, Red Lentil Soup

-Parsley (Petroselinum crispum): A Customable Platter, Artichoke and Broad
Beans, Barley and Dill Soup, Bean Hotpot, Boiled Salad, Broad Bean Soup,
Broccoli Pastries, Brown Lentil Hotpot, Chickpeas Dukkah, Choko Salsa,
Ghee Maitre D'Hotel, Green Topping, Kohlrabi Stew, Macadamia Pesto, Mil-
let and Rice, Multi-Colored Soups, Okra and Pumpkin, Peas, Lettuce, Pota-
toes, Pomegranate Lentil Soup, Potato and Parsnip, Potato Soup, Puy Len-
tils, Red Lentils, Sculpted Aduki Beans, Sesame Seed Salad, Sticky Rice Balls,
Stuffed Potato Patties, Sunchokes and Brussels Sprouts, Thick Vegetable
Soup, Vegetable Sauté, White Beans and Herbs, Wild Rice and Pecans, Yellow
Split Pea Spread

-Parsnip (Pastinaca sativa): Baked Grated Vegetables, Grilled Vegetables, Juniper and Vegetables, Multi-Colored Soups, Oven-Baked Vegetables, Potato and
Parsnip, Potato Soup, Thick Vegetable Soup, White Beans and Herbs

-Pasta (see also Noodles): Kale Soup

-Peaches (Prunus persica): Dried: Dried Fruit in Green Tea
-Fresh: Peach and Cherry Compote, Peach Cake, Stonefruit Spread

-Peas (Pisus sativum): Fresh Green: Filled Flatbread, Peas, Lettuce, Potatoes,
Soft Cheese with Spices, Vegetables Za'atar
Green Split: Green Split Peas and Aubergine, Multi-Colored Soups
Snow: (Pisum sativum ssp. sativum convar. axiphium): (mange tout) A Cus-
tomable Platter, Applesauce Vegetables, Jicama Salad, Lotus Root Salad,
Mung and Okra, Pine Nuts and Vegetables, Soybean Salad, Steamed Rice in
Mugs
Yellow Split: Multi-Colored Soups, Yellow Split Pea Spread

-Pears (Pyrus communis/serotina): Dried: Dried Fruit in Green Tea
   -Fresh: Pears and Anise, Pear Cake

-Pecans (Carya illinoinensis): Nut Slice, Wild Rice and Pecans

-Peppers, Sweet: see Capsicum

-Persimmon (Diospyros kaki): Fruit in Agar-Agar

-Pine nuts (Pinus cembra): Baked Rice and Vine Leaves, Cornbread, Nut Chutney, Pesto Pasta, Pine and Thyme, Pine Nut and Rice Porridge, Pine Nuts
   and Vegetables, Pumpkin Sauce

-Pineapple (Ananas comosus): Dried: Dried Fruit in Green Tea
   -Fresh: Broiled Pineapple, Pineapple and Coconut

-Pistachio Nuts (Pistacia vera): Bean and Rye Patties, Cooked Greens, Cream
   of Rice, Festive Rice, Math Beans, Beets and Kumquats, Millet Berbere, Pistachio Dressing, Quince Spread, Rice and Sweet Aduki Beans, Spice and Nut
   Flatbread
-Plantains (Musa sp.): Curried Plantains

-Plums (Prunus domestica): Plum Sauce, Stonefruit Spread

-Plums, Cherry: Plum Dumplings

-Pomegranate (Punica granatum): Pomegranate Lentil Soup, Roasted Red Pepper Dip

-Potato (Solanum tuberosum): Barley and Dill Soup, Bean and Vegetable Cas-
   serole, Beet and Cabbage Soup, Bzar Potatoes, Chef's Kichuri, Filled Flat-
   bread, Kohlrabi Stew, Mixed Vegetable Soup, Multi-Colored Soups, Oven-
   Baked Vegetables. Peas, Lettuce, Potato, Potato Cakes, Potato and Parsnip,
   Potato Soup, Red Lentils, Sesame Seed Salad, Stuffed Potato Patties, Thick
   Vegetable Soup, Val Vegetable Soup, Vegetables Za'atar

-Prunes (Prunus domestica): Dried Fruit in Green Tea, Prune Chutney

-Pulses: see Lentils

-Pumpkin (Cucurbita maxima): Multi-Colored Soups, Okra and Pumpkin,
   Pumpkin and Fennel, Pumpkin Sauce, Pumpkin Soup
   -Seeds: Broccoli, Okra and Pumpkin, Pumpkin Seeds, Pumpkin Seed Sauce,
   Pumpkin Soup, Red Lentils, Stovetop Cooked Grain, Val Dal, Vegetable Be-
   san

-Purslane or Pigweed (Portulaca oleracea/Montia perfoliata): Cooked Greens, Curried Greens, Multi-Colored Soups
  -Seeds: Seed Crackers

-Quince (Cydonia oblonga): Quince Spread

-Quinoa (Chenopodium quinoa): (Use quinoa in any millet recipe.) Quinoa

-Raisins (Vitis vinifera): Baked Rice and Vine Leaves, Barley-Millet Porridge, Carrot and Milk Pudding, Dried Fruit in Green Tea, Lotus Root Salad, Papaya, Plum Dumplings, Steamed Apples, Stove-Top Cooked Grain

-Raspberries (Rubus idaeus): Berry Stew

-Rhubarb (Rheum rhabarbarum/rhaponticum): Rhubarb and Strawberries

-Rice (Oryza sativa):
  Arborio: Sticky Rice Balls
  Basmati: Chef's Kichuri, Dark Yellow Rice, Festive Rice, Millet and Rice, Rice, Rice Ras el Hanout, Rice and Urad Dal Patties, Steamed Rice in Mugs
  Black: Dark Rice and Sweet Potato
  Brown: Millet and Rice, Potato Soup
  White Long Grain: Baked Rice and Vine Leaves, Lemon Mint Rice
  White Rice Flour: Cream of Rice, Pine Nut and Rice Porridge, Steamed Yam Cake, Sweet Rice Dumplings
  White Short Grain: Multi-Colored Soups, Rice and Sweet Aduki Beans
  Wild (Zizania aquatica): Wild Rice and Pecans

-Rocket (Eruca vesicaria subsp sativa): Barley Dumpling Soup, Multi-Colored Soups, Steamed Sprouted Lentil Salad, Val Vegetable Soup, Yellow Split Pea Spread
-Rose Petals (Rosa spp.): Digestive Teas, Donuts in Rose Syrup, Flower Waters, Yellow Split Pea Spread

-Rosemary (Rosmarinus officinalis): Flowers: Yellow Split Pea Spread
  -Herb: Baked Rice and Vine Leaves, Juniper and Vegetables, Mixed Vegetable Soup, Multi-Colored Soups, Savory Cake with Herbs

-Rutabaga (Brassica napus var. napobrassica): Kale Soup

-Rye flour (Secale cereale): Bean and Rye Patties, Filled Flatbread, Kasha Flatbread, Rye Flatbread, Rye Rounds, Savory Cake with Herbs

-Saffron (Crocus sativus): Barley-Millet Porridge, Basic Gourmet Milk, Broad Bean Soup, Orange Muffin Cakes, Math Beans, Beets and Kumquats, Multi-Colored Soups, Mung Dal Too, Red Lentil Soup, Saffron Crackers, Semolina

Dumplings, Yellow Dal

-Sage (Salvia officinalis/spp.): Cornbread, Green Topping, Multi-Colored Soups, Pumpkin Sauce

-Salad Burnet (Poterium sanguisorba): Yellow Split Pea Spread

-Savory, Summer and Winter (Satureja hortensis/montana): Brown Lentil Hotpot, Puy Lentils, Val Dal, White Beans and Herbs

-Sea Vegetables:
  Agar-Agar: Fruit in Agar-Agar
  Nori (Porphyra sp.): Cabbage Sauté

-Seeds: see individual seeds, also Barley-Millet Porridge, Seed Crackers

-Semolina (Triticum): Semolina Dumplings

-Sesame (Sesamum indicum): Oil: Burdock and Carrot, Cabbage Sauté, Chickpeas Dukkah, Chinese Cabbage and Chestnuts, Eggplant and Basil, Flavorpot, Lotus Root Salad, Noodle Soup, Pancake-Wrapped Vegetables, Pine Nuts and Vegetables, Quince Spread, Steamed Rice in Mugs, Taro and Sorrel Hotpot, Vegetable Parcels
  -Seeds: Beetroot Pudding, Burdock and Carrot, Chickpeas Dukkah, Eggplant and Basil, Honey Shapes, Lotus Root Salad, Math Beans, Beets and Kumquats, Millet and Rice, Multi-Colored Soups, Nut Porridge, Nut and Seed Garnish, Puy Lentils, Red Lentil Soup, Saffron Crackers, Sesame, Almonds and Dates, Sesame Seed Salad, Spice and Nut Flatbread, Spinach Crowns, Steamed Apples, Sticky Rice Balls, Taro and Sorrel Hotpot, Vegetable Parcels, Vegetables Za'atar

-Snow Peas: see Peas

-Sorrel (Rumex rugosus): Cooked Greens, Curried Greens, Multi-Colored Soups, Taro and Sorrel Hotpot, Yellow Split Pea Spread

-Soybeans: see Beans

-Spelt Flour: see Wheat flour

-Spinach, Ceylon (Basella rubra): Cooked Greens, Curried Greens, Multi-Colored Soups
  Egyptian (Malokhia) (Chorchorus olitorius): Cooked Greens, Curried Greens, Multi-Colored Soups
  European (Spinacia oleracea): Applesauce Vegetables, Barley and Dill Soup, Bean Hotpot, Cabbage Sauté, Celeriac with Spinach Sauce, Chef's Kichuri,

Coconut Soup, Cooked Greens, Curried Greens, Leek and Oat Soup, Lentils and Noodles, Multi-Colored Soups, Noodle Soup, Okra and Pumpkin, Pomegranate Lentil Soup, Spinach Crowns

Mountain (Atriplex hortensis) Green or Red: Cooked Greens, Curried Greens, Multi- Colored Soups

New Zealand/Australia (Warrigal greens) (Tetragonia tetragoniodes): Cooked Greens, Curried Greens, Multi-Colored Soups

Water (Kang Kong) (Ipomea aquatica): Cabbage Sauté, Cooked Greens, Curried Greens, Multi-Colored Soups

-Spring Onions (Allium fistulosum): Bzar Potatoes, Cabbage Sauté, Coconut Soup, Flavorpot, Green Beans and Walnuts, Jerk Broth, Multi-Colored Soups, Stuffed Potato Patties, Pine Nuts and Vegetables

-Sprouts:
    Any sprouts: Yellow Split Pea Spread
    Barley: Barley Dumpling Soup
    Fenugreek: Millet and Rice
    Lentil: Steamed Sprouted Lentils
    Mung: Coconut Soup, Kaffir Noodles
    Snow Pea: Lotus Root Salad, Noodle Soup

-Star Anise (Illicium verum): Vegetable Sauté

-Star Fruit (Averrhoa carambola/Psedocydonia sinensis): Steamed Buns

-Strawberries (Fragaria vesca): Berry Stew, Rhubarb and Strawberries

-Sugar, Palm (Palmyra borassus-flabelliformis/Caryota urens) or Cane (Saccharum officinale): Applesauce Vegetables, Avocado, Basic Gourmet Milk, Beetroot Pudding, Berry Stew, Black Beans, Black-Eyed Pea Salad-East, Blueberry Lemon Mini Cakes, Broad Bean Soup, Carob Ginger, Carrot and Milk Pudding, Coconut Cookies, Condensed Milk, Cornbread, Cream of Rice, Custard Apple, Dark Rice and Sweet Potato, Digestive Teas, Donuts in Rose Syrup, Filled Orange Crescents, Flavorpot, Fruit in Agar-Agar, Ginger Syrup, Grilled Vegetables, Hazelnut Biscuits, Jerk Broth, Leek and Oat Soup, Leeks and Rice, Lily-Pillie and Mulberries, Lime-Aid, Lotus Root Salad, Loquat Tart, Marmalade Syrup, Mulberry Tarts, Nut Chutney, Nut Porridge, Oat Biscuits, Orange Muffin Cakes, Pan-Sautéed Eggplant, Papaya and Cape Gooseberries, Peach Cake, Peach and Cherry Compote, Pear Cake, Pineapple and Coconut, Plum Dumplings, Plum Sauce, Potato Cakes, Rice and Sweet Aduki Beans, Roasted Red Pepper Dip, Saffron Crackers, Steamed Apples, Steamed Buns, Steamed Yam Cake, Stonefruit Spread, Sweet Beets, Sweet Mung Soup, Sweet Rice Dumplings, Sweet Walnuts, Tamarind Chutney, Wheat Berry Porridge

-Sultanas (Vitis vinifera): Dried Fruit in Green Tea, Rhubarb and Strawberries

-Sumac (Rhus coriaria): A Customable Platter, Chickpeas Dukkah, Choko, Celeriac and Broccoli Broth, Lentils and Noodles, Pan-Cooked Chickpea Snack, Potato and Parsnip, Red Lentils, Red Lentil Soup, Spinach Crowns, Sticky Rice Balls, Vegetables Za'atar

-Summer Squash: see Zucchini

-Sunchokes (Helianthus tuberosus): Mixed Vegetable Soup, Sunchoke Soup, Sunchokes and Brussels Sprouts

-Sunflower (Helianthus annuus): Oil: Applesauce Vegetables, Buckwheat Besan Crepes, Celeriac with Spinach Sauce, Choko, Lime and Thyme, Cornbread, Fennel, Cucumber and Carrot, Filled Orange Crescents, Grilled Vegetables, Kasha Flatbread, Oatcakes, Peas, Lettuce, Potatoes, Pumpkin Soup, Steamed Buns
-Seeds: Baked Grated Vegetables, Broccoli, Honey Shapes, Lotus Root Salad, Oat Biscuits, Peach Cake, Prune Chutney, Seeds, Figs and Apples, Steamed Buns, Stove-Top Cooked Grain, Toasted Sun Seeds

-Sweet Pepper: see Capsicum

-Sweet Potato (Ipomoea batatas): Dark Rice and Sweet Potato, Grilled Vegetables, Multi-Colored Soups, Pine Nuts and Vegetables, Savory Milk Casserole, Vegetable Besan, Vegetable Parcels

-Tamarillo (Cyphomandra betacea): Papaya and Cape Gooseberries

-Tamarind (Tamarindus indica): Asparagus, East and West, Black Beans, Black-Eyed Pea Salad-East, Coconut Soup, Dark Yellow Rice, Date-Mint Chutney, Fennel, Cucumber and Carrot, Kaffir Noodles, Nuts in Mung Flour, Tamarind Chutney, Taro and Sorrel Hotpot

-Tapioca (Manihot esculenta): Use in Taro recipes or as thickener

-Taro (Colocasia esculenta): Taro Rounds, Taro and Sorrel Hotpot

-Tarragon (Artemisia dracunculus): Asparagus, East and West, Baked Rice and Vine Leaves, Boiled Salad, Broiled Pineapple, Choko, Celeriac and Broccoli Broth, Dried Fruit in Green Tea, Ghee Mâitre d'Hotel, Millet and Rice, Multi-Colored Soups, Val Vegetable Soup

-Tatsoi (Brassica navinosa): Cabbage Sauté, Cooked Greens, Curried Greens, Multi-Colored Soups

-Tea, Green (Camellia sinensis): Dried Fruit in Green Tea

-Thyme (Thymus spp.): Flowers: Yellow Split Pea Spread
  -Herb: Black-Eyed Pea Salad-West, Broccoli Pastries, Chickpeas Dukkah,
  Choko, Lime and Thyme, Choko Salsa, Grilled Vegetables, Jerk Broth, Mixed
  Vegetable Soup, Multi-Colored Soups, Okra and Pumpkin, Pan-Sautéed Egg-
  plant, Pine and Thyme, Soybean Salad, Sunchokes and Brussels Sprouts,
  Vegetable Sauté, Vegetables Za'atar

-Turmeric (Curcuma longa): Basic Gourmet Milk, Bean and Rye Patties, Borlotti
  Beans, Broiled Pineapple, Buckwheat-Besan Crepes, Bzar Potatoes, Chef's
  Kichuri, Chickpea Flour Sauce, Chyawanprash and Milk, Curried Greens,
  Curried Plantains, Dark Yellow Rice, Digestive Teas, Exotically Spiced Veg-
  etables, Festive Rice, Griddlecakes, Sweet and Savory, Lemon Mint Rice,
  Multi-Colored Soups, Mung and Okra, Mung Dal, Mung Dal Too, Noodle
  Soup, Nuts in Mung Flour, Pancake-Wrapped Vegetables, Pan-Sautéed Egg-
  plant, Pineapple and Coconut, Pumpkin Seeds, Red Lentil Soup, Rice, Rice
  and Sweet Aduki Beans, Savory Milk Casserole, Soft Cheese with Spices,
  Stuffed Potato Patties, Toor Dal, Val Dal, Val Vegetable Soup, Yellow Dal,
  Wheat Noodles

-Turnip (Brassica rapa var. rapa): Greens: Cooked Greens, Curried Greens,
  Multi-Colored Soups
  -Root: Kale Soup, Kohlrabi Stew, Oven-Baked Vegetables, Potato Soup, Steamed
  Rice in Mugs, Sunchoke Soup, Turnip, Val Vegetable Soup

-Vanilla (Vanilla planifolia): Condensed Milk

-Violet (Viola odorata/tricolor): Flower Waters and Infusions

-Walnuts (Juglans regia/nigra): Chickpeas Dukkah, Date Slice, Green Beans and
  Walnuts, Green Topping, Roasted Red Pepper Dip, Sculpted Aduki Beans,
  Sweet Rice Dumplings, Sweet Walnuts, Tamarind Chutney

-Watercress (Nasturtium officinale): Millet and Rice, Yellow Split Pea Spread

-Wattle Seeds (Acacia victoriae): Seed Crackers

-Wheat (Triticum sp): Berries: Wheat Berry Porridge
  Wheat Flour: Adaptable Flatbread, Baked Grated Vegetables, Blueberry
  Lemon Mini Cakes, Boiled Salad, Broccoli Pastries, Celeriac with Spinach
  Sauce, Coconut Cookies, Cornbread, Date Slice, Donuts in Rose Syrup, Filled
  Flatbread, Filled Orange Crescents, Griddlecakes, Sweet and Savory, Hand-
  made Pasta, Hazelnut Biscuits, Kasha Flatbread, Loquat Tart, Mulberry
  Tarts, Nut Slice, Oat Biscuits, Orange Muffin Cakes, Pancake-Wrapped Veg-
  etables, Pan-Sautéed Eggplant, Peach Cake, Pear Cake, Pine and Thyme,

Plum Dumplings, Potato Cakes, Saffron Crackers, Savory Cake with Herbs, Seed Crackers, Semolina Dumplings, Spice and Nut Flatbread, Steamed Buns, Stuffed Potato Patties, Sunchokes and Brussels Sprouts

-Winter Squash (Cucurbita maximus): Multi-Colored Soups

-Yam (Dioscorea spp): Pine Nuts and Vegetables, Steamed Yam Cake

-Yuca (Manihot esculenta): use in Taro Recipes

-Zucchini or Summer Squash (Cucurbita pepo ssp. pepo convar. giromontiina): Avocado Soup, Coconut Soup, Exotically Spiced Vegetables, Grilled Vegetables, Steamed Sprouted Lentils, Val Vegetable Soup, Vegetable Besan, Vegetable Sauté

RECIPE INDEX

Recipe

REGARDS

REGARDING THE ILLUSTRATIONS

Photograph details:
Front Cover: Dark Rice and Sweet Potato
Bakery, Savory: Jerusalem, the Old City
Bakery, Sweet: Shwe Dagon, Rangoon, Burma
Beverage: Grandmother and sleeping child, Hill Tribes, Thailand
Dairy: Nepalese girl milking a zhou
Dessert: Uluru and Kata Tjuta, Central Australia
Fruit: Indian sadhu
Nuts and Seeds: Ping Lo Monastery, Lantau Island, Hong Kong
Soup: Man of Northern Pakistan
Staples: Pyramids at Giza, Egypt
Vegetables: Prekerstol, a Norwegian fiord
Reading and Reference: 'Dressed' by Michele Eastwood, artist of Perth, Australia
Appendices: 'Elemental Woman' by Helen Robins, artist of Perth, Australia
Index: Jaisalmer Tea Shop Owner, India
Regards: Jacqueline and parents, outside Lyon, France
Back Cover: Orange Muffin Cakes with Kurrajong Blossoms, Potato and Parsnip and Sweet Rice Dumplings with Amaranth Blossoms.
All photographs by Meta B. and Paul Doherty.

REGARDING YOGA

Both traditional and many contemporary philosophies and studies highlight the mind as a major player in our experiences and their subsequent ramifications. "The mind makes a good servant but a terrible master". What does that mean? There are many modes that it moves in that help us access and integrate our experiences but it also has a mind of its own that runs in small circles and causes us to act upon its misunderstandings. It is a most humbling experience to recognize that your own mind has fabricated information which you believed for a long time! From then on, a compassionate critical literacy develops. The mind is not trying to sabotage us; it is just that its range of thinking is limited, conditioned, automatic. The part of it that produces those patterns is not the part that considers them. Unless we cultivate consideration, the mind runs its own shows and we are the stars. I hope we are getting a good laugh!

The Yoga Sutra-s of Patañjali read for the most part like a psychology primer. They tell us about the incredible things the mind can do when we apply it and the places it can get caught up when we do not. It provides practical methods for gradually moving from distraction to direction, from misunderstanding to clarity. It provides ways to overcome our resistance, our self-imposed obstacles, our frustration and unease, those things that make life bumpy. Not everyone is thrown by the same bumps, which helps us accept that ours must be due to our own concepts and perceptions. When things do not work the way we think they should, we react; let us recognize that mental bias is causing our 'shoulds' in the first place, our reactions to them and our suffering because of them. Develop a pill to alleviate all that and you would make a fortune! But dulling the mind will never reduce our difficulties; observing and clearing the mind will. The recommendations of the yoga sutra-s are based in reality and are available right here, right now.

Mental tension may be more easily recognized as physical tension, illness or tense breathing. It may also appear as uneasiness, incongruence, frustration and depression, both within ourselves and in our relationships. The two mental convictions that cause the most stress, according to the yoga point of view, are "I am the doer" and "It is for me". When we feel stuck, hemmed in, restricted in ideas and actions, when all around us feels to be solid rock and we can see no way out (as Rilke wrote), these convictions have precipitated a chain of thoughts and actions leading to the present. The unease will cause us to want to have things change. It is the natural instinct of all sentient beings to avoid pain. We can thank our unease and rather than ignore, avoid, tolerate or justify it, we can deconstruct it with intent. The freedom that the yoga sutra-s directs us towards is the state of mind where there are no buttons to push. In that state, everything that it apprehends is on its own merit, free from bias. Imagine that.

The mind forms links with ideas, through either attraction or repulsion. Whether we are connected to something we like or something we hate, we are still living in that connection. The stronger the emotional charge, the stronger the link. To facilitate change, we can link to better and better choices. How do we know a choice is better? First, we examine the current choice in depth. To be able to discriminate if something turns out better, we need an initial reference point. Directing awareness is part of the practice of yoga. Acknowledge that some of the responsibility in the current situation may not be yours. Free yourself from excess ownership. By observation, reason or heartfelt feeling, decide if the world is basically good or not. If you choose the former, honor your faith in life and make it an ally. Linking with an overarching intelligence is one of the definitions of yoga.

Make the effort to create a small, consistent change in the direction you think will help. Give it time and assess the difference. Is there more peace, relaxed inner contentment? From where you are now, does it feel like some shift has happened? Are you more in the flow of giving and receiving? Are things easier - your body, breathing, relationships? The application of effort is part of the practice of yoga. Remain aware that there are natural spanners, monkey wrenches, fudge factors and wormholes. Things do not always work predictably, least of all the mind. This asks us to play chess in more than four dimensions and will exercise our intellect as we proceed. Self-study, self-review is part of the practice of yoga.

To change our thinking, reflect on a situation that has been problematical and assess what happened. How and why did that happen? What values caused that, from how long ago? Are those values valid now? Use that understanding for pausing the next time such an occurrence arises, then exercise choice in response. Intending no harm to any sentient being in thought, word or deed is part of the practice of yoga.

To feel inspired, we can share the company of people who are already inspired. We can read or listen to stories from people who have faced similar experiences. We can use contemplative texts to ponder our own thoughts and feelings. This is also a part of self-study.

Carrying out physical movements with the mind coordinating body and breath is the practice of yoga we are most acquainted with. Decreasing physical and mental congestion allows the space to be filled with more natural clarity. Working in this way physically can help us mentally. It is one of the definitions of yoga to be present in the present.

Terrie acknowledges that with her second cup of tea in the morning, she starts to feel her limbs become shaky. She cries easily throughout the day and stops just as easily. There are countless triggers that make her cry and she can name some but not others. She says that tea in the amount she uses is not good for her but cannot manage to decrease it. Ayurveda recognizes willful perversity as the primary cause of disease, when we know something is not in our best interest and yet continue to do it. It is underpinned by the mistake of the intellect, where we believe something, even unconsciously, that is not valid. The mistake of the intellect is also apparent by our belief that the physical plane is the source of everything and perhaps the only plane there is. Drinking too much tea is the tip of the impasse that Terrie faces, so on to the yoga of Patañjali.

Examining the effect of tea on her is something Terrie has already done. She has drawn close to the experience and knows its effects. Ownership is hers in this situation but the willful undermining of her health is perhaps connected to how others have treated her, most notably her family of origin. Terrie believes in an overarching intelligence and has been part of many spiritual groups, traveling the world to link with them. She loves gardening, art and craft, although her art projects accumulate unfinished.

A small change Terrie can make is to leave one quarter of each cup of tea unfinished. Decreasing by quarters is an ayurvedic recommendation. She can celebrate her ability to do so. To act with quality and refinement is one of the definitions of yoga. Faith in the process is her ally. She can assess how this feels for her. After a week or two, Terrie can again decrease the amount of tea she drinks per cup and perhaps eliminate one serving altogether. In its place, she can spend time with her plants, her projects, her connection to spirit, her affirmations or chanting, fortifying her intent to honor herself as much as she honors anyone else. The gesture of namaste in yoga, palms together at heart center, means that we are all equals on earth. No one is more alive than anyone else is; we have each accomplished the same miracle of manifesting a physical body. While this is a mark of respect for others, it also reminds us to respect ourselves. Terrie agrees with the idea of putting something in the newly opened space because in gardening, one would not remove a weed unless prepared to put a plant of choice in its place.

There are myriad avenues of self-study that Terrie can access and this is a most important aspect for her. She can talk to a yoga teacher or other trustworthy professional who can help her clarify her thoughts and feelings. Speaking aloud helps us listen to our own thoughts as we are talking to spirit. It is important to receive feedback from a person who cares so that we do not perpetuate our own erroneous notions. A friend may care but may also have similar justifications and neither person moves forward. Once recognition of her old, emotionally bound links are uncovered, deconstructed layer by layer, the energy released will help Terrie continue. This does take time and requires the help of her teacher along the way. Terrie may resume her beloved practice of physical yoga and breathing and become a support to others. Her beautiful qualities will radiate and her whole demeanor will lighten. The cup of tea, at first a catalyst for change, fades in time; tea has given her up. Yoga can be defined as movement towards and the reaching of a goal.

The paths of yoga include techniques and postures that benefit the body; breathing practices that increase energy, clarity and change body temperature; mental training that focuses, calms and helps develop deep insight and self-reflection; selfless service to all; nurturing love and faith and experiencing unity with the Divine; and chanting, which is joyful and sometimes rigorous, that increases focus, provides mental protection and may prevail over our mental precedents. Specific to the yoga sutra-s is the idea that the overarching intelligence is the ultimate teacher, knowing everything there is to be known, with comprehension beyond human conception and a source of guidance for all. The ultimate is then not a deity and the yoga-sutra-s are not a religion. That is why the teacher-student relationship is so important. A person seeking help is a student rather than a client, patient or disciple.

However many practices there are in yoga, and however many definitions, there is one center, and this includes yoga and everything else. Along a path that we join through choice, which usually involves wanting something better, we understand more, become more content and grow to be a blessing to ourselves and to others. We act with increased integrity, awareness and efficiency, master new endeavors and feel the connection to that which has put everything here. We are as healthy as we can be and experience more enjoyment and sense of purpose. The mind is the facilitator, the higher self is the conductor and the soul is the receiver.

The few yogi-s that achieve the ultimate goal of yoga, freedom, no longer operate via the attributes of nature, sattwa, rajas and tamas.

It has been my experience that T.K.V. Desikachar links the wisdom of his illustrious father, Sri Krishnamacharya, and contemporary examples of the yoga sutra-s, making it useful to all people, even if they do not practice physical exercises. It was Krishnamacharya's intention to open and de-mystify the teachings of yoga, making them accessible, relevant and of worldwide benefit. Mark Whitwell was of great help in this, introducing many westerners to a physical practice that was more than just physical postures. The Krishnamacharya Yoga Mandiram in Chennai, India, started by T.K.V. Desikachar, has given us many caring teachers and is an inspirational place to visit. Desikachar, Desikachar's wife Menaka and son Kausthub, all of whom I have had occasion to meet and learn from, are reaching many people through the transmission of Krishnamacharya's grace. Thanks to the institution of publishing, there are many books written by Krishnamacharya, Desikachar, Kausthub and their students reaching people world-wide. I am one such student. To recall that yoga started its journey out of India in the early part of the 1900's is to be inspired by what has taken place. Take the words of Krishnamacharya with you and find a teacher through whose understanding you can experience them: "The individual does not have to adapt to yoga; yoga adapts to the individual."

REGARDS FROM THE AUTHOR

Born and raised in New York City, playing stoop ball and stick ball in the streets, roller skating eight metal wheels over pebbly sidewalks, being served vegetables out of a can, meat every day, factory-baked goods that later were considered to cause mental aberration and a freely provided supply of junky candy, these are my memories. I was never taught to cook the different cuts of meat and organs and hey, I will never have to learn.

I majored in biology at university and worked in various hospitals as a laboratory technologist until the automated machine started catapulting sample cups containing biological fluids all around the place. Medicine was growing as a big business enterprise and declining in its ability to provide the trust, familiarity and heart that helps healing as found in a family doctor.

Twenty years backpacking and camping around the world, meeting an Aussie who would bring me to the Land of Oz, two children, an ongoing personal and professional practice of yoga and as an ayurvedic lifestyle consultant, I confirm proactive wellness as the easier endeavor, easier to stay well than to get well.

Perth, Australia is a city of light. The clarity here is divine. The sky is shades of pure blue. With many folk of like mind and many more not, and with visits by inspiring people from around the planet, we do not feel like the most isolated city in the western world. Come spring my backyard offers jasmine, orange blossoms and loquats, the first fruits, with mulberries a few weeks later. We watch mangoes from flower to fruit and pick them from our kitchen window.

Our bush property, our homestead at Jarrah Dharma, is towards the northern limit of jarrah-marri open woodland. There are kangaroos, echidnas, reptiles, emus and songbirds. The bush is a living example of non-resistance. Something happens, everything adjusts. With scant water and few nutrients, growing on land called ironstone, sitting above the oldest rock on the planet that all of Australia shares, the jarrah tree is mighty strong. Half a millennium it grows and if fallen it takes another 500 years to decompose.

At Jarrah Dharma, I offer ayurveda cleansing retreats. I also enjoy the work of caretaking the land and sweating as a result of productive activity. There is more living outside in the center of a star-studded universe and less under the roof of a building.

Be ready to discover that recipes with sattwic and doshic guidelines are delicious and satisfying. If this is how you had to eat, it would be easy.

OM SHANTI

Meta B. Doherty
Perth, Western Australia
May 2005

<u>Ayurveda</u>, the teachings of how nature works, are there for us to use so that we can enhance life as we experience it.

<u>Ayurvedic Cuisine</u> is food cooked by a caring person, fresh for each meal, using fresh ingredients and a balance of tastes. It encompasses recipes from all countries which ensures that a healthy diet is available everywhere.

<u>Sattwa</u> is the state of mental clarity and contentment. From this state of mind, what we feel like eating and doing is what benefits us. We are on track effortlessly.

<u>Multicultural Australia</u> is home to people of diverse ethnic origins. We enjoy many styles of cuisine reflecting the traditional wisdom passed through the generations of all populations on this planet.